Taxation in a Sub-N

MW01250445

Taxation in a Sub-National Jurisdiction

RICHARD A. MUSGRAVE AND

PEGGY B. MUSGRAVE

ALBERT BRETON

DOUGLAS G. HARTLE

BRIAN ERARD AND FRANÇOIS VAILLANCOURT

D.A.L. AULD

Edited by

ALLAN M. MASLOVE

Published by University of Toronto Press in cooperation with the Fair Tax Commission of the Government of Ontario

UNIVERSITY OF TORONTO PRESS
Toronto Buffalo London

Printed in Canada

ISBN 0-8020-7456-1 (paper)

Printed on recycled paper

Canadian Cataloguing in Publication Data

Main entry under title:

Taxation in a sub-national jurisdiction

Includes bibliographical references and index.
ISBN 0-8020-7456-1

1. Taxation – Ontario.   2. Federal-provincial
tax relations – Canada.*   I. Maslove, Allan M.,
1946–   . II. Musgrave, Richard A. (Richard Abel),
1910–   . III. Ontario.   Fair Tax Commission.

HJ2460.05T3 1994   336.2'013713   C93-094985-4

Contents

Foreword

The Ontario Fair Tax Commission was established to examine the province's tax system as an integrated whole and, in conjunction with its working groups, to analyse individual components of the system in detail.

It has been many years since the Ontario tax system was subjected to a comprehensive examination. However, a great deal of research on taxation has been undertaken over the past two decades. This work, based in several disciplines, has been both theoretical and applied, and in this context the research program of the Fair Tax Commission was formulated.

The research program has two broad purposes. The first is, of course, to support the deliberations of the commissioners. The second, more novel objective is to inform public discussions of tax matters so that the commission's formal and informal public consultations can be of maximum value. For this reason we have opted to publish volumes in the series of studies as they are ready, rather than holding them all until the commission has completed its work. While our approach is more difficult from a technical and administrative perspective, we believe that the benefits will justify our decision.

The research program seeks to synthesize the existing published work on taxation; to investigate the implications for Ontario of the general research work; and, where required, to conduct original research on the context and principles for tax reform and on specific tax questions. We thus hope to add to the existing body of knowledge without duplicating it. The studies included in these publications are those that we believe make a contribution to the literature on taxation.

I would like to extend my thanks to my fellow commissioners and to the members of the FTC secretariat. I also thank the many members of the working groups and the advisory groups who have contributed to the research program and to the overall work of the commission.

Monica Townson, Chair

Introduction

Discussions of taxation in a multijurisdictional world involve a range of issues that do not arise in the context of a single jurisdiction. In particular, taxation by a subnational unit in a federation raises a number of economic, institutional, and social issues.

The economic issues revolve around the constraints relating to open regional economies and high levels of mobility of capital, goods, and people. While most of these factors also apply to internationally open economies, they tend to be much stronger forces between provinces in a federation than between separate countries. The mobility of people is especially noteworthy in this regard. Among other things, this openness and mobility raise questions of fiscal structure, of the sustainability of differences in taxation among the members of a federation, and of the scope that individual units have to conduct independent fiscal policies, including measures taken through the tax system.

Among the institutional issues are the formal arrangements that exist for the harmonization and collection of taxes, either among the member units of the federation, or between the subnational units and the central government. Such arrangements contribute to the tax system's efficiency by economizing on resources devoted to compliance and administration and by ensuring a large measure of uniformity in tax structure. At the same time, however, these provisions constrain the ability of the individual units to pursue their own public objectives through the tax system; coordination also means coercion.

The social issue of primary concern is the extent to which there are shared values and a sense of community across the units of a federation, at least relative to those that exist across international borders. Concern with equity among individual citizens of the federation raises questions of the allocation of responsibilities for redistribution between central and provincial governments. The related issue is the redistribution of income or wealth among regions, or, as is somewhat different and is more commonly the case, among governments of the regions.

The resolution of these economic, institutional, and social issues is achieved through the allocation of taxation and expenditure (and regulatory) responsibilities to the two (or conceivably more than two) orders of government in the federation. These responsibilities (or powers) for expenditure and tax measures may not be well matched in the sense that one order of government may be over endowed with revenue potential while the other is overburdened with expenditure responsibility (vertical fiscal imbalance). If this discrepancy occurs, some mechanism for intergovernmental transfers will be required. The determination and maintenance of these intergovernmental fiscal arrangements are typically matters of continuing interest in a federation.

The five papers in this volume address many of the key concerns that surface in discussions of these issues. Musgrave and Musgrave explore the dimensions of tax equity in a multijurisdictional setting. Based on the ability-to-pay concept of equitable taxation, they provide an excellent discussion of the pursuit of interpersonal and interjurisdictional equity, the allocation decisions in a federal setting, and interjurisdictional coordination. Elements of Canadian fiscal federalism arrangements are analysed in this framework.

Breton builds on his own work on competitive federalism to discuss some of the same issues, among them the tax and expenditure assignment processes, vertical fiscal imbalance, and intergovernmental transfers. Given his competitive model, one can conclude from Breton's discussion that it is important to focus on the process and competitive structure that generate any federal fiscal arrangement (including tax harmonization agreements).

Hartle addresses the Canadian tax collection agreements (TCA) for personal income tax, which include all provinces and territories, except Quebec, and revisits the recurring question of whether Ontario should leave the agreement and establish its own income tax system. The federal Department of Finance released a discussion paper in 1991 that included a model for the reform of the TCA, which would allow more flexibility for the participating provinces. Hartle uses this paper as the occasion to examine and compare the current arrangements, a reformed TCA, and a separate Ontario income tax.

Erard and Vaillancourt investigate the additional compliance costs of a separate Ontario personal income tax compared with the current situation. The close integration achieved by the current system eases the compliance burdens for taxpayers, employers, and financial institutions. A separate system, or a less integrated combined system, would enhance the ability of the province to use the income tax to accomplish its own policy objectives at the expense of increasing compliance costs and, under some arrangements, administrative costs as well. This paper provides estimates of such additional compliance costs.

In the final paper, Auld reviews the evidence and literature on the efficacy of a provincial fiscal policy. He begins with discussions of several of the main arguments relating to the power of stabilization policy at the provincial level, then reviews the empirical evidence, finding some evidence that policies in the past have been countercyclical. He concludes with a statement of the preconditions upon which successful short-term provincial fiscal policy is likely to depend.

Allan M. Maslove

Taxation in a
Sub-National Jurisdiction

1 Tax Equity with Multiple Jurisdictions

RICHARD A. MUSGRAVE and PEGGY B. MUSGRAVE

Discussion of tax equity is typically pursued in the simplified context of a single and closed jurisdiction; all its residents are subject to the same tax code, and all their economic activities are carried out within its borders. This situation omits the complications and additional considerations that arise in a setting with multiple jurisdictions, be they independent units or joined in a federation.

As economic activity has become increasingly internationalized, these aspects require greater attention. Two new sets of problems arise. First, tax arrangements directed at securing interindividual equity have to be adjusted to allow for multiple taxation by several jurisdictions. In the field of income taxation, how should jurisdiction A treat the income that its residents receive in jurisdiction B, and how should it treat income that originates in its borders but flows to residents of B? In particular, how should A deal with foreign taxes which its residents have paid to B on income derived in B? In the field of commodity taxation, should country A tax what is consumed within its jurisdiction, whether produced at home or imported, or should its taxes apply to consumer goods produced within its borders, whether consumed at home or exported? The answers to these questions will have a bearing not only on the efficiency of resource flows but also on equity in the distribution of the tax burden among residents of any one jurisdiction.

Second, the multijurisdictional setting raises the further problem of how access to various tax bases should be divided among those jurisdictions, posing a problem of interjurisdictional as distinct from interindividual equity. In the field of income taxation, it is generally recognized that the country of residence is entitled to tax the income of its residents on a worldwide basis, whether it originates at home or from foreign sources. But the host, or source country, also exerts a claim to tax income originating within its boundaries, and the two claims have to be harmonized. Similarly, commodity taxation may be applied by both the country of destination and the country of origin, raising once more the question of how the base should be assigned or shared.

These and related problems that arise in the context of independent multiple jurisdictions then reappear in that of federations. Are the conclusions reached for the international setting equally applicable to the relationships between members of a federation, or do they need to be qualified when it comes to jurisdictions that are only semi-independent, such as the Canadian provinces or the American states? Moreover, there is now the additional problem of equitable relations between members of the federation and their central government. Depending on the nature of the federation, the issues of tax treatment may no longer be separable from the assignment of expenditure functions, thus rendering the problem of intermember equity one of fiscal, not tax equity only. This issue, as we shall see, becomes of particular importance in the context of fiscal equalization schemes. The answers greatly depend on how the nature of the federation is viewed.

Resolution of these equity issues, as in all matters of tax equity, calls for judgement on what is fair and thus cannot be dealt with in categorical terms, as can matters of efficiency. At the same time, the two are related, and efficiency as well as equity aspects must be given consideration. While our primary assignment is to address the former, the latter will also be allowed for as we go along.

Tax Equity in the Closed Economy

By way of introduction, it is well to review briefly the principles of tax equity as they arise in the simpler setting of a closed jurisdiction (see Head 1993 for a comprehensive discussion; see also Musgrave and Musgrave 1989). A background will therefore be given against which to view the modifications and additions needed for the multijurisdictional case.

Over the years, the idea of equitable taxation has been pursued along two lines. One of these, referred to as benefit taxation, calls for a distribution of the tax burden so as to match that of expenditure benefits. It thus follows a principle of fiscal, not merely tax, equity. The other disregards expenditure benefits and, looking at the tax side only, aims to secure a fair distribution of the resulting losses. Both are relevant to equity in the multi- as well as the single-jurisdictional setting.

Benefit Taxation

We begin with the concept of equity underlying benefit taxation. It is based on the classical premise that a person is entitled to his/her earnings and their use. Fair taxation, therefore, means that the beneficiaries of public services should be charged for their cost. Analogous to the way in which the market charges the consumers of private goods, they should pay in line with their marginal evaluations. The fiscal process, in this setting, is a matter of quid pro quo and has no redistributional function. Everyone should get what he/she pays for and everyone should pay for what he/she gets. The principle is similar to that of the market, but for certain reasons "public provision" is called for. The use of that term here implies that a political process is needed to decide what is to be supplied and that it has to be financed through the budget. Whether the government itself is to be the producer (as with the services of the courts) or whether it purchases the services from private producers (e.g., highways installed by a construction company) is a different issue, which does not concern us here.

The principle of benefit taxation, as a rule for equitable sharing in the cost of public services, is simple enough, but its implementation is not. If the values consumers place on such services were known to government, the tax price could simply be assessed accordingly for each taxpayer. But this is not the case. In order to induce consumers to reveal their preferences, the availability of the service must be made contingent on their willingness to pay a price. Such is the case with private goods when provided in the market, but not with public goods. Their nature may be such that exclusion is undesirable because A's enjoyment of the benefits does not interfere with B's; or they may be such that exclusion, though desirable, is not feasible. Availability of weather information illustrates the former, the benefit of traffic lights at crowded intersections illustrates the latter, while protection given by national defence has both characteristics. Then there are other public services provided free of direct charge, even though they are excludable and their consumption is rival. This is the case with items like education or health facilities, which are viewed as "merit goods" and are to be made available to all. Other situations arise, especially in the context of local government, where facilities like golf courses are maintained publicly and where, in the absence of such justification, fee rather than tax finance would be in order.

Such abuses aside, our concern here is with situations where benefits of public services must or should be made available free of direct · charge. Consumers then have no reason to reveal their preferences, so that the appropriate level of provision along with who pays must be decided upon by vote. Individuals seeking an outcome to their liking then have an incentive to record their preferences. In this way, a solution will be approximated that is both efficient and equitable in outcome. It will tend to be efficient, because resources are used and services are provided in line with consumer preferences; and it will tend to be equitable, because each consumer shares in the cost in line with his/her evaluation of the service provided.

Here, a further difference from the case of private goods arises. With private goods purchased in the market, all consumers pay the same price. Those who value the product more buy a larger amount. With public goods, the same level of provision is enjoyed jointly and by all. In order to equate price with marginal evaluation, as is the case in the market, consumers who value the product more highly should therefore pay more. Differential evaluation now calls for different tax prices. Ideally, each consumer would be charged a tax price in line with his/her own evaluation, but at the more practical level it would be impossible to fit individual tax prices to millions of consumers. Rather, individuals have to be grouped, based on an index that reflects their evaluation. Thus public services whose benefits accrue to the residents of a particular region should be paid for by members of that region – a consideration that will prove important later when equity is viewed in a multijurisdictional context. The cost of some public services, mostly of the local type, may also be assigned in relation to beneficiary characteristics (e.g., the use of property taxation in the finance of fire protection services). But for the larger part of the budget, such use-related specification of beneficiary groups is not possible, and a more general index of benefit accrual is needed. This may be provided by a general measure such as total income or consumption.

Taking income as the index and assuming that people have similar preferences, those with similar incomes may then be expected to pay the same, while those with higher incomes may be expected to pay more. The tax schedule will then relate the amount of tax payable to the taxpayer's income. A person with higher income will be taken to place a higher value on the given public service and thus be charged a higher tax. The tax bill will rise with income, depending on how rapidly evaluation increases. In the economist's language, the rate schedule will be regressive, proportional, or progressive, depending on whether the price elasticity of demand exceeds, equals, or falls short of its income elasticity.

Tax equity, as seen in this approach, is thus a matter of quid pro quo. Given the distribution of income available to consumers, it is considered fair for them to pay in line with their evaluation, as they do with regard to private goods. Whether or not this calls for progressive taxation is a matter of consumer preferences, not of a desire to correct the prevailing distribution of income. A system of benefit taxation thus separates equity as it applies to the financing of public goods from considerations of equity in the distribution of income, whether used for the purchase of private or of public goods. At the same time, use of the budgetary mechanism for adjusting the distribution of income is not incompatible with use of the benefit rule for the financing of public services. The two are then viewed as separate budget functions (Musgrave and Musgrave 1989, ch. 1).

Tax Equity and Ability To Pay

We now turn to a second and more widely applied approach, where tax equity is seen not in relation to expenditure benefits, but as a matter of fairness in the distribution of the tax burden only. The problem, therefore, is related more closely to that of distributive justice, seen not in terms of entitlement to earnings and their use, but as based on what society considers a fair state of distribution.

As the matter was put in the literature from Adam Smith on, a person's contribution to the tax bill should be in line with his/her ability to pay. Taxable units with equal ability should contribute the same. Equals, as required by the principle of "horizontal equity," should be treated equally. But taxpayers with higher ability, in order to satisfy the principle of "vertical equity," should pay more. The idea that people in equal positions should be treated equally is readily accepted, but the pattern of differentiation among unequals remains controversial. The problems to be considered are thus (1) how to define equals, and (2) how to let the tax contribution differ among unequals.

Defining Equals

Defining equals calls for an index by which to measure equality in position or differences therein. Next, the appropriate taxable unit must be defined.

Choosing the Index of Equality.   Equal ability to pay has to be defined in terms of measurable economic characteristics, such as income, consumption, or property. Traditionally, income has been viewed as the most appropriate index. Defined in terms of accretion to a person's wealth, all forms of income are to be included, whether from labour or capital, whether paid out or accrued, whether realized or held in the form of appreciation of assets, whether earned or received as gifts or bequests. Similarly, all sources of income use are covered, whether applied to current consumption or saved for future use. Since ability to pay depends on the real value of a person's income, the ideal income definition should be in real terms, with correction for inflation. Moreover, not only should all sources of income be included, but they should be combined in a global base before tax rates are applied.

Taxpaying ability thus measured rests with individuals, with all income traced to the final recipient. Where income is received via legal entities, the resulting ability to pay is vested with the individuals by whom the legal entity is owned, not by the entity as such. Ideally, all business income should be imputed to the owner, and there would be no additional tax on the business unit as a separate taxpayer. Tax collection at the corporate level would serve only as withholding of the shareholder's tax at source. Such at least would be the case in the unitary setting, although, as we shall see later, additional considerations enter in the multijurisdiction case.

While the rationale of defining income as accretion is clear enough, its implementation encounters numerous difficulties. Given the intricate business structure of modern society, measuring income and identifying its flows is exceedingly complex, the more so as the presence of taxation provides an incentive to hide it. Implementation of tax equity, therefore, involves a perpetual struggle and is achieved in only an incomplete fashion. But unfortunately, such is the case with most desirable goals.

More recently, economists have been attracted to consumption as an alternative and perhaps superior measure of ability to pay. The value of receiving income, it is argued, lies in its consumption. People who consume more should be taxed more, but there is no reason why those who consume early should be favoured while others who save and consume later should be discriminated against. Such discrimination comes about under the income tax because the taxation of interest may be seen to involve double taxation. This outcome is avoided either by exempting interest from the income tax or by taxing consumption only when it occurs.

The case for the consumption base is not without merit, although it raises some problems. For one thing, not all income is consumed during the recipient's lifetime; for another, future consumption is not the only gain from saving. The holding of wealth also carries benefits in status, power, and independence, and bequests are passed on. As a matter of application, the consumption base avoids some of the difficulties involved in the measurement of income, but others arise (such as drawing a distinction between consumption and investment and keeping track of financial transactions), and it is not evident that shifting to a consumption base would bring great simplification.

Defining the Taxable Unit.   A second aspect of defining equals involves the taxable unit. The taxable capacity of a unit with a given income will differ depending on whether that unit is single, married, or married with dependants. Appropriate allowances, granted in the form of exemptions or credits depending on differentials in the cost of living, will have to be made to secure horizontal equity. Beyond these considerations, one might argue that handicaps that raise additional needs should be allowed for, thus adding further dimensions to the equity concept.

Differential Treatment of Unequals

Notwithstanding difficulties in implementation, the call for horizontal equity, that is, for equal treatment of equals, has general acceptance. But determining the appropriate differentials in tax to be paid by people in unequal positions is highly controversial, which is not surprising, since it involves the issue of equity in income distribution.

Equal Sacrifice.   A traditional position, taken from John Stuart Mill on, was that people in unequal positions should be taxed so as to leave them with an equal burden or sacrifice. Thinking in terms of an income tax, and taking the utility derived from the last dollar of income to fall as income rises, meant that a person with a higher income should pay more. How much more would depend on how rapidly that utility is taken to decline. On that basis, the pattern of effective tax rates (ratio of tax to income as income rises) that will equalize burdens may then be determined.

The prescription of equity as calling for an equal level of sacrifice is not without appeal, but when it comes to application, serious difficulties arise. For one thing, the utility of income schedule is not known and is hardly measurable. For another, the schedule may not be the same for different people, and there may be serious obstacles to drawing comparisons between them. Analysts thus came to replace the concept of an "observed" and comparable utility schedule with that of a politically agreed upon pattern of social evaluation, referred to as a "social welfare function." As usually viewed by society, this function then assigns declining weights to successive units of income as income rises.

Minimum Welfare Loss.   Rather than aiming at equalizing the level of *total* sacrifice, later economic analysis adopted the goal of equating the level of *marginal* sacrifice. The tax burden distribution should now be such as to equalize the sacrifice incurred from the last tax dollar. Viewed as an equity rule, this result may have no evident appeal, but economists found it attractive because by equating marginal sacrifice, the tax burden assignment will also yield the efficiency goal of minimizing total sacrifice or welfare loss. Assuming the value placed on the marginal dollar of income to fall as incomes rise, this readily follows.

As before, the premise of an agreed-upon social welfare function has to be stipulated; and given that function, the rate schedule designed to minimize total sacrifice may be derived. Assuming the schedule to assign decreasing utility to additional income as income rises and taking total income to be fixed, minimizing total sacrifice or welfare loss now calls for maximum progression, that is, for securing the needed revenue by levelling income down from the top.

This conclusion has to be qualified, however, because the process of taxation, and of taxation at high marginal rates in particular, will initiate adverse taxpayer responses, such as the substitution of leisure for labour or consumption for saving. These responses add to the burden, so that the taxpayer loses more than government gets in revenue. This additional or "excess" burden (also referred to as "deadweight loss") rises with the marginal tax rate. If it is allowed for in measuring the taxpayers's burden, the pattern of tax rates that minimizes total sacrifice or welfare loss calls for a flatter schedule and more moderate progression.

Choosing the pattern of burden distribution that minimizes the aggregate loss for taxpayers as a group is now generally accepted by economists as the appropriate rule. This is not surprising, since they make it their business to advocate an efficient conduct of economic affairs. But though the goal of least total sacrifice is economically efficient, it is not evident why it should also be viewed as equitable and fair. As distinct from the equality of marginal sacrifice that it implies, why should not a rule of equal absolute sacrifice, or some other variant, be just as or more plausible?

To establish least total sacrifice or welfare loss as *the* equity rule, it has to be argued that (1) contrary to the setting of the benefit principle, income distribution is a matter for social judgement and is not necessarily set by entitlement to earnings; and (2) individuals in a civilized society should take an impartial view of matters of distribution.[1] They should value the utility of others as if it were their own. Given that premise, X not only agrees to a rearrangement that improves the position of Y without affecting her own, she will also approve a change that will add more to the welfare of Y than it detracts from her own. This ethic of impartiality thus supports the conclusion that a distribution of tax payments that minimizes total loss will be the just or equitable solution.

Equity and Efficiency

In concluding this brief survey of interindividual equity, we once more note that considerations of equity and efficiency may conflict. To be fair, in the context of this approach, taxes have to be imposed in line with the taxpayer's ability to pay, which requires that they be related to his economic position, whether in terms of income received or outlays made. As a result, the taxpayer will respond, which introduces an efficiency cost or burden. This burden would be avoided if taxation were imposed without reference to the taxpayer's economic activity (e.g., as a head, or lump-sum tax), but that would be unacceptable on equity grounds. The requirement of horizontal equity, taken by itself, will tend to reduce this cost. By calling for a comprehensive definition of the tax base, including all income sources or uses, tax-induced shifts in what to buy or sell are minimized. Such, at least, is the case in the single-jurisdiction setting. But considerations of vertical equity, especially when progression and high marginal rates are called for, may interfere with efficient resource use and thus create costs that need to be considered in the pursuit of ability-to-pay taxation. Tax equity, as with all good things in life, carries its cost.

Extension to Net Benefits

Before leaving this approach to tax equity, the question may be raised: Why does the principle of fair distribution apply to tax burdens only, while the expenditure side of the budget and its resulting benefits are disregarded? A good case can thus be made for extending the analysis to include benefits, with the application of distributive fairness to the resulting pattern of *net* benefits or burdens, an idea to which we return below, under "Extending Equity across Member Jurisdictions."

Conclusions

Finally, having considered the benefit and ability-to-pay approaches, the reader may wonder which is to be taken as the correct one. The answer is that views of tax equity, like views on justice in distribution, depend on the value set of the beholder. Some may view just distribution as given by entitlement to earnings, in which case benefit taxation is the entire answer. Others will hold that justice in distribution depends on how society feels about equality and inequality, in which case ability-to-pay considerations enter. But the intelligent observer need not make an exclusive choice between the two. He/she may choose what constitutes a fair balance of the two.

Equity with Independent Multiple Jurisdictions

Setting the rules of tax equity in a single jurisdiction is not a simple task, and further complications are added as taxation by multiple jurisdictions is allowed for. Two additional problems arise. First, tax-payers in the international setting may now be exposed to taxation by more than one jurisdiction, thus requiring some reconsideration of the meaning of interindividual equity. At the same time, when tax rates differ across jurisdictions, the movement of goods and factors as well as the choice of residence may be interfered with by tax differentials. Second, more than one jurisdiction may now have access to parts of the same tax base, thus raising a problem of interjurisd-ictional equity (as distinct from interindividual equity), that is, of determining entitlements to tax.

Conceptually, both problems would be resolved under a regime of benefit taxation. The jurisdiction by which the services are rendered would be entitled to tax its beneficiaries. Services in the nature of final goods would be charged directly to the consumer. Others that enter into production would be charged at the point of input and then be passed on to the final user. These charges would apply whether the product is consumed in the jurisdiction of service, or whether it is exported to consumers in other jurisdictions. Where the public service benefit goes to increase earning power, as in the case of education, the cost would be charged to the earner. In all these cases, the charge would be in line with the services received, independent of distributional considerations. Such an arrangement would extend benefit-based interindividual equity to the multijurisdiction setting, as well as secure a corresponding division of tax bases among jurisdictions.

But, as noted before, interindividual equity is usually not viewed in benefit terms. Rather, it is seen as a fair distribution of tax burdens independent of benefits. On this basis, taxation by multiple jurisdictions complicates interindividual equity. It must now be decided whether any one member jurisdiction should define the equal treatment of its equals in terms of its own taxes only, or whether and how the taxes paid to other jurisdictions should be allowed for in equity determinstion. Similarly, how should the central government treat taxes paid to member jurisdictions? Moreover, without benefit taxation of individuals, should that principle be reintroduced when an equitable assignment or division of tax bases among jurisdictions is determined?

Intertaxpayer Equity

We begin with the intertaxpayer aspect of equity. Jurisdictions are territorially limited units within which each seeks to apply its own tax code. But economic activities extend across borders and the question is how the potential to extend the jurisdiction's tax authority outside its own borders should be exercised. Under a rule of benefit taxation, taxpayers would pay tax to whatever government provides services to them with intertaxpayer equity provided by this rule. No issue of multiple taxation would arise. But such is not the case under an ability-to-pay approach.

Personal Income Tax

A distinction has to be drawn between wage income earned abroad and capital income received from abroad.

Wage Income Earned Abroad.   As a matter of global income taxation, wage income earned abroad has to be included in the earner's global base, a fact that places primary responsibility for intertaxpayer equity with the country of residence. While nationality would be an alternative possibility, its implementation is hardly feasible, so that residency is generally accepted as the test of tax allegiance. But the jurisdiction of residence is confronted with the fact that the foreign-source income of its residents may also have been taxed abroad by the jurisdiction of source and must thus consider how to deal with the latter.

Our earlier conclusion was that income should be assessed on a global basis, including all sources of income. That is to say, the logic of income taxation calls for the inclusion of foreign-source income of residents. Unless this is done, the residency-imposed tax liability would depend on whether income is earned at home or abroad, thereby offending the principle of horizontal equity. But, as noted before, S, the jurisdiction of source, may already have taxed foreign-source income and various possibilities may be distinguished as to how R, the jurisdiction of residence, may treat such taxes. R may (1) disregard such taxes, (2) permit their deduction from taxable income, or (3) permit them to be credited fully or partially against its own tax. The choice depends on how horizontal equity is to be defined, specifically, in terms of own taxes only as under (1) or in terms of total taxes as under (3), or whether foreign-source income should be defined on a net basis as under (2). As a matter of tax equity, and seen from the perspective of the country of residence, there is much to be said for (2), that is, the treatment of foreign taxes as a cost. As a matter of worldwide efficiency, however, (3) is the preferred solution. Here, the resident of A will pay the same combined tax wherever his/her earnings are received. Distorting effects of taxation on temporary labour location are neutralized. As a matter of international practice, crediting is thus widely applied, permitting considerations of efficiency to be decisive.

But whichever of the three approaches is taken by the country of residence, taxation by the country of source has left the former with a national loss. Granting a credit to the resident of A who derives income from abroad merely means that the revenue is forgone by R and must be recouped elsewhere. Hence, the question arises whether a jurisdiction should be entitled to tax the income that non-residents derive from within its borders – an issue to which we return, below.

Capital Income Received from Abroad.   Capital income received directly from abroad should similarly be included in the shareholder's global base. Such income may have been subject to taxation abroad not only via a withholding tax but also via a corporation tax. Whereas the withholding tax can be credited against the shareholder's tax, it typically falls far short of the corporation tax which, as a matter of practicality, cannot be so treated. Thus, integration of the foreign corporation tax remains, at best, incomplete.

If the foreign-source capital income is received via a domestic corporation (as is usually the case), the foreign corporation tax can be credited against the domestic corporation tax, however, and can thus be accounted for in the shareholder's ultimate liability. We now turn to this case.

Corporation Tax

In the closed economy setting, we argued that the role of the corporation tax from a normative point of view is to serve as a mechanism of source collection for the shareholder's personal income tax. Seen in the international context, that relationship becomes more complex. In addition, the corporation tax now receives a further rationale based on entitlement for the country of source to take a share in the income derived by foreign capital within its boundaries. Leaving the latter aspect for later consideration, our concern here is with extending the residence principle to the corporation tax and its relationship to the shareholder-integration issue.

Whether the corporation tax is viewed in "absolute" form or as a device for source withholding of the individual shareholder's personal income tax, it is necessary to identify the jurisdiction in which the corporation is "resident," that is, to which it owes its primary tax allegiance. Here, general custom is to use the place of incorporation for that purpose. The corporation's country of residence, in turn, may permit an allowance for corporate tax paid by its affiliates abroad. This allowance may take the form of a deduction or a credit. The credit is the correct procedure in order to permit integration of the foreign corporation tax with the personal income tax of the shareholder in the domestic parent corporation. From the point of view of the country of residence, however, the foreign tax involves a national loss. This loss remains, whatever the treatment of the foreign tax by the country of residence. From the point of view of national efficiency, however, something may be said in favour of stemming this loss by disregarding or not fully allowing for the foreign tax, since doing so will keep capital at home. Taking a worldwide view of efficiency, the crediting approach is to be preferred (P. Musgrave 1986a). Given that any one country's practice will also affect how other countries respond, it is therefore not surprising that general practice has tended towards the crediting of outside taxes on foreign-source income.

In following these ground rules, major difficulties of implementation arise. One problem arises because income earned abroad by foreign-incorporated subsidiaries tends to be taxed only when it is received by the parent corporation, but not if it is retained. As a result, the parent may find it advantageous to retain income abroad where taxes are lower and to engage in transfer pricing so as to allocate profits to subsidiaries in low-tax jurisdictions. The division of profits between parent and affiliate thus becomes a matter of controversy, and the enforcement of source rules has been problematic. In the case of foreign branches, this problem of tax avoidance does not arise, since there is usually no deferment, although there is now the issue of determining source in connection with how much foreign tax is creditable to the parent.

We have presented a simplified picture of an intricate technical problem. Seen in detail, the applicable tax treatments differ according to the form that the foreign investment takes, whether undertaken directly by the shareholder, or through a domestic corporation which itself invests abroad in portfolio or majority-owned form (P. Musgrave 1969, 121–30).

Consumption and Product Taxes

We now turn from income to consumption as the alternative tax base. To begin with, the previously noted distinction arises between taxing consumption on a personal basis, namely, via a potentially progressive expenditure tax, and taxing it at a flat rate on an *in rem* basis. In the former case, equitable taxation would again require a global base approach, with primary assignment to the jurisdiction of residence, as for personal income taxation. There would then be similar adjustment problems for foreign taxes on consumption abroad (P. Musgrave 1989).

This option need not be pursued here, since, in practice, consumption taxes are not applied on a personal but on an *in rem* basis. Charged at a flat rate, general consumption taxes may be imposed on the producer of consumer goods, or on the consumer. In the open economy, it may thus be imposed by the country of origin where the product is produced (e.g., as an origin-based value-added tax); or it may be imposed by the country of destination (e.g., as a destination-based value-added tax); or, what is essentially the same, as a retail sales tax. As will presently be seen, this distinction becomes of major importance in the context of source entitlement but presents no need for adjustment in the context of intertaxpayer equity.

Interjurisdictional Equity

Next, we consider the problem of interjurisdictional equity, specifically, the question of which jurisdiction should tax cross-border economic activities, and by how much. The question could be readily answered in the context of benefit taxation, where each jurisdiction covers its costs by taxing its respective beneficiaries, but the resolution is less evident in the more usual context of ability-to-pay taxation.

Income Taxation

We have seen that the country of residence, in the ability-to-pay context, should tax the entire income of its residents, of both domestic and foreign source, and that this practice is justified on grounds of taxpayer equity. The country of source, however, may also claim an entitlement on different grounds. One rationale for that claim might be offered by applying the rule of benefit taxation in the interjurisdictional (as distinct from the intertaxpayer) context. Foreigners should pay for public services rendered to them by the country of income source. That point is not without merit, but it is not the entire story and would hardly justify the prevailing scope of source taxation. A second, and distinct, rationale adheres to the advantages that residents of X gain from operating in Y, and in sharing in the use of the host country's resources. Such may be the case, especially for developing countries, where labour is relatively cheap and natural resources are ample. Given these advantages, the host country feels entitled to seek a share in such rents by placing an *in rem* tax on domestic-source income accruing to foreign owners. This may take the form of various *in rem* taxes such as the corporation tax, the payroll tax, and the so-called withholding taxes on payments made abroad (P. Musgrave 1984).

In implementing any source-based entitlement to taxation, whether based on the benefit rule or on entitlement to rent sharing, it must again be decided how income is to be imputed to various jurisdictional sources, a problem noted already in the parent-affiliate relationship.

Where income is earned by clearly defined separate business entities without shared overheads and other interdependencies, the tax base may be divided among source countries simply by the process of separate accounting. But usually this is not the case, so that a formula approach may be used such as division in line with sales, payroll, and property shares (P. Musgrave 1984; R. and P. Musgrave 1972). Implementation of an orderly division of tax bases in the international context thus raises complex technical problems, but they need not be pursued here.

The problem of source-country entitlement, furthermore, involves the question of just how much the source country may take in tax. Since source taxation implies an *in rem* tax, this question cannot be answered with reference to the rate at which the country applies its residency taxation. In the absence of an international, legal settlement, which sets common rates for source taxation, it is reasonable to rely on bilateral reciprocal agreements. A flaw in international tax treaties is that such reciprocity is usually applied only to the withholding taxes, not to the underlying income taxes that, in principle, should be separated from those on residents. In concluding, it may be added that the role of the corporation income tax, which we have seen to be questionable within the context of taxpayer equity, becomes meaningful and necessary as an instrument for implementing source entitlement. An ideal scheme would indeed contain a uniform-rate corporation tax, with each jurisdiction crediting that tax against a fully integrated domestic corporation tax, along the lines of the *avoir fiscale* system.

Consumption and Product Taxes

We now turn to the question: Who should tax the consumption base? Should it be the country of origin, or the country of destination? As in the case of income taxation, it is generally agreed that the country of destination is entitled to tax its residents on their consumption within its borders. This may take the form of retail sales taxation of final goods, or of a destination-type value-added tax, namely, a value-added tax that grants export rebates and thus excludes exports from the base. Such an arrangement will also be trade neutral. The situation differs, however, with a value-added tax of the origin type, that is, a value-added tax that includes exports in its base. Provided the country of origin is sufficiently potent to affect prices in the world market and if perfectly flexible exchange rates are absent, the country of destination will then suffer a national loss. If the country of destination permits the exporter's tax to be credited against its own tax, trade neutrality will be restored and its internal burden distribution will be rearranged, but it will not recoup its national loss.

The question remains: Should the country of origin be entitled to tax consumption in the country of destination? A rationale for such taxation may again be made on benefit grounds to the extent that exports have benefited from the input of intermediate public goods, but the case for rent sharing seems less convincing in this context than in that of income taxation. Application of such benefit taxation would not depend on whether production is for export or for domestic use, however, but would be applied in line with benefits received whether consumed domestically or exported. Such benefit taxation should be limited in amount to the value of benefits received and should not be permitted to be used as a cover for export of tax burdens.

Coordination versus Competition

In the closed economy, or with a single jurisdiction setting, residents operating through the political process of democratic institutions are free to formulate their tax laws in line with what they consider an equitable arrangement. The freedom to choose and implement that arrangement may be severely limited in a setting with multiple jurisdictions. Individuals, residents of jurisdiction A where tax rates are high, may choose to move to B, where rates are low; or, more important, they may choose to invest in B rather than in A. Corporations may also choose to incorporate where tax rates are low. The resulting tax-base flight then imposes a national loss on A. As as result, the pattern of taxation chosen by B will restrain the freedom of A to set its rates and vice versa. Given the high mobility of capital, these considerations are of particular importance for the corporation income tax. Moreover, since the weight of capital income tends to rise with movement up the income scale, competition for low tax rates is especially powerful in limiting the choice of any one jurisdiction to exercise progressive taxation.

It may be argued that this line of reasoning overlooks the expenditure side of the budget. If tax rates are higher, so will be the level of expenditures and the resulting benefits. The taxpayer should account for both when choosing location of residency or investment. This point has merit, but it also assumes that tax expenditure systems follow the benefit rule. With ability-to-pay taxation and redistributional objectives of tax and expenditure policy allowed for, net benefits or burdens may differ substantially and affect the location of tax bases.

In the absence of coordination, the capacity of any one jurisdiction to implement what it considers an equitable tax system is severely limited. Given the premise that the policies of a sovereign jurisdiction should be set by its residents rather than by the trading bloc, this is an unfortunate constraint, especially in the context of developing countries (P. Musgrave 1986b). A partial remedy, as we have noted, is available via the crediting of foreign taxes paid on foreign-source income, but this does not prevent tax-base flight via movement of residency of persons and place of incorporation. As international mobility increases further, the implementation of tax equity and the formulation of equity norms, by necessity, increasingly become an international matter.

Two qualifications to this line of reasoning may be added. First, allowance should be made for expenditure as well as tax differentials. If tax rates are higher, so will be the level of expenditures and the resulting benefits. The taxpayer should account for both when choosing location of residency or investment. Second, the case for coordination is based on the premise that any one jurisdiction and its voters can be trusted to operate an equitable and efficient fiscal system if left to their own devices. Postulating that an innate tendency for over-expansion of the budget and excessively progressive taxation exists (Buchanan 1975), international competition for low tax rates may be viewed as a corrective device. Tax coordination now becomes undesirable, since it deters the penalizing loss of tax base arising from excessive taxation. This case for tax competition, however, rests on the questionable premise of Leviathan government (R. Musgrave 1981) and the debatable proposition that tax competition offers the appropriate remedy. As long as the international order allows for separate and independent jurisdictions, each entity should be allowed to implement its own view of equitable taxation, and coordination via crediting should be used to dampen double taxation of foreign source income (P. Musgrave 1991).

Equitable Tax Design in a Federation

The discussion now turns to equitable tax design within a federation, a setting that falls somewhere between the unitary state and truly independent jurisdictions. With the federation – an association of member jurisdictions wherein each continues to operate its own tax systems – the problem of interaction again arises. These problems are multiplied, since any one taxpayer may now be exposed to taxation by four sets of jurisdictions, including his/her place of residency, other member jurisdictions, the central government, and foreign countries. Moreover, since the members are now joined in a federation, the further problem of securing an equitable sharing of benefits and obligations among them arises. This opens up a new dimension of fiscal equity, now in interjurisdictional rather than intertaxpayer terms.

Diversity of Federalism

How these relationships work out depends upon the compact by which the various jurisdictions are linked. A distinction is drawn by political scientists between "confederation" or "Staatenbund," as a union of sovereign states combining to seek certain common but limited objectives, and "federation" or "Bundesstaat," as a closer union where larger aspects of sovereignty are surrendered. Whereas the founding debate over union in the United States was in terms of federation, Canada's basic law speaks of confederation, thereby reflecting the image of a less centralized union.

Various degrees of surrender or retention of sovereignty may thus enter the terms of federation. Much depends on how the federation has come into existence, whether out of the collapse of imperial rule, as with the United States and Canada, the incorporation of newly conquered territory, as with Bismarck Germany, or voluntary joining to achieve certain common objectives, as in the European Community, which may eventually become a European Union. The appropriate fiscal relations must fit the origin and objectives of the particular federation, with no single answer to what form they should take. What constitutes fair and equitable interjurisdictional arrangements within any one federation depends on the political, economic, ethnic, and cultural forces that moulded it. Moreover, the structure of federations is subject to change, as was so vividly evidenced in the Canadian context and its recent attempts at constitutional reform.

Nevertheless, there are certain basic issues that will have to be confronted, beginning with the assignment of expenditure responsibilities for the provision of public services, along with a corresponding access to revenue sources. Next, the appropriate fiscal arrangements will depend on how responsibilities for distributional issues are viewed within the federation. Then there is the further problem of how interindividual equity is to be seen and implemented in such a multijurisdictional, yet federation-linked, system.

Assigning Service Responsibilities and Resources

Modelling fiscal equity and efficiency within the federation, as economists see it, begins with the spatial nature of jurisdictions – combining groups of people within a territorially constrained set of fiscal rules. The problem of fiscal federalism may thus be seen as one of spatial fiscal arrangements.

Provision of Public Services

Different public services have different benefit ranges, so that returning to the spirit of benefit taxation, it will be fair for services with federation-wide benefits (such as national defence) to be provided centrally and to be financed on a federation-wide basis, while more spatially limited services will be provided and paid for by smaller units. Such an arrangement is fair, because the respective costs will be shared by recipients of the benefits. It is also efficient, because the respective beneficiary groups know best what they want and should be allowed to determine the provision thereof. Moreover, where the supply involves social goods benefits shared in a non-rival fashion, local provision permits residents of equal preferences to move together, thus sharing in the common benefit of services most suitable to their tastes (Tiebout 1956; 1961).

The model of spatial benefit taxation thus offers a basic rationale for an equitable and efficient assignment of expenditure responsibilities and tax claims within a federation. Even though each jurisdiction may arrange its internal taxation along ability-to-pay lines, the interjurisdictional arrangement is essentially along benefit lines: each jurisdiction finances its services by drawing on the residents of the region in which benefits are received. But though the Tiebout model offers a basic rationale for an equitable and efficient sharing of responsibilities in a federation, real world federations, as they emerge in the historical process, are not constructed according to such rules. They are formed by previously independent units that reluctantly surrender their previous fiscal prerogatives. Moreover, they are typically so large that they do not correspond to local benefit regions. For this reason, the spatial model is more applicable when it comes to assigning local expenditure and revenue functions within a member jurisdiction than for dividing functions and obligations between member jurisdictions themselves. Nevertheless, the spatial model remains of some use in that context as well.

Thus, it is efficient for services with federation-wide benefits to be provided by central government, since duplicating provision at the member level would not yield an efficient outcome. Given such central provision, it is then equitable to have the cost borne on a federation-wide basis. Typically, this takes the form of direct central finance. Individuals, as citizens of their member jurisdictions, are also citizens of the federation. Acting in the latter capacity, they vote on the provision of such services and their finance through central taxation. This is the usual pattern, exemplified by those most closely knit federations, such as Canada and the United States, where the individual acts as both citizen of the nation and citizen of his/her member jurisdiction. Under an alternative procedure, such as that followed in a loose federation of the Common Market type, the citizens of the various member jurisdictions will instruct their respective governments to determine the level of services and then finance their contribution from their own tax systems, thus obviating the need for central taxation.

As we turn to services rendered by the member jurisdictions to their own residents, both efficiency and equity considerations again call for the costs to be borne by them. In the absence of spillovers of benefits across the border, burden export is inappropriate. For reasons noted previously in the international context, product taxation at the member level should thus be on a destination basis so as to exclude exports. In the income tax field, the issue of source entitlement again arises. As we have argued in the international context, the country and now member of source is entitled to take some share of the income earned by outside factors within its borders. As in the international case, this again justifies use of an *in rem* corporation tax and again raises the bothersome problems of assigning profits between affiliates and parent, and of determining source.

Issues of Distribution

As we noted above in the context of a unitary setting, the concerns of fiscal policy are not limited to the equitable finance of public services, but they may also be designed to address issues of income distribution. The same considerations may also be taken to apply in a federation. Acting as citizens of the federation and voting on central taxes, individuals may express their views regarding the state of federation-wide distribution. But as residents of their member jurisdiction, they may also have views regarding the state of distribution within their unit. It would not be inconsistent to apply different standards in the two settings. The choice will be constrained, however, by the high mobility of factors and residents among members of the federation. Progressive taxation thus has to be primarily a central government function. It is not surprising, therefore, that attitudes towards progressive taxation enter into the political debate over centralized versus decentralized finance.

Tax Assignments

Tax equity within a federation requires that member jurisdictions have adequate access to revenue bases, but it does not follow that the various tax bases need be divided for exclusive use by one level of government or the other. Some taxes, to be sure, are more appropriate at one level than at another. Thus, we just noted that progressive income taxation is more appropriate at the central level. Property taxation (especially in the benefit context) is also particularly appropriate at the local level, and gasoline taxes used for highway maintenance are especially appropriate at the member level. At the same time, there is no reason why income or broad-based consumption taxes should not be used at both the central and the member level, provided that there is appropriate coordination between them. To this matter we now turn.

Tax Equity within the Member Jurisdictions

As initially independent jurisdictions form a federation rather than join in a unitary state, they do so because they wish to maintain freedom to arrange major aspects of their public affairs to their own liking. This also applies to the design of their own tax structures. While all may be expected to value the rule of horizontal equity, their desired levels of taxation may differ, as may their views on vertical equity – the distribution of the tax burden among unequals. Membership in the federation, therefore, should not require adoption of a uniform pattern of taxation. At the same time, distorting effects of tax differentials on tax equity and economic choices should be avoided. As before, the resolution should be through harmonization rather than through downward equalization through low-rate competition. Problems similar to those previously discussed in the context of independent jurisdictions again arise but in somewhat different form, and central taxation adds a new factor.

Personal Income Tax

Personal income taxation at the member level varies widely. In Canada, the process begins by letting provinces express their own tax as a flat per cent of the federal tax. However, the province may then add a surtax or low-income credit. After federal collection, the tax is then returned to the provinces on a residency basis. A possible change in the system, now under discussion, may call for use of a common base, while replacing the piggyback system by separate rate structures for each province. The freedom to choose differential rates is limited, however, by tax competition.

In the United States, most states use the adjusted-gross-income base, and some use the taxable-income base, both with minor adjustments and application of their own rates, while two states proceed independently. Another two states piggyback at a flat per cent on the federal tax. The question thus is: Should taxes already paid on such income to other members be disregarded, deducted, or credited? From an equity point of view, the treatment of outside taxes again depends on how the tax burden for purposes of equal treatment is to be defined. From the point of view of efficiency, however, there is a strong case for crediting, as a harmonizing means of permitting diversity in member tax rates while avoiding distorting effects. The usual practice is to credit the tax paid to another state.

We now turn from intermember tax relationships to those existing between central and member governments. Beginning with central treatment of member taxes, if the central government credited income taxes paid to members, the latter would obtain a free ride, and receive costless revenue by raising their rates up to the central level. If the central definition of the base permits deduction of the taxes of members, as is done in the United States, this effect is greatly reduced but its impact is more valuable to high-income taxpayers who are subject to high marginal rates. Deductibility of a flat-rate member tax thus reduces the progressivity of the overall system. At the same time, such deductibility serves to reduce effective rate differentials among the member jurisdictions (the umbrella effect). Canadian practice permits neither deduction nor crediting at the federal level, but its use of tax "room" has a similar effect, since the federal government may reduce its rate by a number of percentage points in response to the provincial rate. Turning to the treatment of federal taxes at the member level, crediting would wipe out their income tax as a revenue source, since central tax rates are typically higher. Deduction of central tax would be less painful but would now substantially reduce the progressivity of the member income tax. For these reasons, it is not surprising that member taxation usually disregards the central tax. Other arrangements, such as mutual deductibility may be made, but they need not be considered here. Suffice it to say that the pursuit of globally based and progressive income taxation at the member level not only is limited by tax competition but also encounters considerable difficulties in tracing the global base and in dealing with the deduction problem.

Corporation Tax

When initially considering the corporation income tax in a unitary setting, we argued that its role should essentially be one of assisting the coverage of corporate source income in the individual income tax base. This meant that there should be integration with the personal income tax. Proceeding to the international setting, we noted that corporations are treated as residents and are thus taxed by the country of incorporation on their worldwide income. Since foreign shareholders cannot be reached, the role of the corporation tax as a withholding device thus came into question. Applying these considerations to the member level in a federation, it would be impracticable for member jurisdictions to operate a corporation tax so as to reach the worldwide income of resident corporations. Not only would it be difficult to determine the full base, but with the choice of location of incorporation readily adaptable, extreme tax competition would result, leading to a highly arbitrary distribution of the remaining revenue.

We also noted, however, that in the international setting there is a good case to be made for an absolute corporation tax, calling for taxing domestic-source profits of foreign capital, be it on benefit or other entitlement grounds. Applicable equally to the case of members in a federation, this levy takes the form of a source-based tax under which the member jurisdiction will share in the tax base of corporate profits that are judged to arise in its jurisdiction. As with branch taxation in the international setting, the tax is imposed independently of where the parent corporation is located. Taking an *in rem* form, it is applied at a flat rate to the jurisdiction's share of the base. The problem of source attribution is much more severe than we had previously noted arising in the international context, because there is much more crossing of jurisdictions in business operations within the federation. Source attribution, by means of a commonly used formula, thus becomes crucial. A further issue then arises of whether foreign-source profits should be included in the apportionable base or whether such apportionment should stop at the "water's edge."

There is much to be said for the same rate being used by the various member jurisdictions so as to achieve reciprocity. With a uniform rate and a uniform source formula, the tax might then be administered in a central fashion, with revenue being returned to the member jurisdictions according to source. Whereas states in the United States are free to proceed as they wish, subject only to the limitations set by the commerce clause of the constitution, the Canadian arrangement provides for a measure of coordination. Under the dominion-provincial agreements applicable to seven provinces, the provinces may apply their own rates to the common dominion tax base, but they are required to abide by a central and uniform apportionment formula based on payroll and sales. Surprisingly, property is excluded from the formula (Boadway, Cromb, and Kitchen 1988), perhaps so as to avoid the difficulties involved in allowing for it. The remaining three provinces (Ontario, Quebec, and Alberta) determine their own base and administer their own taxes, though they abide by the common apportionment rule. The 10 per cent federal tax abatement as an inducement to harmonization might also be noted.

Some observers have argued that taxation of corporate profits should be given no place at the level of member jurisdictions. This view is correct in that a worldwide income-based corporation income tax, as used at the central level, does not fit the member tax system. At the same time, the case for a source-based *in rem* tax may be seen as stronger here than at the central level, because such a large proportion of corporate income arising within a member jurisdiction will be earned by corporations resident in other jurisdictions.

Payroll Tax

Extending the principle of source entitlement to the labour income of foreign residents, member jurisdictions in the United States follow the practice of taxing the labour income of non-residents working in their jurisdiction. Since they are not taxed as residents, the tax is applied in *in rem* form, specifically, as a flat rate applied to their income earned within the guest jurisdiction. This source taxation of wage income is often referred to as a commuter's payroll tax and, based on the source rule, is to be viewed as a legitimate feature of interjurisdictional equity.

Consumption Taxes

We previously noted the basic rule that interjurisdictional equity in the federal setting requires that member jurisdictions pay for their own services and do not impose taxes whose burden is exported. Since a personal expenditure tax would not be feasible at the member level, *in rem* product taxes on consumer goods have to be relied on. If levied in the form of retail sales tax, the burden will be borne at home. If levied in the form of a value-added tax, absence of burden export calls for either exclusion of exports from the base or tax rebate by the jurisdiction of origin. Since border tax adjustments that require fiscal frontiers are highly complex within a federation with many members, there is a strong case for implementing the tax at the retail level rather than via a value-added tax. Such, at least, is the case in developed countries where retail establishments are sufficiently substantial and permanent to permit this approach.

Whereas a country in the international setting may tax products on a destination basis without too much concern regarding comparable levels of taxation in other countries, this may not be the case for member jurisdictions in the federation, especially where heavy concentrations of population along the border permit widespread cross-border shopping. This is but another aspect of the general principle that the choice of tax instrument becomes increasingly constrained as we move from centre to federation members to local jurisdictions. While a strong case can be made for decentralized taxation in the context of benefit taxation, decentralization complicates tax design on both efficiency and equity grounds when the direct relationship between tax contributions and benefits received is broken. Member use of origin taxes at unequal rates has the further disadvantage of causing inefficiencies in production location. Unlike the international setting, where rate differentials can be neutralized by adjustment in exchange rates, such an adjustment cannot occur within the federation where a common monetary regime applies, so that the differentials will result in factor flows.

Depending on whether the central government uses an origin- or destination-type tax, a larger share of the revenue will be collected in high-value-added or high-consumption jurisdictions. This result, however, should not be taken to suggest that one set of jurisdictions should favour the origin and another the destination approach. Fol-lowing the usual assumption of forward shifting, the VAT, if consumption based, will fall on the consumer in either case. Alternatively, if it were argued that the tax is shifted back to factor incomes, that outcome would also hold equally for both types.

Property Tax

As we turn to the property tax, we must take into account the fact that the problem of federation, broadly interpreted as one of regional fiscal arrangements, is concerned not only with the division of functions between the central and middle (provinces-states-Länder) level, but also with the division of responsibilities between the middle and local jurisdictions. Indeed, the spatial benefit rationale for regional fiscal organization, as we noted before, has special merit when it comes to the local level. It also explains why property taxation is typically used at the local level, since it permits a linkage between the kind of services that usually are rendered locally (e.g., police, sanitation, street lights), and the economic base of the beneficiary population. With ability-to-pay considerations left largely to the higher levels, benefit taxation assumes a primary role. Moreover, the burden of taxation, especially in the case of land, tends to remain within the local jurisdiction and cannot be escaped readily by moving out. Frequently, property taxation also heavily figures in education finance, which tends to be considered a special local concern. Finally, local tax administration is more familiar with local property values, thus facilitating the task of assessment, and property is a base to which it has ready access.

This local role of property taxation as an *in rem* tax has to be distinguished from the taxation of wealth, which might be appropriate at the central level. Viewed in that context, it would be applied as a personal tax and in conjunction with ability-to-pay based income or expenditure taxation.

Extending Equity across Member Jurisdictions

Next, we examine various views of equity in the federation that apply equity norms across jurisdictions thereby calling for transfers between members. As distinct from central collection of member taxes with return of revenue to source, such transfers involve gains and losses across jurisdictions and thus express the underlying philosophy of fiscal federalism. Subject to special attention in the United States in the 1960s, the topic has been of lively concern in Canada from the beginning and has remained so ever since. Traditionally, such grants have been seen as a matter of interjurisdictional equity, calling for the equalization of fiscal capacities or the reduction in fiscal disparities among rich and poor member jurisdictions. More recently, the rationale for Canada's equalization grants, as adopted in the Economic Council of Canada's (ECC) statement, *Financing Confederation* (1982), has been reinterpreted as a federation-wide extension of horizontal equity among individuals, so as to secure equal member tax treatment, independent of residence. The case for intergovernmental grants may thus be approached in a variety of ways and may be directed at different objectives.[2]

Equalizing Fiscal Capacity of Jurisdictions

Beginning with the more traditional perspective, concern is with the fiscal capacity of the various member jurisdictions. Where members differ greatly in per capita income, so will their fiscal capacity to provide public services. Residents of high-income jurisdiction H, acting as citizens of the federation, may then wish to make a transfer to low income jurisdiction L so as to raise or equalize its fiscal potential. The purpose of fiscal capacity equalization (FCE) is thus to enable member jurisdictions with different levels of per capita tax base to obtain the same per capita revenue and, hence, to provide the same per capita levels of public services when applying a uniform, specified (usually average) tax rate.

This approach is widely followed in such countries as Australia, Switzerland, Germany, and, in more limited form, in some aspects of grant programs in the United States (Bird 1986). This philosophy was also adopted at the outset by Canada's Royal Commission on Dominion-Provincial Relations (1940), in calling for a National Adjustment Grant "to the less fortunate provinces in order to give them the opportunity to bring standards of services in those provinces up to the national average" (ECC 1982b, 4). This goal of fiscal capacity equalization appears also in the 1982 Constitution Act, which states that the federal government is committed to making equalization payments "to ensure that the provincial governments have sufficient revenue to provide reasonably comparative levels of public services at reasonably comparative levels of taxation" (Constitution Act 1982, 3.36.2).

Grant Design.   Strictly applied, capacity equalization calls for jurisdictions with above-average per capita tax bases to make transfers to jurisdictions with below average bases, in an amount sufficient to equalize the revenue obtainable from a stipulated (usually defined as average) tax rate. For this purpose, an equalization formula is developed that computes the revenue each jurisdiction would derive from applying a standard rate to its base. That standard, not unreasonably though not necessarily, is then defined as the ratio of aggregate revenue to the aggregate base, that is, a weighted average of actual rates. Jurisdictions with above-average per capita revenue would then be called upon to transfer the surplus to jurisdictions with a revenue deficiency, so that per capita yields are equalized. To determine the revenue under a standard level of taxation, major components of the base, such as income, sales, and property, are distinguished, and the average of the respective rates used by various jurisdictions are applied to each part. The formula may then be refined in various ways, including allowance for differential costs of providing stipulated service levels. In practice, the procedure may be simplified by determining the claims of deficient jurisdictions and then financing the payment out of central revenue, rather than requiring differential contributions from jurisdictions with excess revenue. Thereby, the intent of equalization is somewhat blurred, but the procedure is simplified and the need for direct interjurisdictional transfers is avoided.

In most cases, the resulting grant to deficient jurisdictions is rendered unconditionally, permitting the recipients to use the proceeds as they wish, whether for additional programs or as a substitute for own taxation. This is usual practice, even though the logic of FCE would require the former. If the intent was to shift income available for private use, claims and contributions should not be linked to the average level of tax effort. Going a step further, the grant may be made contingent on the recipient's undertaking a tax effort of its own (e.g., taxing at least at the average rate), reflecting the willingness of the donor jurisdictions to render support only if the recipients do not act as free riders but also do their part. Other provisions, such as directing the grant at specific programs may be added, with certain specific services (rather than public services at large) viewed as "merit goods" at the central level.

Natural Resource Differentials.   In many instances, and particularly in the case of Canada, differences in the potential per capita income and tax base among jurisdictions reflect differences in natural resource endowments. Since the taxation of natural resources is less burdensome than wage or capital income, such differentials, above all, should enter into the equalization mechanism. But where such resources are publicly owned and/or (as in Canada's case) subject to constitutional protection, the income they generate may be excluded from the base, thus leading to a deficient level of equalization. The (ECC) report struggles bravely with this problem, a difficulty that arises under FCE as well as under horizontal equity and corresponding equalization (HEE). While it is not difficult to understand that high capacity jurisdictions may wish to set a limit on their required contribution, such limitation, it would seem, should refer to their total capacity rather than give privileged treatment to particular items such as natural resources.

Group Equity.   These details (R. Musgrave 1961) need not be pursued here, but the view of equalization grants as based on considerations of interjurisdictional equity has been challenged. Equity, it has been argued, must address the welfare of individuals, and cannot be applied to jurisdictions. The implied critique is that treating jurisdictions or governments as creatures in their own right smacks of a totalitarian view of society (Buchanan 1950, 190; Boadway 1986, 9; ECC 1982a, 26) and is thus unacceptable. On these grounds, an alternative interpretation has been proposed and will be considered below. Here, we merely express our view that, whatever the merits of that approach, rejection of the FCE's view as "undemocratic" is invalid. Individuals, for purposes of deciding on common matters, operate not independently, but as members of a jurisdiction. The very problem of federation derives from the premise that individuals wish to relate to each other as members of more than one jurisdiction. They thus perform a double function, acting as citizen-voters in their own member jurisdictions and as citizen-voters of the federation. As a federation is formed, individuals as citizens of their particular jurisdiction do not surrender that role as they would when joining a unitary state; rather, acting through their representation in their member government, they agree with individuals acting similarly in other jurisdictions to let their jurisdictions accept certain rights and obligations. These may involve acceptance of an equalization scheme requiring richer jurisdictions to support the fiscal capacity of the poorer ones. Outcome of an individual-based decision process, this does not imply that benefits or burdens are enjoyed or suffered by rich and poor jurisdictions as a "whole," thereby suggesting a totalitarian view. Rather, what happens is that one set of individuals, operating through their decision-making process, agrees to share in obligations to bestow benefits on another set of individuals grouped within other jurisdictions.

Extending Horizontal Equity across Member Jurisdictions

We now turn to an alternative rationale for interjurisdictional grants based on the proposition that interindividual equity should be extended across member jurisdictions rather than, as taken for granted above (see "Tax Equity within the Member Jurisdiction"), be viewed as an internal affair by each jurisdiction. The principle of extending horizontal equity across jurisdictions may be interpreted in various ways, calling for (1) equalizing tax burdens only, (2) equalizing total net fiscal benefits, and (3) equalizing only those net benefits that arise from higher levels of average income in the jurisdiction. While it is this third approach that has been given special attention in the Canadian debate, our discussion begins with the first two.[3]

Tax Burden Equalization.   With various member jurisdictions having different tax regimes, taxpayers with equal incomes will be left with different member tax burdens, depending on where they reside. This might be considered unfair practice for a federation, thus suggesting an equalizing adjustment.

A simple illustration shows what would be involved. Suppose jurisdiction *J'* consists of taxpayers *A* and *B* with incomes of $1000 and $2000, respectively. Taxed at a rate of 10 per cent, they pay $100 and $200 and are left with post-tax incomes of $900 and $1800, respectively. Next, let jurisdiction *J"* include taxpayer *C* with an income of $1000, and taxpayers *D* and *E* each with incomes of $2000. If taxed at the same rate, *C*'s post-tax income would be similar to *A*'s, just as *D*'s and *E*'s post-tax income would be similar to *B*'s. Horizontal equity would prevail and no transfers would be needed. But now, suppose that *J"* taxes at 20 per cent, raising the liability for *C* to $200 and for *D* and *E* to $400 each, leaving post-tax incomes of $800, $1600, and $1600, respectively. In order to equalize the treatment of equals, *A* should pay $50 to *C*, so as to leave both with $850. Similarly, *B* should pay $67 each to *D* and *E*, so as to leave all three with $1667. Theoretically, these transfers could be made directly on an intertaxpayer basis or channelled via their respective member governments.

It will be noted that such tax equalization would direct the flow of transfers from low-rate to high-rate jurisdictions, regardless of the average level of incomes. If poor jurisdictions have lower tax rates to permit needed private outlays, the direction of transfers may be contrary to that arising from FCE. Moreover, any one jurisdiction would find it advantageous to impose higher rates and, thereby, claim equalization payments from low-rate jurisdictions. To avoid rate wars, a mutually acceptable common set of tax rates would have to be negotiated among member jurisdictions, thus depriving jurisdictions of the freedom of setting their own rates, a solution hardly compatible with the spirit of a federal (as distinct from a unitary) fiscal setting.

Net Benefit Equalization.   The principle of horizontal equity, as just examined, fits the spirit of ability-to-pay taxation, viewing taxation separately from the expenditure side of the budget. But in principle, there is much to be said in favour of allowing for expenditure benefits as well. In the absence of strict benefit taxation, net benefits may be positive or negative at various points of the income scale, and it might well be argued that horizontal equity, the equal treatment of equals, should be restated in net benefit terms. Surprisingly, this principle has not been followed up in the single-jurisdiction context, although it has now been suggested for the interjurisdictional setting.

To simplify matters, suppose that the use of tax revenue is shared so as to yield equal per capita benefits for all residents of the jurisdiction. As before, we assume that residents A and B of J' receive incomes of $1000 and $2000, respectively, while residents C, D, and E of J'' receive $1000, $2000, and $2000. With a tax rate of 10 per cent, total revenue in J' will be $300, and per capita benefits will be $150. In J'', a tax rate of 20 per cent will yield revenue of $1000 and per capita benefits of $333. Net benefits for A and B would thus be $50 and −$50, respectively, while those for C, D, and E would be $133, −$67, and −$67. Equalization would call for a transfer of $41.5 from C to A, so that each would be left with net benefits of $91.5 and the same "real" income (including benefits) of $1091.5. Similarly, equalization would call for a transfer of $11.3 from B with $5.7 each going to D and E, leaving all three with net benefits of −$61.3 and real incomes of $1938.7. Combining the interindividual transactions, a net transfer of $30.2 from J'' to J' would be called for, with the flow now from the high- to the low-tax rate jurisdiction; but, depending on income and tax rate differentials, the flow could also be in the other direction.

Such a comprehensive equalization scheme would encounter much the same difficulties as those incurred with equalization of tax differentials only, and thus it remains incompatible with the spirit of a federation that permits member jurisdictions to conduct their own fiscal affairs in their own way.

Horizontal Equity Equalization. In line with an approach developed first by James Buchanan (1950; 1961), a more limited view may be taken of the appropriate scope of net benefit equalization. Only those differentials that result from differentials in the average income of jurisdictions are viewed as unjustified, not those due to differences in their tax rates. An individual's net fiscal benefit should be independent of the average income of the jurisdiction in which he/she resides. This view of HEE was recently taken up in the Canadian discussion (Boadway and Flatters 1982; Boadway 1986) and proposed in the ECC's 1982 report, *Financing Confederation.* Moreover, it was suggested that the results under HEE would be the same as those under FCE, so that the HEE view could be seen as a superior rationale underlying Canada's FCE-type equalization payments.

To show how differences in average income alone will result in unequal treatment of equals, we now assume that both jurisdictions tax at the same 10 per cent rate. As before, individuals A and B in jurisdiction J' receive incomes of $1000 and $2000, respectively, and, with a tax of 10 per cent, pay $100 and $200. Assuming again that the revenue of $300 provides equal-value services of $150 to each, A enjoys a net gain of $50, while B suffers a net loss of $50. Residents of jurisdiction J'', C, D, and E again receive incomes of $1000, $2000, and $2000, respectively, and now pay $100, $200, and $200, respectively, in tax. With total revenue of $500 and per capita benefits of $167, C is left with a net benefit of $67 as against $50 enjoyed by A, his equal in J'. D and E are left with net losses of $33, as against $50 suffered by B, their equal in J'. Even though tax rates are the same, this result comes about because the average or per capita income in J'' is higher and, with a given tax rate, per capita benefits, which are assumed to be shared equally, rise with per capita income. In the ECC report, such differentials are viewed as unfair and violating horizontal equity in a federation. They should thus be corrected for, so that the net benefit received from the fiscal systems of the member jurisdictions is independent of their average income levels.

This would call for a transfer of $8.3 from C to A, so that both are left with net benefits of $58.3 and a total real income of $1058.3.

Similarly, it would call for transfers of $5.6 each from D and E to B, so that all would be left with a net loss of $38.9 and a total real income of $961.1. These transfers could again be made directly on an intertaxpayer basis, they could be introduced as credits against or additions to the central income tax, or they could be implemented by an interjurisdictional transfer from J'' to J' of $19.4, leaving it to the paying jurisdiction to assess the appropriate revenue collection from its residents, and the receiving jurisdiction to pass on the receipts.

The outcome of this HEE adjustment may now be compared with that under FCE. That comparison is of interest, since the ECC report suggests that Canada's prevailing and traditionally FCE-based equalization grants may be seen as implementing its HEE goal (ECC 1982b, vol. 2, 30, 35; Boadway 1986, 15). Computing the transfer needed under FCE, the combined tax base for both jurisdictions equals $8000 and the combined revenue at the 10 per cent rate is $800, leaving a per capita revenue for the five residents of $160. With per capita revenue in J' of $150, the per capita shortfall is $10, thus calling for a total transfer from J'' of $20. J'', in turn, enjoys a per capita revenue of $166.7, so that with an excess of $6.7, a total payment to J' of $20 is due. The required total transfer of $20 is thus close to the $19.40 called for under FCE procedure. If now J' raised its expenditures by $20 while J'' made a similar cut, the net budgetary benefits of both A and B would be raised by $10, while those of C, D, and E would be reduced by $6.66 each. As a result, both A and C would receive similar net benefits of $60 and $60.33, respectively, while B, D, and E would be left with similar net positions of -$40, -$39.66, and -$39.66, respectively. The outcome would then be roughly similar to that derived under the FCE procedure. As in that case, the purpose of the exercise, now HEE, will be accomplished only if these expenditure adjustments do in fact occur.

This conclusion, that the same results will obtain under the FCE and HEE procedures, holds only on the quite unrealistic assumption that both jurisdictions use the same tax rate. If we return to our earlier example where J' taxes at 10 and J'' at 20 per cent, the transfer required under FCE is compared now at a weighted average tax rate of 16.25 per cent and calls for a transfer of $32.50. How to determine the corresponding transfer under HEE is puzzling. The difference in average incomes (which should be corrected for) and tax rates (which should not be corrected for) makes it impossible to separate the differential in the treatment of equals. Both effects are interdependent. Different transfers would be required if both rates were at 10 and 20 per cent. Only if the same average rate of 16.25 per cent is assumed to apply in both jurisdictions will a transfer of $31.50 (similar to that applicable under FCE) be required. But rate levels do differ – not to mention possible differences in the pattern of progression – so that there is no obvious way to allocate the gains and losses among individuals so as to correct for only those differences that result from income differentials. Whereas, in the case of FCE the use of an average rate offers a sensible standard for setting the degree to which equalization should be carried, this does not hold for HEE and its objective.

Finally, it should be noted that both procedures take public services to be in the nature of private goods. This is obvious in the above HEE illustrations, where the benefits from public services are clearly treated as rival. But, it also follows under FCE procedure, where the required transfer is a function of the per capita service level. Rethinking the problem in terms of non-rival public goods offers an interesting exercise, but it will not be undertaken here. There is a difference, however, in that the HEE procedure requires benefits to be distributed equally among residents, whereas under the FCE procedure that choice is left to each jurisdiction.

More generally, the two approaches differ in orientation and spirit. Under HEE, concern is with securing a horizontally equal treatment of equals residing in different jurisdictions. Under FCE, concern is with equalizing public service capacities among jurisdictions. Focus is on an interjurisdictional or group-based concept of equity in its vertical dimension. Setting aside the previously examined and invalid charge that equity considerations can be applied meaningfully to individuals only, the question is not which is the correct formulation. Both are valid in their own context; but, given their different objectives, they should not be considered similar, because they may be shown to yield similar results only under rather unrealistic assumptions. Given the sharp differences in average income levels across Canada's provinces and the latter's strong sense of identity, the FCE perspective seems to us the more appropriate view of Canada's equalization payments.

Efficiency Aspects

The preceding pages have addressed the merit of equalization schemes from the equity perspective; but efficiency effects also enter. The effect of fiscal differentials on location choice not only may result in inequities, but also may lead to inefficient location of economic activity. As was observed above, under "Equity with Independent Multiple

Jurisdiction," crediting adjustments may be made that will neutralize
the impact of tax differentials on the location of investment choices.
But most labour earnings originate in the jurisdiction of residency, so
that fiscal differentials continue to affect labour location. FCE and HEE
will be of help in this respect, but to a limited degree only, since tax
rate differentials are not neutralized by the equalization processes of
FCE and HEE and cannot simply be assumed to be washed out by
corresponding benefit differentials. Deductibility of member taxes from
the central government's tax base may narrow the differentials, but
it does not remove them. Full horizontal equalization of tax liabilities,
on the other hand, would require uniform fiscal operations and would
thus be incompatible with the spirit of federation that calls for diversity. A federal as opposed to a unitary form of fiscal organization
has its advantages, but it also carries its costs, the more so the larger
the share of fiscal operations at the member as against the central
level.

Summary and Conclusions

This paper has explored how the principles of tax equity, usually seen
in the context of a single jurisdiction, may be extended to a setting
of multiple jurisdictions. With initial focus on an international setting
of multiple and independent jurisdictions, we then proceeded to the
further case where semi-independent jurisdictions are joined within
a federation.

Independent Jurisdictions

As the problem of tax equity was viewed in the international setting,
two distinct problems arise. One is the problem of interjurisdictional
equity, namely, of defining the scope within which any one jurisdiction is permitted to tax. The other is how any one jurisdiction is to
preserve equity in the tax treatment of its own residents who may be
involved in international transactions.

Interjurisdictional Equity

Transferring the principle of benefit taxation from the individual to
the interjurisdictional setting, a first rule is that each jurisdiction may
impose a benefit charge for services rendered to economic activity
within its jurisdiction. This entitles J' to charge income earned by J''

residents within J', as well as J' products exported to J''. But such charges would be in the form of *in rem* charges, held strictly within the limits of benefits rendered, while leaving general income taxation on a residency and commodity taxation on a destination basis. These limitations imposed by the benefit rule may be broadened by permitting J', the country of source, to impose a charge on income earned within its boundaries by J'' residents so as to retain a share in the advantages or rents derived from their activities in J''.

Interindividual Equity

Operating within these largely benefit-principle-based ground rules of interjurisdictional equity, the country of residence is then confronted with how to operate ability-to-pay taxation of its residents in this open economy setting. The major issue, not present in the closed economy setting, is how to treat taxes paid by its residents on income earned abroad. Depending on the residence country's view of equity, such taxes may be disregarded, deducted, or credited; but whichever is done, the country of residence will not recoup the burden imposed by taxation in the jurisdiction of origin.

Federations

Turning to the case of the federation, the initial problem exists of securing an equitable and efficient allocation of functions between the various parties. Proceeding once more on the basis of the benefit rule, there is a persuasive case for letting each level provide those services whose benefit incidence falls within its borders and for being responsible for charging its residents to defray their cost. Thus, central services would be financed on a nationwide basis, while member services would be financed within the borders of each member jurisdiction. That finance would then be subject to the same rules of good tax manners as is applied in the international case. There would be further complications, but basically the same rules would hold.

In addition, the federation case opens a new dimension of interjurisdictional (now intermember) equity. Whereas, in the international setting, each jurisdiction is on its own (except for arrangements to provide a fair set of mutual tax relationships), any one member of the federation may well be concerned with the fiscal well-being of other member jurisdictions. This concern may call for measures to equalize fiscal capacity across jurisdictions. Alternatively, member jurisdictions may agree to void what are considered to be unfair fiscal advantages of residing in high-income jurisdictions and to provide for interjurisdictional transfers needed to implement such corrections.

While these two approaches – FCE and HEE – may, under restrictive assumptions, call for similar interjurisdictional transfers, such concurrence does not hold in the general case. The two approaches differ in spirit and objectives. Canada's equalization scheme, as we conclude, is more realistically interpreted in terms of fiscal capacity equalization.

While our discussion of equitable fiscal arrangements has been mainly in normative terms, it must be realized, of course, that implementation of these criteria is impeded in the real-world setting by many other factors. This fact holds true for the closed economy case, where the interaction of political and institutional forces may yield fiscal arrangements different from what these norms would call for. The same applies to the international setting, where fiscal arrangements between nations will be subject to variations in bargaining power and policy objectives. Finally, such limitations apply to the fiscal arrangements in federations. That federations are not formed in the image of equity and economic efficiency, but are conditioned instead by historical, ethnic, and political circumstances needs to be recognized, and normative considerations have to be applied within these institutional constraints. Nevertheless, it is necessary to have such considerations in mind in order to secure the best arrangements within these limitations.

Notes

The first draft of this paper was prepared for the Ontario Fair Tax Commission and completed in March 1993.
The authors wish to acknowledge the helpful suggestions provided by Richard M. Bird, Robin W. Boadway, Allan M. Maslove, Wayne R. Thirsk, and others associated with the Ontario Fair Tax Commission.
1 The principle of impartiality may be interpreted as calling for choice under uncertainty, where individuals will choose among alternative states of distribution without knowing what their own position will be (Rawls 1971; Arrow 1973; R. Musgrave 1992). Allowing for risk aversion and assuming total income to be fixed, they will then opt for maximum progression; but allowing for adverse tax effects that impose deadweight losses, the agreed upon solution will again call for a more moderate pattern.

2 For a comparative evaluation and extensive literature references, see Grewal, Brennan, and Matthews, eds (1980), particularly part IV. For a broader view of the role of federalism, see also the contribution by Albert Breton (1965). Also, see the essays in R.M. Bird, ed. (1980).

3 The reader may wonder why this type of equalization, which refers to horizontal equity among individuals, is included here rather than in the preceding section. The reason for doing so is that this type of equalization, like that of fiscal capacity equalization, results in interjurisdictional transfers and that, as shown in the text, the HEE approach has been suggested as similar to the FCE approach.

Bibliography

Arrow, Kenneth. 1973. "Some Ordinalist-Utilitarian Notes on Rawls' Theory of Justice." *Journal of Philosophy*, 70: 245–65
Bird, Richard M. 1986. Federal Finance in Comparative Perspective. Toronto: Canadian Tax Foundation
– ed. 1980. *Fiscal Dimensions of Canadian Federalism.* Toronto: Canadian Tax Foundation
Boadway, Robin. 1986. "Federal-Provincial Transfers in Canada." In *Fiscal Federalism*, ed. M. Krasnick, Vol. 65, Royal Commission on the Economic Union and Development Prospects for Canada. Toronto: University of Toronto Press
Boadway, Robin, and Frank Flatters. 1982. "Efficiency and Equalization Payments in a Federal System of Government: A Synthesis and Extension of Recent Results." *Canadian Journal of Economics*, 15: 613–33
Boadway, Robin, I. Cromb, and H. Kitchen. 1988. "The Ontario Corporate Tax and the Tax Collection Agreement." Memorandum to the Ministry of Treasury and Economics. Toronto
Breton, Albert. 1965. "A Theory of Government Grants." *Canadian Journal of Economics and Political Science*, 31: 175–87. Reprinted in *The Economics of Federalism*, ed. B.S. Grewal, G. Brennan, and R.L. Mathews, 9–24. Canberra: Australian University Press, 1980
Buchanan, James M. 1950. "Federalism and Fiscal Equity." *American Economic Review*, 40: 583–99. Reprinted in *The Economics of Federalism*, ed. B.S. Grewal, G. Brennan, and R.L. Mathews, 183–200. Canberra: Australian University Press, 1980
– 1961. "Comments." In *Public Finances: Needs, Sources and Utilization*, 122–31. National Bureau of Economic Research. Princeton, NJ: Princeton University Press
– 1975. *The Limits of Liberty.* Chicago: University of Chicago Press

Canada. Royal Commission on Dominion-Provincial Relations. 1940. *Report*. Book II. Ottawa: Queen's Printer

Economic Council of Canada. 1982a. *Financing Confederation – Today and Tomorrow*. Ottawa: Economic Council of Canada

– 1982b. *Financing Confederation – Summary and Conclusions*. Ottawa: Economic Council of Canada

Grewal, B.S., G. Brennan, and R.L. Mathews, eds. 1980. *The Economics of Federalism*. Canberra: Australian University Press

Head, John G. 1993. "Tax-Fairness Principles: A Conceptual, Historical, and Practical Review." In *Fairness in Taxation: Exploring the Principles*, ed. Allan M. Maslove, 3–62. Fair Tax Commission, Research Studies. Toronto: University of Toronto Press

Musgrave, Peggy B. 1969. *United States Taxation of Foreign Investment Income: Issues and Arguments*. International Tax Program: Harvard Law School

– 1984. "Principles for Dividing the State Corporate Tax Base." In The *State Corporation Income Tax*, ed. C.E. McLure, Jr, 228–46. Palo Alto, CA: Hoover Institution Press

– 1986a. "Interjurisdictional Coordination of Taxes on Capital Income." In *Tax Coordination in the European Community*, ed. S. Cnossen, 197–226. Deventer: Kluwer Law and Taxation Publishers

– 1986b. *Coordination of Taxes on Capital Income in Developing Countries*. World Bank: Report No. DRD286

– 1989. "International Coordination Problems of Substituting Consumption for Income Taxation." In *Heidelberg Congress on Taxing Consumption*, ed. M. Rose, 453–90. New York: Springer-Verlag

– 1991. "Fiscal Coordination and Competition in an International Setting." In *Retrospectives on Public Finance*, ed. L. Eden, 276–305. Durham, NC: Duke University Press

Musgrave, Richard A. 1961. "Approaches to a Fiscal Theory of Political Federalism." In *Public Finances: Needs, Sources and Utilization*, 97–134. Princeton NJ: National Bureau of Economic Research. Reprinted in *The Economics of Federalism*, ed. B.S. Grewal, G. Brennan, and R.L. Mathews, 209–33. Canberra: Australian National University Press, 1980

– 1981. "Leviathan Cometh – or Doth He?" In *Tax and Expenditure Limitations*, ed. H. Ladd and N. Tidemann, 77–120. Washington, DC: The Urban Institute Press. Reprinted in R. A. Musgrave, Collected Papers, 1986. *Public Finance in a Democratic Society*, vol. II, Fiscal Doctrine, Growth and Institutions, 200–32. Brighton: Harvester Press

– 1992. "Social Contract, Taxation and the Standing of Deadweight Loss." *Journal of Public Economics*, 49: 369–81

Musgrave, Richard A., and Peggy B. Musgrave. 1972. "Internation Equity." In *Modern Fiscal Issues*, ed. R.M. Bird and J.G. Head, 63–85. Toronto: University of Toronto Press

– 1989. *Public Finance in Theory and Practice*, 5th ed. New York: Mc-Graw-Hill

Rawls, John. 1971. *A Theory of Justice*. Cambridge MA: Harvard University Press

Scott, A.D. 1950. "A Note on Grants in Federal Countries." *Economica*, 17: 416–22. Reprinted in *The Economics of Federalism*, ed. B.S. Grewal, G. Brennan, and R.L. Mathews, 201–7. Canberra: Australian National University Press, 1980

Tiebout, Charles M. 1956. "A Pure Theory of Local Expenditures." *Journal of Political Economy*, 64: 416–24. Reprinted in *The Economics of Federalism*, ed. B.S. Grewal, G. Brennan, and R.L. Mathews, 59–70. Canberra: Australian National University Press, 1980

– 1961. "An Economic Theory of Fiscal Decentralization." In *Public Finances: Needs, Sources, and Utilization*, 79–96. Princeton, NJ: Princeton University Press

2 Fiscal Federalism in a Competitive Public-Sector Setting

ALBERT BRETON

Introduction

Not only are the topics usually discussed in the subdiscipline of public economics known as fiscal federalism numerous, but each one is interesting and challenging in its own right. Indeed, fiscal federalism wrestles with the question of why powers are divided between levels of government,[1] and examines how that division is (or should be)[2] determined at a given point in time, and how it changes over time. Discussions of expenditure, regulatory, redistribution, stabilization, and taxation responsibilities flow naturally into the analysis of harmonization in respect of all these powers. Problems related to vertical fiscal imbalance as reflected in intergovernmental grants also receive a great deal of attention. The attention given to fiscal imbalance and grants is not an accident. Indeed, as will become apparent, all problems of fiscal federalism can be discussed in a model of fiscal imbalance and intergovernmental flows of funds.

The work done over the last 40 years or so by a large number of economists has taught us much that is worth retaining. However, the subdiscipline of fiscal federalism still lacks a consistent unified treatment. Too many propositions are exclusively normative, that is, lack any descriptive or real-world basis; too many are based on the premise that agents who are assumed to be rational, among them governmental decision makers, systematically misallocate resources and cause inefficiencies; too many cannot be applied to governmental systems made up of three or more jurisdictional tiers – virtually all existing systems; and too many, if they are not inconsistent with each other, must live separate lives because bridges that would help us go from one to the other do not exist.

From this study's perspective, the questions raised by vertical fiscal imbalance are central to the theory of fiscal federalism. For example, why does it exist? How is it remedied? What are the effects of these remedies? It will help to give concreteness to the criticisms of the last paragraph as well as serve as an introduction to "Fiscal Federalism in a Competitive Public Sector Setting" if I begin with a discussion of the state of the art with regard to fiscal imbalance. The literature and the models are well known. I shall therefore do no more, in the next section, than provide a brief outline of the models having the widest circulation. This approach will provide sufficient background for a critical assessment, also undertaken in the first section, and for the alternative approach suggested in the second section. The third section concludes the paper.

The Standard Explanation

The existence of vertical fiscal imbalance – the mismatch of own revenues and expenditures of governments located at different juris-dictional tiers – and the consequent flow of funds between govern-ments are often (sometimes implicitly or tacitly) assumed to be given or, technically speaking, to be exogenous. When this assumption is made, analysis, of necessity, concentrates on the *effects* of the im-balance and of the intergovernmental money flows. Exogeneity, in other words, is a way of disregarding origin or motivation and of focusing on consequences, on the (tacit) assumption that effects are unrelated in any way to origin or motivation. I note three effects on which the standard view of fiscal imbalance has concentrated. A first line of analysis has focused on the distortions in the spending prior-ities of recipient jurisdictions (the first, and still among the best model is Scott 1952; see also Wilde 1971 and Gramlich 1977). A second has stressed the incentive to fiscal irresponsibility on the part of the same governments resulting from the separation of expenditure and taxa-tion decisions which the money flows imply (see, e.g., Hicks 1978 and Walsh 1991, 1992). A third has underlined the promotion of fiscal illusion in citizens, and/or the encouragement to bureaucratic ma-nipulation also caused by the separation of revenue and spending decisions (see, e.g, Courant, Gramlich, and Rubinfeld 1979; Romer and Rosenthal 1980; and Winer 1983).

Words like distortion, irresponsibility, illusion, and manipulation, if they do not automatically speak of intrinsic evil, do not signal much that should be encouraged and nurtured either. Indeed, whenever those who focus on the effects of vertical fiscal imbalance, and on the money flows between governments choose to jettison the exogeneity assumption – not systematically, but as a prelude to sagacious *obiter dicta* – they almost invariably decry vertical imbalance and the consequent flows of intergovernmental funds. The limit of the exogeneity assumption has been widely recognized,[3] however, which has led to the formulation of a variety of models aimed at explaining why vertical imbalance and intergovernmental flows of funds exist in all multi-tier governmental systems.

One group of explanations derives from welfare economics, and Keynesian macroeconomics, or from Musgrave's (1959) translation of these traditions into the allocation (efficiency), redistribution (equity), and stabilization functions and branches of governments. The efficiency argument rests on the assumption or observation that there are uneven spillover flows between jurisdictions consequent on the supply of goods and services by "junior" governments, and that in the absence of what are, in effect, Pigouvian subsidies,[4] these spillovers would lead to non-optimal provisions of goods and services. The Breton (1965) study is the first formulation of this argument, although the most often quoted source is Oates (1972). However, the argument is now entrenched in many textbooks.

The equity argument has two strands. According to one of them, if the level of income in a jurisdiction is so low that its government cannot match the "fiscal residuum"[5] (Buchanan 1950) ruling in other jurisdictions without provoking destabilizing mobility, the central government – necessarily less affected by this type of mobility because of the spatial dimension of its jurisdiction – should equalize fiscal residuums by using income redistributive intergovernmental transfers. The second strand is based on the assumption or the fact that fiscal capacities, needs, or both differ between jurisdictions, and that these differences call for some form of equalization payments from governments situated at one jurisdictional level to those inhabiting another.

Straddling the standard efficiency and equity arguments just outlined and, in a way, intersecting both the argument is advanced by Flatters, Henderson, and Mieszkowksi (1974) and extended by Boadway and Flatters (1982a, 1982b). They argue that if junior governments provide goods and services whose "span" (to use Breton and Scott's (1978) word)[6] is less than national – namely, goods and services that are private and/or congestible – and if per capita residence-based public revenues are larger in some jurisdictions than in others because of, let us say, an uneven endowment of taxable marketable natural resources, intergovernmental transfers should be used to eliminate inefficient mobility between jurisdictions. The central government, then, should tax the jurisdictions that are rich in natural resources and transfer the proceeds to those that are poor, thus permitting both to adopt taxation and expenditure patterns that eliminate the inter-jurisdictional mobility of labour that would otherwise occur. These efficiency grants, incidentally, would also contribute to an equalitarian equity objective because they lead to transfers from rich to poor jurisdictions.

In their monograph on the division of powers and the assignment of these powers to governments at different jurisdictional tiers, Breton and Scott (1978) argued that it was unlikely that the minimization of organizational costs – the cost of public administration and of intergovernmental coordination on the one hand, and the cost of signalling preferences and of mobility incurred by citizens to ensure that their preferences would be attended to on the other – would lead to an assignment of powers that would guarantee to all governments revenues and expenditures that, in equilibrium, would match each other. A cost-minimizing-constituent assembly or a social-welfare-maximizing ethical observer or planner would have to create a degree of vertical imbalance and a corresponding flow of funds between governments to ensure that the organization of the governmental system economizes on the use of scarce resources.[7]

To complete the discussion, let me note that stabilization of overall economic activity may call for cyclical budgetary imbalance at the national level, but, as a matter of logic, it precludes a corresponding converse imbalance at other jurisdictional levels. It is not, therefore, related[8] to the problem of vertical imbalance and will not, as a consequence, further retain my attention in this paper.[9]

Let me begin my critique of the above explanations of vertical fiscal imbalance and the derived intergovernmental money flows by remarking that even if these two phenomena are features of all democratic federal systems of government, they are also attributes of democratic unitary states, all of which – the word unitary notwithstanding – are multi-tier governmental systems (see fn 1). Vertical imbalance is not, therefore, a reflection of a constitutionally entrenched division of powers that is too costly to change, either because of rigidities in the amending formula, or because of a lack of sufficient consent among decision makers. In unitary states, the power to alter the division of powers is unambiguously nested in the central government – that is why they are called unitary – so that interjurisdictional spillovers could be easily removed by reassigning the provision of the goods and services that cause the externalities to governments higher up in the system, thus eliminating, in one swoop, the need for intergovernmental transfers and the concomitant vertical fiscal imbalance.

Moreover, as Breton and Fraschini (1992) have documented, some unitary states, such as France and Spain, for a decade or so, have been doing exactly the opposite. Their central governments have significantly reduced the degree of expenditure concentration[10] in their respective governmental systems. We should conclude, therefore, if we adhere to the welfare economics credo, that they have wilfully created interjurisdictional spillovers that demand intergovernmental transfers that "cause" vertical imbalance and, one should no doubt add, that foster distortions, irresponsibility, illusion, and manipulation. Such long-term all-pervasive irrationality on the part of central governments cannot be presumed. It is imperative, therefore, that we ask why interjurisdictional spillovers exist or, more to the point, why they appear to be created by the multiplication of jurisdictional tiers.

The Breton-Scott (1978) model of the assignment of powers can be adopted easily and used to answer such a question. The argument would be developed along the following lines. A constituent assembly, attempting to minimize organizational costs – to repeat, the costs of administration and intergovernmental coordination as well as the costs of gauging the preferences of citizens, not the costs of producing and supplying goods and services – would sometimes elongate the governmental system by adding jurisdictional tiers. It would also increase vertical fiscal imbalance by assigning expenditure responsibilities to these new tiers, while maintaining all revenue responsibilities at the national level because that would economize on organizational resources. That line of reasoning is not only attractive, it is also, from a certain perspective, correct. The problem with it is that the postulated constituent assembly – like the planners and ethical observers who maximize social-welfare functions and the decision makers who operate behind veils of ignorance – does not have any empirical or institutional counterpart. It is possible to dispense with the notion of a constituent assembly by adopting a theory of competitive governmental systems of which the theory of competitive federalism is a special case (see Breton 1989b). I shall sketch that theory below; I make reference to it at this point to introduce the second criticism I wish to level at the explanation of vertical imbalance erected in the presence of interjurisdictional spillovers.

Assume, to begin, that there are at least two levels of government in a particular governmental system and that all the governments of the system – let me call them federal and provincial whether they be the governments of federal or of unitary states – provide goods and services[11] to citizens from whom they raise revenues to pay for these supplies. Assume, further, that all these governments maximize a well-behaved index of political power that increases as the volume of expected votes granted by citizens increases. As a consequence, they are led to compete with each other.[12] Competition will force each government to specialize in the supply of the goods and services in which it is relatively efficient, that is, in the supply of the goods and services it can provide at tax prices[13] that the other governments cannot match. We should, therefore, expect the goods and services whose "benefit spans" exceed the domain or territory of a particular government – but are within the domain of the whole governmental system – to be supplied by the federal government or by one or more "coalitions" of provincial governments. Such action would enable supply tax prices to be brought to their competitive level in the same way that in competitive markets economies of scale that are external to firms, but internal to the industry, are internalized and the supply of goods and services made to reflect the opportunity cost of resources. In a competitive model of that genre, vertical imbalance and inter-governmental transfers could exist (see the following section), but they would not be generated by interjurisdictional spillovers.

The foregoing should not be understood to imply that in competitive governmental systems all externalities are always internalized. There are costs to the formation of "coalitions"; they may degenerate into colluding oligopolies; barriers to entry to coalitions may exist and so on. Still, the presumption cannot be that provincial governments will deal with spillovers only if they are paid to do so by a perfectly informed and disinterested higher-level planner. On the contrary, the presumption must be that competition will force them to act and, as the script says, force them to "do the right thing."

To summarize, the efficiency argument for vertical imbalance and intergovernmental transfers derived from welfare economics is based on three assumptions. First, an exogenously given or institutionally vacuous division of powers; second, the existence of interjurisdictional spillovers consequent on that division of powers; and third, the absence of intergovernmental competition. The way I have stated it, the third assumption is too vague. It is not only that competition is ruled out in the welfare economics paradigm, but that either cooperation, or a master-servant relationship between the federal and provincial governments is required. Indeed, the senior government, after having estimated the size of the externalities – more precisely, the size of the marginal damages (and/or of the marginal benefits) generated by the spillovers – must raise, in the most neutral way possible, the revenues required to deal with them and enter into an agreement with the provinces that will permit an implementation of the decision to internalize the spillovers. In unitary states, because master-servant rules often obtain, the "agreement" may reflect instructions of senior governments. In federal states, the agreement must presumably be cooperative because the federal government cannot, in general, impose its decisions on provincial or junior governments (see below, however, "The 'Constitutional' Dimension"). The third assumption, therefore, speaks of instructions from above, or of cooperation. Welfare economics begets autocracy or cooperation, at least as long as the division of powers begets spillovers.

These comments on competition and cooperation bring me to what may be called the Queen's explanation of vertical imbalance and transfers (both Henderson and Mieszkowksi were at Queen's when working on the problem, and Boadway and Flatters still are). This particular explanation is based on the view, acknowledged by some of its originators (see Boadway and Flatters 1982b, 6), that, from an economic perspective, the "ideal" form of government – that is, the one that is most conducive to efficiency and equity – is the single-tier unitary state (which, as has been noted already, does not exist). It is a simple matter to go from that view to the argument that in real-world governmental systems, any specific advantage that improves the relative efficiency of a junior government in supplying goods and services, and thus makes it more competitive, should be suppressed by taxing the advantage away and by transferring the proceeds to less well-endowed jurisdictions. The resulting vertical imbalance and flow of funds will inhibit the mobility of labour that the advantage, left untaxed, would have provoked. The argument can be put differently: the supply of goods and services and their tax prices should be exactly the same in a multi-tier as it would be in a single-tier system of government, and the role of intergovernmental transfers is to ensure that this result obtains.

Vertical imbalance and intergovernmental transfers, though they extinguish intergovernmental competition, are not, in the Queen's approach, motivated by that objective. They have a different purpose: to recapture (capture?) the efficiency and equity properties of markets and of single-tier unitary states. Intergovernmental competition is not needed for this goal, nor is cooperation. In this case, welfare economics begets only itself. It is worth adding that if intergovernmental competition is required for efficiency in governmental systems, the Queen's approach to vertical imbalances and to transfers, by sacrificing that competition to achieve efficiency in labour markets, can make society worse off than it would otherwise be.

The income redistribution argument for vertical fiscal imbalance and intergovernmental transfers that derives from welfare economics can be sustained only if it is assumed that senior or "donor" governments suffer from systematic chronic irrationality. Why? Because intergovernmental transfers are not an efficient instrument for redistributing income in comparison with interpersonal transfers, namely, transfers from person to person mediated by a government, or another agency.

It is well to recall at the outset that, in most societies, income redistribution policy is embodied in a variety of welfare programs based on: the age; the employment situation; the family status; the health conditions and other characteristics of the individuals; families; and groups that are recipients. Proposals to "streamline" these programs often have been made by academics and others on the basis of research that shows, one supposes, that they are inefficient. Akerlof (1978) has shown, however, that a strong case can be made that the patchwork of programs forming the income redistribution policy of societies is more efficient than some proposed "streamlined" systems would be, because, for any given volume of redistribution, the excess burden[14] of the revenues needed to pay for it is smaller in the patchwork than in the streamline systems. What Akerlof calls "tagging," namely, the use of certain characteristics to identify the individuals and groups in need, is simply a device that ensures that resources are not transferred to those who are not in need.

On the basis of the foregoing, one would have to conclude that, from an income redistribution point of view, intergovernmental transfers are inefficient because some governments of jurisdictions in which rich and poor citizens reside receive funds, whereas other governments of jurisdictions in which rich and poor citizens also reside do not receive any funds only because average per capita income, for example, is lower in the first than in the second. Intergovernmental transfers, in other words, are inconsistent with "tagging" and, therefore, with efficient behaviour. Before concluding that governments are irrational, however, it is well to consider the possibility that intergovernmental transfers are not used for the purpose or goal of redistributing incomes between persons. That objective is pursued through the use of interpersonal redistribution programs, while intergovernmental transfers are a response to a different set of forces. If that is the case, welfare economics would beget nothing.

If the achievement of a particular distribution of income has to be left, on grounds of efficiency, to interpersonal transfers (which, also for reasons of efficiency, will be effected by governments), the need to equalize the capacity to compete between governments may sometimes call for intergovernmental transfers. (The need to distinguish between "fiscal capacity" and redistribution is also recognized by Walsh 1992). Breton (1991) has shown that horizontal or intra-tier competition (see fn 11) between governments can lead to unstable equilibrium outcomes. Intergovernmental transfers are one way of achieving stability. In general, these transfers should be unconditional (see, however, the second section, second subsection). Breton (1991) and Breton and Fraschini (1992) have called these transfers "stabilizing payments" (not to be confused with the stabilization grants, discussed in fn 7) and distinguish them from "revenue payments," introduced and analysed in the next section. To put the matter differently, in equilibrium, there are *only* two types of transfers from senior to junior governments: stabilizing transfers and revenue transfers. In Canada, at present, the equalization payments are of the first type, while the Established Programs Financing and the Canada Assistance Plan are of the second type. Incidentally, it is the stabilizing transfers that are entrenched in section 36 of the Canadian Constitution (1982). Both types of transfers have income redistribution effects, but, in a model of competitive governmental systems, it is not these effects that motivate their existence. I pay no further attention to stabilizing transfers in this paper (I have examined them in Breton 1991).

An Alternative Explanation

To be sure that it is not an exogenously given, constitutionally entrenched division of powers that creates vertical imbalance and intergovernmental transfers, I rule out such entrenchment. I also exclude all divisions of powers imposed by constituent assemblies of any kind or by the central governments of multi-tier unitary states. In other words, I assume that there are no barriers, legal or otherwise, to the emergence of any divisions of powers called forth by the competition of governments engaged in producing and supplying goods and services to the citizens of a particular country. (I look at these barriers briefly, below under "The 'Constitutional' Dimension.") To establish this proposition, I will make use of and ask the reader to refer to two closely related developments in microeconomic theory. The first examines the forces that lead competitive firms to specialize, that is, to distribute functions among themselves. The second is concerned with some of the implications of incomplete and implicit contracts between persons who, for whatever reason, cannot trust each other; these contracts, in such circumstances, must be self-enforcing.

These two models of microeconomics can, I shall attempt to show, generate a division of powers between "spatially" positioned governments that will, in general, display vertical imbalance and the consequent flow of funds. These models will also explain why the intergovernmental transfers have a number of the characteristics they possess.

The Technical Dimension

More than forty years ago, Stigler (1951), on the (implicit) assumption (made explicit in Stigler 1966, ch. 9; 1987, ch. 10) that the costs of market and of intraorganizational transactions were given, suggested that the division of functions between firms and industries is determined by "the extent of the market" or by the volume of production.[15] The argument is simple. A raw material is subjected to a large number of transformations on its way to becoming a final product. Each of these transformations is associated with a production process or function. To understand how they are divided among firms, assume that some functions are subject to increasing, others to decreasing, and still others to increasing and then to decreasing returns to scale. As the size of the market grows, firms will "seek to delegate decreasing and increasing cost functions to independent (auxiliary) industries" (Stigler 1987, 172). Why? Because such "delegation" will reduce the unit cost of the firm's output. Consider the case of decreasing costs. Given that a number of functions in a firm are subject to increasing costs, that firm will not be able to exploit the economies of scale of a decreasing cost function because expanding the output would cause the aggregate average cost of that output to rise. However, by "delegating" the decreasing cost function (i.e., by specializing) to another firm, the "delegator" can allow the "delegatee" to concentrate on that function for the whole market, that is, for a larger number of firms – indeed, from an increasingly large number of firms as the "extent of the market" increases – and, thus, reduce the average cost of its output. Ceteris paribus, competition, then, induces the delegating firm to an ever greater degree of specialization as output increases.

I would like to suggest that the de facto division of powers in the kind of governmental system that I am, for the moment, postulating is governed by similar forces. The average costs of goods and services and of revenue collection are determined, in part, by the same kind of factors determining the average costs of market-provided goods and services, which I shall call "technical," and, for another part, by considerations peculiar to governmental delivery that have to be brought into the picture, which I shall call "institutional." Focusing on the technical factors, we should expect that for some functions or powers (i.e., expenditure, regulatory, redistribution, stabilization, and revenue collection) unit costs will rise, while for others they will fall. For others still, they will fall and then, after some point, rise as the volume of output or the size of jurisdiction varies. Ceteris paribus, competition will lead to specialization in governmental systems as it does in market systems, owing to increases in the size of systems.

With reference to the more conventional or technical factors affecting the behaviour of average cost as size varies, consider, by way of illustration, the case of tax collection. The administration (assessment and collection), enforcement (random auditing), and compliance costs related to the performance of this function are influenced, to a significant extent, by the need for large initial set-up expenditures (e.g., personnel, computers, storage facilities) and by "learning by doing" – all factors that imply decreasing costs as output increases (see Alchian 1959 and Arrow 1962). To illustrate for other functions, it is sufficient to evoke the large variance in the distribution of the technical "spans" of the goods and services provided by governments – a variance that implies that the behaviour of average costs as output flows vary will also vary, decreasing for some goods and services, remaining constant for others, and increasing for still others.

When we turn our attention from the technical factors determining the behaviour of the average costs of providing the goods and services historically associated with the expenditure, regulatory, redistributive, stabilization, and tax collection functions of governments towards the factors that are institutional and specific to non-market[16] and particularly to governmental supplies, two appear to be especially important: (a) the capacity to reduce utility losses originating in public provision,[17] and (b) the ability to control free-riding.

To simplify, assume that the tax price of a good or service (marginal equals average) must be taken as given by any government, in the same way that prices are taken as given in competitive markets. It is then easy to show that the size of the utility loss (or excess burden) of the provision of a good or service – different from the optimal quantity for each individual at the given tax price – increases as that difference increases. If we also assume that the expected votes that citizens grant to a particular government increases as utility losses inflicted by that government decrease and falls as the losses inflicted by other governments rise, and if we assume that governments maximize expected votes, we have to conclude that they compete with each other to provide goods and services in quantities that match as closely as possible the quantities desired by citizens.

We could say that competition makes governments responsive to the preferences of citizens. Remember, however, that all governments are assumed to be maximizing an objective function. If, therefore, there is any difference in the responsiveness of governments – as is assumed when it is asserted that local governments are more responsive than governments higher up in the jurisdictional structure – such difference cannot be imputed to motivation or to effort, but must be the result of constraints operating differentially on the objective functions (e.g., the fact that the preferences of the citizens inhabiting the jurisdictions of senior governments are generally less homogeneous than those of the citizens living in the jurisdictions of junior governments). Another factor consistent with the model outlined above pertains to the cost of obtaining information about the preferences of citizens. Such information does, indeed, allow governments to reduce the size of the utility losses inflicted on citizens and, in this way, increases expected votes. Relative inefficiency on the part of a government in supplying a particular good or service could arise, therefore, from relatively greater difficulties in obtaining information about the preferences of citizens.

It is possible that lower-level governments (local and provincial) can obtain information more easily about the preferences of citizens. It is important to stress, however, that this supposition is an assumption, not an empirically established proposition. It appears that there are, significant economies of scale in polling, canvassing, and consulting generally, and there could be economies of size in interest groups or demand lobbies whose function, among many, is to offer information to governments on the preferences of citizens (see Pross 1986). All this runs counter to the "closer to the people" argument. Furthermore, cliques, family compacts, and other cabals that discriminate against some individuals or groups may be easier to create at the local level. The point of the foregoing is not that lower-level governments are not responsive or are less responsive to the preferences of citizens than other differentially located governments, but instead that the ability to obtain and to use information about preferences is likely to vary with governments, with time periods, and with levels of operation.

Before going on to the problem of free-riding, let me note that the factors identified so far will generally lead to a very complex, and efficient, division of powers between governments. Competition is not likely to generate a neat, airtight assignment of functions such as that called for by Wheare (1963). Instead, we should expect different governments to be involved in different aspects of functions such as police protection, road building, international affairs, arts and culture, financial regulation, administration of justice, housing, day care, education, and health care. And, indeed, to the extent that collusion has not erected barriers to competition, that is, in fact, what we observe to be the case. Under competition, concurrency – joint occupation of powers – is the rule.

It is possible to be brief on the matter of free-riding. Buchanan (1967) has shown that when "tax institutions" such as tax rates, tax brackets, exemptions, and credits are given, individuals do not free-ride by misrepresenting their preferences. Buchanan was preoccupied with strategic behaviour in the presence of public goods; as a consequence, he did not consider that with given "tax institutions," individuals free-ride by engaging in tax avoidance and evasion. If, recognizing that fact, we now assume that the incidence of tax avoidance and evasion increases with the mobility of tax bases, and that the mobility is greater the larger the number of jurisdictions in a given territory, it follows that the capacity to control free-riding increases with the size of jurisdictions. Put differently, there are economies of size in controlling tax avoidance and evasion. Some tax bases are easier to move than others, so that the economies of size will differ between bases, but, as a general proposition, under competition there will be pressures to economize on resources allocated to tax collection by exploiting size economies (for a more detailed discussion, see Breton and Fraschini 1992).

The picture emerging from the foregoing discussion is one in which competitive pressures lead to the vertical integration of some functions, and to the vertical "disintegration" (Stigler's (1968, 135) word) of others. More specifically, the picture taking form is one of more concentration in revenue collection than in the provision of the goods and services associated with the expenditure, regulatory, and redistribution powers. We must recognize, however, that a high level of revenue concentration can be achieved in one of two ways: (a) lower level – local and provincial – governments can "delegate" (making use again of Stigler's (1968, 172) language) all or part of the revenue-collection function to a more senior government and, through this choice, give rise to a governmental system characterized by vertical imbalance and intergovernmental flows of funds from the "top" to the "bottom"; or (b) they may decide to create their own tax collection agency. If economies of scale in tax collection are at all significant, the first alternative will, ceteris paribus, be chosen because the second – though it leads to the exploitation of some economies of scale – results in one that is necessarily less than what is possible when the collection of the senior government's revenue is also part of the package. The ceteris paribus assumption refers to problems of tax harmonization and will be addressed in the next subsection.

Lower-level governments will "delegate" the revenue collection function to a more senior government *only* if doing so makes it possible for them to deliver goods and services to their citizens at lower unit costs and, through the consequent reduction in (marginal) tax prices, to minimize the utility losses inflicted on these same citizens. That course of action, I suggest, will be possible only if senior (sometimes federal and sometimes provincial) and junior governments (sometimes provincial and sometimes local) can enter into contractual agreements that make it possible for the first to guarantee that taxes will be efficiently collected *and* efficiently transferred to the second. In other words, if an enforceable contract cannot be drawn up, the competition driven by the technical and institutional factors calling for a greater degree of revenue concentration than of expenditure concentration will not be allowed to yield its beneficial effects. The outcomes of competition, then, must be embedded in enforceable contracts.

Putting the problem of enforceable contracts aside for a moment, let me conclude the present discussion by asking whether vertical imbalance and intergovernmental transfers should be analysed, as I have done, as a manifestation of competition operating to exhaust the benefits of technical and institutional factors or, following Brennan and Buchanan (1983), as manifestations of cartelization (cooperation?) and monopoly? Brennan and Buchanan conceive of a situation in which lower-level governments *"cede* their powers to tax to a higher level of government in return for an appropriate share in the total revenue: the whole intergovernmental grant/revenue-sharing structure can then be treated as a means of sharing the profits from political cartelization" (62, my italics). As a consequence of the reassignment of the power to tax, the higher level of government becomes a monopolist; lower-level governments, therefore, will no longer engage in beneficial tax competition.

It is always difficult to decide whether a particular phenomenon is a reflection of competition, or of monopoly. Take the celebrated cases of resale price maintenance and exclusive territories that, for a long time, were taken to be prima facie evidence of monopoly in the marketplace but are now seen as consistent with, nay, called for by, competition (see, for example, Klein and Murphy 1988). Stigler (1968, 133) recognized that the "delegated" decreasing cost process would make the receiving firm, the delegatee, at least temporarily, into a monopolist. He also noted, however, that it would be a monopoly facing very elastic demands because it could not charge a higher price for its output than the average cost of that output to the firm ceding it. Lower-level governments are in the same kind of relationship with the higher-level monopoly one.

As the language used by Brennan and Buchanan (italicized above) makes clear, the monopoly of the federal government is not achieved by force or capture, but by cession of, or delegation from, junior governments. In such a model, as distinguished from that of Brennan and Pincus (1990), to which I return below, the lower-level governments are (implicitly) identified, in my view correctly, as the principals, and the federal government as the agent in a principal-agent relationship. That kind of modelling, except of the most fragile variety and of a kind that brings about a more efficient allocation of resources, is inconsistent with cartelization and monopoly (see below, however, "The 'Constitutional' Dimension").

The Contractual Dimension

It is central to a proper understanding of intergovernmental arrangements, when the relations between the governments of multi-tier systems are competitive, to recognize that all governments stand to gain, that is, stand to increase the volume of the expected votes granted them by citizens, only if a contract can be drawn up effectively. In other words, the impossibility of a contract that makes it possible for senior governments to collect taxes, and for junior governments to spend the proceeds, would mean that both the senior and junior governments would be granted fewer votes by citizens, because the size of the utility loss inflicted on them (the citizens) would increase with regard to the goods and services supplied by both groups of government.

Before we discuss the nature and characteristics of intergovernmental contractual arrangements, it is important to note that when efficient low-cost provision of goods and services requires that revenue concentration exceed expenditure concentration, the resulting vertical fiscal imbalance can be accommodated in at least two ways. First, the senior government can act as a revenue collection agency for the junior governments, much in the way the federal government in Canada, through the tax collection agreements, does for the provinces (except Quebec) in respect of the personal income tax. Henceforth, I shall call the sums thus collected by senior governments and returned to junior governments *remittances*. Second, the senior government can raise revenues that it delivers to the junior governments as conditional transfers. I shall call these second sums *revenue transfers*.[18]

Intergovernmental contracts relating to vertical fiscal imbalance and to the resulting flow of funds between governments are both incomplete and implicit. A complete contract would specify all relevant contingencies over the life of the contract, foresee a course of action for each of these contingencies, deny the signatories the possibility of renegotiation so as not to deprive the original agreement of its credibility, and provide for each contingency before the contract is signed – a dispute settlement mechanism that is satisfactory to all parties. Given these requirements, most contracts are incomplete. If incomplete contracts are supplemented with unarticulated and generally shared expectations and understandings, they are said to be implicit.

The idea that relations between governments, regarding intergovernmental flows of funds, possess characteristics that place them (the relations) in the category of incomplete and implicit contracts is not new. It can be traced back at least to the work of McGuire (1975, 1979) and to that of Zampelli (1986). Recently, Brennan and Pincus (1990) have argued that contracts regulating grants from federal to provincial governments contain tacit "provisos, riders, or contingencies" (129) and that, as a consequence, all grants are conditional. The tacit "provisos, riders, or contingencies" imply, in other words, that in the conventional framework of analysis, all grants possess substitution as well as income effects. Brennan and Pincus, in effect, tell us that "donors" are neither disinterested nor neutral regarding the sums they grant. They do not tell us, however, why these "donors" are concerned and interested in the behaviour of recipients. Indeed, Brennan and Pincus, like McGuire and Zampelli, though they allude to or make use of the concept of implicit contracts, do not use the rich economic theory that has developed regarding these contracts.

In the present context – where senior governments are hired, in effect, by junior governments to collect their revenues – incomplete and implicit contracts have two facets. First, even if the principals, the junior governments, monitor their agent, the senior government, and observe a degree of shirking in tax collection, they cannot demonstrate to a third party, such as a court, that the senior government has, indeed, breached the contract and caused them damages. It is in this sense that the contract is said to be non-verifiable. Incompleteness and implicitness can also mean – and that is the second facet of these contracts – that reverse cheating is possible: principals can breach contracts just as well as agents. Specifically, junior governments can renege on contractual undertakings – specified below – as much as senior governments can.

If, as is dictated by the assumption of non-verifiability, enforcement by third parties is not possible, and if trust is ruled out on the ground that intergovernmental relations are too sporadic and short term for trust to form the basis of long-term enforcement, contractual relations will be possible only if contracts are self-enforcing. Self-enforcement requires that both principals (in the case under analysis, junior governments, namely, provincial or municipal) and agents (federal or provincial governments) credibly commit to perform the tasks specified in the implicit contractual agreement. Put differently, each must be seen by the other as having something to lose from the termination of the contract consequent on non-performance.

If junior governments choose to rely on a self-enforcing contract, they must be able to create a valuable stream of (political) quasi-rents[19] and deliver that stream to the senior government. The capital loss the principals can then impose on the agent by extinguishing that stream will be sufficient to induce the latter to perform as long as the present value of the delivered stream exceeds the present value of the advantages of non-performance. Can junior governments create such streams of quasi-rents? The answer to this question is "yes"; a demonstration of the affirmation requires, however, that we distinguish between remittances and revenue transfers.

In the case of remittances – the sums returned by the senior to the junior governments on the basis of some revenue collection agreement – the quasi-rents are created, as already noted, by the exploitation of economies of scale consequent on the greater capacity of senior governments to control tax avoidance and evasion.[20] Indeed, to a considerable degree, avoidance and evasion are functions of the mobility of tax bases – personal and corporate incomes, capital, sales, etc. – and that mobility will, in general, be less the larger the size of jurisdictions. I have examined earlier, with Fraschini (1992), that facet of economies of scale in some detail; I shall pay no further attention to it here. Instead, I shall focus on a second aspect of these economies of scale, namely, that associated with the institutions and technologies of tax collection proper. Before turning my attention to this matter, I note that the quasi-rents created by remittances will be greater the larger the fraction of their own tax revenues that junior governments delegate for collection to the senior government. Indeed, given the presence of the economies of scale, the unit cost of tax funds *to the senior government* will diminish as that fraction increases.

The size of the economies of scale associated with the institutions and technologies of tax collection will depend on the extent to which common definitions for variables such as income, tax brackets, deductions, exemptions, and credits can be adopted by the contracting parties – or the extent to which the junior governments, in Walsh's (1991, 11) words, choose to "piggyback" on the tax system of the senior government. The size of economies of scale will, in fact, depend on the degree of *tax harmonization*.

Notwithstanding the existence of a sizeable, though largely normative-prescriptive literature on the subject, tax harmonization remains a poorly understood phenomenon. For example, the marginal cost to the federal government of administering special provisions in the income tax act for each province is not likely to be large – depending on nothing more than a little more complexity in computer programs and on the addition of a few extra clerks and tax auditors – so that the federal government could easily administer a separate rate for every deduction, credit, or special provision it currently has in its personal income tax by simply mailing different forms to people depending on their province of origin.[21]

The relationship between the size of economies of scale in tax collection and tax harmonization, though real, does not appear very strong. Still, as Winer (1992) remarked, in discussing the likelihood that Ontario would harmonize its own retail sales tax with the federal government's Goods and Services Tax (GST), it is not "expensive for [the government of] Ontario to selectively grant sales tax relief to any Ontario firm that finds itself under increased pressure from a Quebec competitor. Such fine-tuning of a tax base is far cheaper than the establishment of an entirely new tax, and, it is normal practice for precisely this reason" (359). Winer's point that the short-term marginal costs of fine-tuning the tax base are low must, however, be contrasted with the fact that the long-term marginal benefits of harmonization, resulting from the substantial reduction in marginal compliance costs,[22] would be significant. What then prevents harmonization of the sales taxes?

Tax harmonization has benefits – the reduction in the average and marginal costs of tax revenues to both the federal and the provincial governments – but it also has costs:

- it is the product of an exercise in coordination and, as such, absorbs scarce resources;
- it constrains junior governments by reducing or even suppressing their autonomy to exploit monopolistic or quasi-monopolistic advantages[23] and/or to overcome idiosyncratic disadvantages; and
- it inhibits the capacity of junior governments to compete with other governments located at the same jurisdictional level.

The costs of coordination depend on the number of jurisdictions that have to be party to an agreement to make that agreement worthwhile. These costs will increase, possibly more than proportionally, as numbers increase. Coordination costs will also depend on precedents, on conventions derived from historical compromises, and on the distance initially separating the contracting parties. Loss of autonomy will be small, possibly nil, for a jurisdiction that possesses no "natural" advantage that could be exploited, or no "natural" disadvantage that could be surmounted by adopting tax measures that departed from those incorporated in a tax harmonization agreement. But if a jurisdiction possesses a real monopolistic advantage that it could exploit, or a specific disadvantage that it could void by special tax measures, the loss in autonomy caused by tax harmonization could be a significant cost. The capacity to compete which, as Winer (quoted above) reminds us, depends on a host of factors – including the ability to fine-tune tax bases as well as credits, deductions, exemptions, and other provisions of the tax code – will be reduced by tax harmonization. This diminished capacity could impose much heavier costs on some jurisdictions than on others. The need to compete and, therefore, the cost of tax harmonization may also be less in the presence of efficient regional development policies implemented by senior governments.

The decision to harmonize and the degree of tax harmonization, as a consequence, will be the outcome of a balancing of discounted benefits and costs. Countries and/or jurisdictions in which the expected benefits from the economies of scale in tax collection are large may still rationally shun tax harmonization completely if the number of jurisdictions having to coordinate is large, and/or the costs of lost autonomy and the hindrance to competition are significant. These countries and jurisdictions will be characterized by a low degree of revenue concentration. At the other end of the spectrum, countries and/or jurisdictions in which the benefits from harmonization are small may still rationally harmonize if the number of jurisdictions is small, and if none possesses significant unique advantages or disadvantages and a specific capacity to compete. In these countries and jurisdictions, the degree of revenue concentration will be relatively high.

These considerations can explain why, in the presence of significant economies of scale resulting from the greater capacity of senior governments to control the avoidance and evasion that depend on the mobility of tax bases, junior governments may not delegate tax collection to senior governments. It would be relatively easy to document, I believe, that the refusal of the Canadian provinces to harmonize their sales taxes with the GST, the decision of the governments of Alberta, Ontario, and Quebec to collect their own corporation income taxes and, in part (for the rest of the explanation, see below), the decision of the government of Quebec to withdraw from the tax collection agreements in respect of the personal income tax can be explained by one or more of the above factors. For example, in the opinion of Strick (1985, 93), and of Musgrave, Musgrave, and Bird (1987, 381), whom I quote, Alberta, Ontario, and Quebec "tend to consider them [the corporate tax rate differentials] a major factor [in location decisions] and therefore engage in low-rate competition to attract capital."

The same kind of considerations can explain why, in recent years, in the words of Bird and Mintz (1992, 24), "the provinces have become increasingly critical of the income tax collection agreements and have sought autonomy in the income tax field." The drive to compete has been growing, in good measure, as a result of the virtual elimination of regional development policies, itself a consequence, on the one hand, of an ideological bias against regional policies on the part of the federal government and, on the other, of the reinforcing ban on such policies inscribed in the free-trade treaty with the United States.

In delegating tax collection to the senior government, the junior governments create a stream of quasi-rents that *can* benefit that senior government. It *will* benefit that government, however, only if a particular condition is satisfied. To appreciate what that condition is, consider what would happen, in an admittedly extreme case, if the institutional and technical factors discussed in the previous subsection called for a division of powers that demanded the tax revenues of the entire governmental system be raised by the senior government and that all of them be spent by the junior governments. The only expense of the senior government under these circumstances would be remittances to the junior governments. As a consequence, the value of low-cost tax funds to the senior government would be zero, and so would the value of the stream of quasi-rents. In other words, only if the senior government provides some goods and services to citizens can it itself benefit from the low unit cost of tax funds. Indeed, these benefits will rise as the volume of goods and services supplied increases, or, in other words, the value of the stream of political quasi-rents increases as expenditures concentration increases.

More generally, if the institutional and technical factors governing the division of powers call for a low degree of expenditure concentration, and if there are economies of scale in tax collection that could technically be exploited, the required volume of remittances may be so large, and the value of the stream of political quasi-rents accruing to the senior government consequently so low, that that stream would be unable to ensure performance on the part of that government. To guarantee performance – to prevent or, more precisely, to control shirking, negligence, and other forms of inefficient behaviour in tax collection – the volume of remittances will have to be reduced below the level that would be technically possible in a world in which the cost of ensuring performance was zero. Differently worded, the inherent conflict between the benefits of a high degree of revenue concentration and the benefits of a low degree of expenditure concentration implies that there are limits in the extent to which remittances can be used to create a stream of valuable political quasi-rents that can be delivered to the senior government to ensure performance.

The volume of remittances will be determined, therefore, by two factors: (a) the benefits, net of costs of tax harmonization to the junior governments; and (b) the value of reductions in the unit cost of tax revenues to the senior government. If, for example, the expenditures of the senior government on own goods and services decline significantly, so that low-cost tax funds generate only a limited stream of quasi-rents, and, if the cost of harmonization increases, senior and junior governments may not be able to enter into contractual arrangements in respect of remittances that would permit much exploitation of the economies of scale in tax collection called for by the technical and institutional factors alone.

Does that limit on the volume of remittances imply that relevant economies of scale in tax collection cannot be exploited and/or that the degree of expenditure concentration has to be greater than that called for by the division of powers reflecting the relative technical and institutional supply efficiency of competing governments? The answer is "no." All economies of scale in tax collection can be exploited, and the competitively determined, optimal division of powers can be achieved by making use of what I have called earlier revenue transfers. These transfers, then, permit the exploitation or, if remittances already exist, the further exploitation of economies of scale in tax collection, and they allow junior governments to spend the sums transferred on goods and services that they produce and deliver relatively efficiently.

The revenue transfers must be conditional, however, and the conditions have to be specified in terms of particular goods and services supplied. Why? Remember that the problem remains one of ensuring that the senior government finds it in its own interest to abide by the terms of an implicit contract and to act as an efficient tax collector for the junior governments. That can happen only if the revenue transfers create a sufficiently large stream of political quasi-rents or, in other words, can generate a sufficiently large stream of expected votes for the senior government that it will not want to risk losing it through non-performance. In the first instance, therefore, these conditions will attach the revenue transfers to goods and services in high demand and for which demand is relatively easy to estimate, thus reducing the utility losses resulting from supply. Typically, these goods and services will be educational services, health and hospital care, vocational and other forms of training, transportation services, care of the blind and of other disabled persons, and so on. Of course, as times and circumstances change, the demand for goods and services may change, and/or the volume demanded may become more difficult to appraise – thus increasing the chances of providing quantities and qualities that differ more markedly from those desired – and the conditions that attach to the revenue transfers may also change.

Two complementary points should be made. First, the conditions that attach to the transfers are willed by the junior governments; these are the governments who wish to create the stream of political quasi-rents for the benefit of the senior government. Second, the senior government will, as a rule, have a say in the formulation of the conditions, and will monitor how well the conditions are adhered to simply because the conditions are the factors that cause the stream of quasi-rents accruing to them to be created. The available evidence indicates that the conditions are, indeed, negotiated as suggested above. (See, e.g., Bella 1979; Chernick 1979; and Strick 1971).

Two other problems must be addressed to complete the analysis. The above discussion tells us that junior governments are capable of creating a stream of political quasi-rents to induce the senior government to exploit the relevant economies of scale in tax collection, and to pay the sums collected to junior governments either as remittances and/or as revenue transfers. That discussion did not tell us, however, why the senior government could expect the junior governments to abide by their side of the contract. First, it did not tell us why the senior governments should expect the junior governments to continue to deliver the stream of quasi-rents they are capable of creating if circumstances change in such a way that it becomes advantageous for them not to deliver. Second, it did not tell us why junior governments would be efficient suppliers of the goods and services to which the conditions of the revenue transfers attach. Both problems are easily dealt with; I consider them in turn.

Junior governments must not only be able to create a stream of political quasi-rents for the benefit of the senior government, they must also be able to make a credible commitment that they will continue to deliver that stream, provided the senior government does not shirk tax collection. Such a commitment is possible for both remittances and revenue transfers if the costs to the junior governments of raising their own revenues – forgoing the economies of scale in tax collection – exceed the sums that have to be paid to the senior government for the collection service *plus* the costs, expressed in comparable monetary units, of creating the political quasi-rents.

We therefore have some more reasons for the possibility of what may be called "contractual failure" in addition to those suggested in the earlier discussion of the benefits and costs of tax harmonization to the junior governments and of the value of lower tax revenues to the senior governments. Indeed, if economies of scale in tax collection are relatively small, if the supply price of tax collection is relatively high, and/or if the costs of creating quasi-rents are relatively high, it may not be possible to achieve the optimal division of powers that the institutional and technical factors discussed in the last subsection dictate. For example, in some federations, at certain times, because of widespread negative feelings vis-à-vis the senior government in one or more junior units, the costs of creating a flow of political quasi-rents for the benefit of that senior government are so high that these units will choose to forgo the benefits of a technically optimal division of powers. That situation, I suggest, is what led the government of the province of Quebec, as early as 1947, to seek control of the personal and corporate tax fields and to continue to stay out of the collection agreements. In general, such decisions inflict losses on the whole federation – the supply price of goods and services is higher for all – but the losses are larger for the unit or units choosing to collect their own taxes.

Turning to the second problem, specifically, the efficient performances of junior governments in supplying the goods and services to which the conditions of revenue transfers apply, it is sufficient to recognize that if the stream of political quasi-rents is appropriately divided between the senior and junior governments or, put differently, if the conditions that attach to the revenue transfers generate large enough political quasi-rents for both levels of government, junior governments will have an incentive to perform efficiently. To see why, consider what would happen if the whole stream of quasi-rents accrued to the senior government. Under such circumstances, the junior governments would have no incentive to be efficient providers of the goods and services "financed" by the revenue transfers. An appropriate division of the political surpluses is needed to deal with the reverse cheating problem.

The conventional model of intergovernmental grants based on the assumption that the origin of grants is exogenous to the analysis makes a prediction that has been tested empirically by a number of scholars (the classic paper is Gramlich 1977; see also, for a good survey of the empirical literature, Fisher 1982). The prediction is the following: if $X is received by a junior government in the form of an unconditional transfer, a fraction of $X will be spent on the goods and services supplied by that junior government, and the rest will serve to reduce taxes and thus lead to an increase in private- or market-supplied goods and services bought by citizens, as long as privately and publicly provided goods are normal goods.[24] When tested, the evidence indicated that if not all of $X, at least a larger fraction than expected is spent by junior governments and, as a consequence, relative to expectation, little takes the form of tax reductions. Gramlich (1977) called the anomaly the "flypaper effect," a colourful expression designed to describe the "fact" that money appears "to stick where it hits."

This paper does not deal with unconditional grants proper – with stabilizing transfers that I have associated earlier with equalization payments and revenue-sharing. Because of the position taken by Bird and others (see Musgrave, Musgrave, and Bird 1987, 512, and Bird and Mintz 1992, 22–23, from which I quote) that, in Canada at least, "so-called conditional grants programs (such as grants for education) actually have few conditions attached to them,"[25] it is legitimate to discuss the various views taken regarding the flypaper effect and to state what the model proposed here implies about it.

Early explanations of the flypaper effect appealed to fiscal illusion and to bureaucratic empire-building. More recently – in recognition, no doubt, of the inherent weakness of explanations based on assumptions of irrationality and inefficient behaviour – analysts have been arguing that, whatever the legal and formal terms in which grant programs are embodied, there are always provisos, often only implicit, that ensure all grants are matching conditional grants. In other words, in the conventional analysis, all grants have substitution effects. This is true whether they are formally unconditional or effectively untied as is the case – except for "corner" solutions or outcomes – with specific-purpose grants. Therefore, it becomes unnecessary to appeal to a flypaper effect to explain why money "sticks where it hits."

More recently still, Brennan and Pincus (1991), building on an earlier discovery of Fisher (1982), have argued that, because the citizens of a federation are citizens of both the junior and senior governments and, a fortiori, are taxpayers and consumers of the goods and services at the two jurisdictional levels, intergovernmental grants have no net income effects whatsoever, only substitution effects. Put differently, the positive income effect enjoyed by an individual in his or her role as a citizen of a grant-receiving junior government is cancelled by the negative income effect suffered by that same individual as a citizen of the grant-paying senior government. Redistributional effects may exist, but overall, the positive and negative income effects will cancel each other out to yield a zero net income effect. Brennan and Pincus (1991, 2) claim that the conventional model of intergovernmental grants is really a model of international aid, not one of federal aid.

The difficulty with the first "new" explanation of intergovernmental money flows – that based on implicit adjustments by recipients à la McGuire, or on implicit provisos by donors à la Brennan and Pincus – is that it provides no rationale for these flows (grants are exogenously determined), and it assumes that the decision-maker is always and exclusively the senior government. In the McGuire (1975; 1979) and Zampelli (1986) explanations, the junior governments, unhappy to be victims of particular grant programs they do not like, seek redress by disguised manipulations of the terms of the contract, and a hapless senior government does nothing about it. In the earlier explanation by Brennan and Pincus (1990), the senior government, unwilling to give funds without attaching strings to them, covertly ties conditions to the grant. Why a senior government would behave in this way is unclear; the simplest explanation is that they behave like empire-building leviathans. If so, the presumption must be that the outcome is socially inefficient.

According to Brennan and Pincus (1991), the existence of intergovernmental grants derives from the preferences of median voters, and from the assumption that the excess burden of federal tax funds is smaller than the excess burden of provincial tax funds. The explanation for the existence of unconditional grants rests on the assumption that there is a unique median voter – the same at the federal and provincial levels of government – who, through grants, economizes on the cost of tax revenues. These grants are, therefore, efficient. For matching grants, two different median voters are needed – one at each jurisdictional tier. It is assumed that the median voter at the federal level makes the grant. The resulting expenditure level and tax mix is inefficient. Brennan and Pincus appear to be headed in the direction of producing results not much different from those of conventional models, except that the income effect has been removed.

The model suggested in this study is based on an accepted theory of implicit contracts that rests on the assumption that all agents are rational and use resources efficiently. It does away with the assumption that federal-provincial relations, at least regarding intergovernmental flows of funds, are necessarily master-servant relations. It does not assume that intergovernmental flows of funds are Pigouvian subsidies aimed at interjurisdictional spillovers – a plus in a world in which that policy instrument is rarely, if ever, used. It does not assume that Pigouvian subsidies could not be used to deal with interjurisdictional spillovers. It is able to explain why the degree of expenditure and revenue concentration varies between governmental systems, and from period to period. It is able to explain why revenue and expenditure concentration usually differ and, therefore, why vertical fiscal imbalance and the accompanying flows of funds exist. It is capable of explaining why transfers from senior to junior governments are often conditional and efficient.[26] It is consistent with the observed fact that governmental systems are sometimes lengthened and sometimes contracted. It can explain why the degree of tax harmonization varies from time to time and from context to context. Finally, it establishes naturally that the flypaper effect is not an anomaly of the real world, only an anomaly of a particular theory.

The "Constitutional" Dimension

So far, in proposing an alternative hypothesis for understanding the problems of fiscal federalism, I have assumed that there were no barriers in the form of entrenched constitutional provisions or other legal or de facto arrangements to impede creative competitive responses to exogenous changes in technological, institutional, and contractual opportunities.[27] Barriers do, however, exist. Some of these may have a positive role to play regarding matters not related to the efficient provision of goods and services, but, as valuable as they may be in the pursuit of these other objectives, their negative effects on competition, on contracting, and on other matters, if such exist, must be recognized in a discussion of the efficient supply of goods and services. In what follows, I shall disregard the possible positive elements that may attach to some of the provisions and arrangements that act as barriers to competitive efficiency of supply to focus exclusively on the negative effects of these provisions and arrangements on the supply of goods and services by governmental systems. In addition, I shall be brief and schematic, because a complete treatment of the subject would require considerably more space than is at my disposal.

Consider the division of powers as it pertains to the expenditure, regulatory, and redistribution functions. Constitutional entrenchment in respect of these powers can become barriers if, for example, the assignment is so rigidly interpreted by the courts and the governments involved that the interpretation becomes an insuperable impediment to competition (and to de facto concurrency). Focus on the power pertaining to education as it has been interpreted by the Canadian courts and governments. Two things have resulted from that interpretation: first, a virtual monopoly of the power at the provincial level – it is true that the federal government supplies some component parts of educational services, but that is done through the provinces. Second, intergovernmental competition has been extinguished in this vital area, no doubt one reason the quality of educational output is so low in the country. (Recall that I neglect possible positive effects of that monopolization. If positive effects exist, the low quality of education is the price paid, presumably willingly, for these effects).

Rigid interpretation of assignments is only one barrier. Extremely detailed and precise assignments that, by their very nature, cannot be retailored easily to accommodate changing circumstances is another. Constitutionally entrenched asymmetric assignments, over which Canadians, lacking a theory of federalism, have so feverishly consulted their entrails in recent years, is yet another. The list could go on to include defective constitutional amending formulas, use by the courts of "inappropriate" constitutional doctrines, and so on.

By way of conclusion, let me mention one barrier that has been the occasion of much debate in Australia, namely, the monopoly of the commonwealth government over the income tax. This monopoly, many scholars have already remarked (see, e.g., Bird 1986 and Walsh 1992), has been the source of large flows of funds from the commonwealth to the state governments. The monopoly, which in what follows I presume to be complete, means that the transfers of funds are not the product of a voluntary contractual arrangement between the two levels of government. To be more precise, the transfers do not emanate from a verifiable contract that would stipulate that a less risk-averse (possibly risk-neutral) commonwealth government would ensure the more risk-averse state governments against unfavourable conditions of nature by promising a steady flow of funds in exchange for a premium. Nor do the transfers derive from an implicit (non-verifiable) contract of the type described in the preceding subsection and assumed to be the product of competitive intergovernmental relations.

Indeed, the (implicit) contract between the commonwealth and the states is of a kind that belongs to the class of master-servant contracts. In such a contract, the conditions that attach to the transfers are "imposed," no doubt very gently, on the junior governments by the senior government. The conditions are not there to produce a stream of political quasi-rents whose purpose is to induce the senior government to perform. Rather, they are "imposed" to generate a stream of monopoly rents with no political or economic purpose except exploitation. I believe that a very careful reading of the first Brennan and Pincus (1990) paper will reveal that they are, indeed, describing this kind of master-servant contract. On that reading, it is highly appropriate that the paper should have been included in an issue of *Publius* dedicated to Australian federalism!

Finally, one should note that if the Australian commonwealth's monopoly over that power was somehow broken, and if, by a strange turn of events, the flow of funds from the commonwealth to the states remained, as it is now, reflecting by accident the same assignment of powers under competition as under monopoly, the shift from a master-servant to a voluntary, though implicit, contract would be reflected in a multitude of changes in the conditions attached to the transfers, some barely ponderable, that would signal the passage to a more efficient organization of supply for the whole of the Australian governmental system.

Conclusion

This paper has attempted to do two things. First, to show that there is not much that can be retained from standard theory – which is largely derived from welfare economics – to understand fiscal federalism problems and, in particular, to explain vertical fiscal imbalance and intergovernmental transfers. This point is now widely recognized. Second, to offer an alternative explanation. The paper suggested that the way to look at imbalance and transfers in competitive governmental systems is as a reflection of specialization dictated by relative technical and institutional efficiencies in the delivery of goods and services, and by competition. The paper also suggested that the benefits of specialization derive from the possibility of contractual arrangements between governments. It was further argued that these contracts were necessarily non-verifiable and had, as a consequence, to be self-enforcing; that property was used to explain some of the more salient features of intergovernmental transfers and some of the problems in the subfield of fiscal federalism. It was finally argued that barriers to competition will diminish the benefits of specialization.

Notes

The first draft of this paper was prepared for the Ontario Fair Tax Commission and completed in January 1993. I am grateful for very helpful comments on an earlier draft of this paper to Michele Bernasconi, Geoffrey Brennan, Angela Fraschini, Brian Galligan, Emilio Gerelli, Allan Maslove, Kimberly Scharf, Cliff Walsh, and an anonymous reviewer.

1 As emphasized below, all democratic governmental systems have two, three, four, or even more levels of jurisdiction. Many of these systems are not federal under any moderately rigorous definition of this word. Indeed, countries like France, Italy, Spain, and the United Kingdom are generally presented as prototypical unitary states, yet most of them, the first three, have four tiers of elected governments. Because many of the principles governing the assignment of powers in a theory of competitive governmental systems apply to both federal and unitary states, however, the lack of rigour in the definition of the word federal is of small consequence. That is not the case, however, in standard discussions based on some presumed technical properties of public goods. The point will become clearer as we proceed.

2 Whenever economists are unable to explain how a real-world phenomenon is generated, they treat their models as normative and assert that the world should be organized along the lines suggested by them. Many discussions of topics in the theory of fiscal federalism alternate between descriptive and normative considerations without apparent difficulty.

3 This recognition has sometimes, notably in textbooks, produced strange results: for example, it has led to the presentation of one theory of intergovernmental grants based on a "welfare economics" rationale (see below) *and* another describing the effects of grants on the assumption that they are exogenously motivated, without emphasis on the disparity of approaches!

4 Pigouvian subsidies are sums equal to the (marginal) benefits or damages, depending on whether the spillovers are beneficial or harmful, that eliminate the effects of the spillovers.

5 A fiscal residuum is the difference between the utility that a citizen attaches to the goods and services provided by governments and the utility that attaches to the private goods and services that that citizen sacrifices when paying his or her taxes.

6 The span of a public good is simply the number of persons who "benefit" from the goods. If the seeding of a cloud generates rain over the

city of Kingston, then the span of the public good we may call weather modification is equal to the population of Kingston (including visitors). The span of a private good is equal to one person.

7 Breton and Scott's (1978) monograph contains an "institutional model" of the assignment of powers, but that model is based, in good part, on a theory of bureaucracy, borrowed from Niskanen (1971), in which politicians (sponsors or principals) are totally passive. Niskanen tried to remove this passivity, but he was not successful. Breton and Wintrobe (1982) made that removal one of the central tasks of their own model of bureaucracy. The Breton-Scott model of the assignment of powers has never been sifted through the Breton-Wintrobe model of bureaucracy. My suspicion is that few of the institutional propositions of the Breton-Scott model would survive. It is on this basis that I currently restrict the Breton-Scott model to its canonical version based on a cost-minimizing constituent assembly and, as a consequence, take the model to be institutionally empty.

8 Rabeau (1986) provides an excellent survey of the various proposals that have been made in which the senior government, through one scheme or the other, seeks to achieve regional macroeconomic stability, by making use of what are, in effect, stabilization grants.

9 The argument that macroeconomic stabilization of the Keynesian variety calls for permanently larger revenues than expenditures at the national level and, therefore, for vertical imbalance is logically untenable. For a good discussion, see Walsh (1992).

10 Expenditure concentration can be defined as the share of the total expenditures of the entire governmental system undertaken by the national government. Because that variable is not always an unbiased index of overall concentration, it may sometimes be appropriate to work with a vector definition that incorporates the share of governmental expenditures at each jurisdictional level separately. The concept of revenue concentration is *mutatis mutandis* similarly defined (see Breton 1989b).

11 Governments supply more than the standard public goods. In addition to these, they supply censorship, war, racial discrimination, affirmative action, oil exploration, and many more. An expansive definition is needed to understand their behaviour.

12 In governmental systems, competition is horizontal *and* vertical. The first pertains to the relations of governments located at a particular jurisdictional tier, whereas the second relates to the relations of governments that inhabit different jurisdictional levels. The discussion in the text focuses on vertical competition without paying attention, except in

the analysis of tax harmonization, to the interrelationships between vertical and horizontal competition. I look at competition in more detail in the second section.

13 A tax price is defined as the increment in total taxes paid by a taxpayer when the quantity of a good or service is increased by one unit. Though sometimes difficult to measure, it is, at the theoretical level, always a tractable concept.

14 Conventional tax theory shows that a tax has two components: a burden, and an excess burden. The first component of a $1 payment in taxes is the $1 sent to the exchequer. If, in addition, the taxpayer moves away from consuming a given quantity of a good because of the tax, his or her utility, or welfare, is reduced. The loss in utility is the excess burden of the tax.

15 To economize on space, I restrict myself to Stigler's model of the competitive forces making for specialization. A more complete analysis would also build on models from the theory of international trade that have sought to study the patterns of specialization between countries. Some of these models, but not all of them, have interesting things to say about the problem of the division of powers between different jurisdictional tiers in competitive governmental systems.

16 These same factors operate in families, churches, guilds, cooperatives, charitable organizations, and other organizations of the sort (see Breton 1989a).

17 There is a loss in utility every time the quantity of a good or service provided is greater or smaller than the quantity desired at a given tax price.

18 Recall that this paper is not concerned with stabilizing transfers (equalization payments). It is limited to revenue transfers, that is the Established Programs Financing arrangements and the Canada Assistance Plan. Recall also that, in equilibrium, stabilizing and revenue transfers, to which we must add remittances, exhaust intergovernmental flows of funds.

19 A quasi-rent is a sum in excess of the minimum needed to prevent a firm from exiting an industry. If the average variable cost of output x is $\bar{q}$ and if the price received per unit of x is $\bar{q}$, then the quasi-rent is $(\bar{q}-)x$. (Remember that if the average variable cost $\bar{q}$ is less than q, the firm will close down). The makeup of political quasi-rents will become clear as we proceed.

20 Avoidance is legal, while evasion is illegal. In a framework in which governments are assumed to be maximizing expected votes and, as a result, responsive to interest groups, however, it is often possible for

individuals and groups to avoid paying taxes by obtaining changes in the tax laws. What, before the change, was evasion becomes, after the change, avoidance. Hence, the use of the two words in the text.

21 This point was made by an anonymous reviewer.

22 For a masterful survey of the literature and for new estimates of all collection costs with an emphasis on compliance costs, see Vaillancourt (1989). The evidence, such as it is, appears consistent with the view that unit costs fall as the size of jurisdictions increases.

23 These advantages are of the same kind as those that give substance to the theory of the optimum tariffs (see, among many discussions, Johnson 1953–54).

24 A good is said to be normal whenever an increase in disposable income does not lead a consumer to reduce his or her purchase of that good.

25 The view of Brennan and Pincus (1990) that (in Australia, at least) unconditional grants always have implicit conditions attached to them seems contradictory to the position of Bird and Mintz (1992) that (in Canada, at least) conditional grants are really unconditional. I suspect that the contradiction is apparent and will dissolve once a robust economic model of fiscal federalism is generally accepted.

26 Because of space limitations, I have not analysed the case where tax funds flow from junior to senior governments, but the model can be adapted relatively easily to that case, even if not in a straightforward manner.

27 For a good description of some of the exogenous factors that have shocked federal-provincial-local fiscal arrangements in Canada in the last 60 years or so, see Winer (1992)

Bibliography

Akerlof, George A. 1978. "The Economics of 'Tagging' as Applied to the Optimal Income Tax, Welfare Programs, and Manpower Planning." *American Economic Review*, 68: 8–19

Alchian, Armen. 1959. "Costs and Outputs." In *The Allocation of Economic Resources*, ed. Paul A. Baran, Tibor Scitovsky, and Edward S. Shaw, 23–24. Stanford: Stanford University Press

Arrow, Kenneth. 1962. "The Economic Implications of Learning by Doing." *Review of Economic Studies*, 29: 155–73

Bella, L. 1979. "The Provincial Role in the Canadian Welfare State: The Influence of Provincial Social Policy Initiatives on the Design of the Canada Assistance Plan." *Canadian Public Administration*, 22: 439–52

Bird, Richard M. 1986. *Federal Finance in Comparative Perspective*. Toronto: Canadian Tax Foundation

Bird, Richard M., and Jack M. Mintz. 1992. "Introduction." In *Taxation To 2000 and Beyond*, ed. Richard M. Bird and Jack M. Mintz, 1–28. Toronto: Canadian Tax Foundation

Boadway, Robin, and Frank Flatters. 1982a. "Efficiency and Equalization Payments in a Federal System of Government: A Synthesis and Extension of Recent Results." *Canadian Journal of Economics*, 15: 613–33

– 1982b. *Equalization in a Federal State: An Economic Analysis*. Ottawa: Supply and Services Canada

Brennan, Geoffrey, and James Buchanan. 1983. "Normative Tax Theory for a Federal Polity: Some Public Choice Preliminaries." In *Tax Assignment in Federal Countries*, ed. Charles E. McLure, Jr, 52–65. Canberra: Centre for Research on Federal Financial Relations, Australian National University

Brennan, Geoffrey, and Jonathan Pincus. 1990. "An Implicit Contract Theory of Intergovernmental Grants." *Publius: The Journal of Federalism*, 20: 129–44

– 1991. "A Minimalist Model of Federal Grants." Typescript

Breton, Albert. 1965. "A Theory of Government Grants." *Canadian Journal of Economics and Political Science*, 31: 175–87.

– 1989a. "The Growth of Competitive Governments." *Canadian Journal of Economics*, 22: 717–50

– 1989b. "The Organization of Governmental Systems." Typescript

– 1991. "The Existence and Stability of Interjurisdictional Competition." In *Competition Among States and Local Governments*, ed. Daphne A. Kenyon and John Kincaid, 37–56. Washington, DC: Urban Institute Press

Breton, Albert, and Angela Fraschini. 1992. "Free-riding and Intergovernmental Grants". *Kyklos*, 45: 347–62

Breton, Albert, and Anthony Scott. 1978. *The Economic Constitution of Federal States*. Toronto: University of Toronto Press

Breton, Albert, and Ronald Wintrobe. 1982. *The Logic of Bureaucratic Conduct*. New York: Cambridge University Press

Buchanan, James, M. 1950. "Federalism and Fiscal Equity." *American Economic Review*, 40: 583–99. Reprinted in *Readings in the Economics of Taxation*, ed Richard A. Musgrave and Carl S. Shoup, 93–109. Homewood, IL: Irwin, 1959

– 1967. *Public Finance in Democratic Process. Fiscal Institutions and Individual Choice*. Chapel Hill: University of North Carolina Press

Chernick, Howard A. 1979. "The Economics of Bureaucratic Behavior: An Application to the Allocation of Federal Project Grants." In *Fiscal Federalism and Grants-in-Aid*, ed. Peter M. Mieszkowski and William H. Oakland. Washington, DC: Urban Institute

Courant, Paul, N. Edward, M. Gramlich, and Daniel L. Rubinfeld. 1979. "The Stimulative Effects of Intergovernmental Grants: Or Why Money Sticks Where It Hits." In *Fiscal Federalism and Grants-In-Aid*, ed. Peter M. Mieszkowski and William H. Oakland, 5–21. Washington, DC: Urban Institute

Fisher, Ronald C. 1982. "Income and Grant Effects on Local Expenditure: The Flypaper Effect and Other Difficulties." *Journal of Urban Economics*, 12: 324–45

Flatters, Frank, R., J. Vernon Henderson, and Peter M. Mieszkowski. 1974. "Public Goods, Efficiency, and Regional Fiscal Equalization." *Journal of Public Economics*, 3: 99–112

Gramlich, Edward, M. 1977. "Intergovernmental Grants: A Review of the Empirical Literature". In *The Political Economy of Fiscal Federalism*, ed. Wallace E. Oates, 219–39. Lexington: D.C. Heath

Hicks, Ursula, K. 1978. *Federalism: Failure and Success*. London: Macmillan

Johnson, Harry G. 1953–54. "Optimum Tariffs and Retaliation." *Review of Economic Studies*, 21: 142–53. Reprinted in *International Trade and Economic Growth*, ed. Harry G. Johnson, 31–55. Cambridge, MA: Harvard University Press, 1958.

Klein, Benjamin, and Kevin M. Murphy. 1988. "Vertical Restraints as Contract Enforcement Mechanisms." *Journal of Law and Economics*, 31: 265–97

McGuire, Martin C. 1975. "An Econometric Model of Federal Grants and Local Fiscal Response." In *Financing the New Federalism: Revenue Sharing, Conditional Grants, and Taxation*, ed. Wallace E. Oates, 115–38. Baltimore: Johns Hopkins University Press for Resources for the Future Inc.

– 1979. "The Analysis of Federal Grants into Price and Income Components." In *Fiscal Federalism and Grants-in-Aid*, ed. Peter M. Mieszkowski and William H. Oakland, 31–50. Washington, DC: Urban Institute

Musgrave, Richard A. 1959. *The Theory of Public Finance. A Study in Public Economy*. New York: McGraw-Hill

Musgrave, Richard, Peggy B. Musgrave, and Richard M. Bird. 1987. *Public Finance in Theory and Practice*. Toronto: McGraw-Hill Ryerson

Niskanen, Jr, William A. 1971. *Bureaucracy and Representative Government*. Chicago: Aldine-Atherton

Oates, Wallace E. 1972. *Fiscal Federalism.* New York: Harcourt Brace Jovanovich

Pross, A. Paul. 1986. *Group Politics and Public Policy.* Toronto: Oxford University Press

Rabeau, Yves. 1986. "Regional Stabilization in Canada." In *Fiscal and Monetary Policy*, ed. John Sargent, 151–97. Toronto: University of Toronto Press

Romer, Thomas, and Howard Rosenthal. 1980. "An Institutional Theory of the Effect of Intergovernmental Grants." *National Tax Journal*, 33: 451–58

Scott, Anthony D. 1952. "The Evaluation of Federal Grants." *Economica N.S.*, 19: 377–94

Stigler, George J. 1951. "The Division of Labor Is Limited by the Extent of the Market." *Journal of Political Economy* 59: 185–93. Reprinted in George J. Stigler *The Organization of Industry*, 129–41. Chicago: University of Chicago Press, 1968

– 1966. *The Theory of Price.* 3rd ed. New York: MacMillan

– 1987. *The Theory of Price.* 4th ed. New York: Macmillan

Strick, John C. 1971. "Conditional Grants and Provincial Government Budgeting." *Canadian Public Administration*, 14: 217–35

– 1985. *Canadian Public Finance.* 3rd ed. Toronto: Holt, Rinehart, and Winston

Vaillancourt, Franois. 1989. *The Administrative and Compliance Costs of the Personal Income Tax and Payroll Tax System in Canada, 1986.* Toronto: Canadian Tax Foundation

Walsh, Cliff. 1991. *Reform of Commonwealth-State Relations – "No Representation Without Taxation."* Canberra: Federalism Research Centre Discussion Paper No. 2

– 1992. *Fiscal Accountability, Vertical Fiscal Imbalance and Macroeconomic Management in Federal Fiscal Systems.* Canberra: Federalism Research Centre Discussion Paper No. 7

Wheare, Kenneth, C. 1963. *Federal Government*, 4th ed. London: Oxford University Press

Wilde, James A. 1971. "Grants-In-Aid: The Analytics of Design and Response." *National Tax Journal*, 24: 143–55

Winer, Stanley, L. 1983. "Some Evidence on the Effect of the Separation of Spending and Taxing Decisions." *Journal of Political Economy*, 91 (1): 126–40

– 1992. "Taxation and Federalism in a Changing World." In *Taxation to*

2000 and Beyond, ed. Richard M. Bird and Jack M. Mintz, 343–69. Toronto: Canadian Tax Foundation

Zampelli, Ernst M. 1986. "Resource Fungibility, The Flypaper Effect, and the Expenditure Impact of Grants-in-Aid." *Review of Economics and Statistics,* 68: 33–40

3 The Federal-Provincial Tax Collection Agreements: Personal Income Tax Coordination

A Background Report

DOUGLAS G. HARTLE

Introduction

Brief History

The British North America Act of 1867 established the basis for joint occupancy of the most important tax fields by assigning to the provinces the power to levy direct taxes within their boundaries and by assigning to the federal government the power to raise money "by any mode or system of taxation."

Income taxes are direct taxes because they are levied against the persons who are expected to pay them. Because provincial sales taxes in Canada are legislated as consumer purchase taxes, with retailers designated as the crown's agents for purposes of collection, they too are direct taxes for constitutional purposes. Thus, in Canada both orders of government are constitutionally empowered to levy the two kinds of taxes that are the major sources of revenue for most governments in most developed countries.

Joint occupancy of the direct tax field gives each order of government the flexibility of finance its spending obligations; it also raises the possibility of conflicts between the federal government and provincial governments as well as among provincial governments. It can also entail costly duplication for taxpayers when the tax systems require different returns for different governments because coordination has been lacking.

Since 1917 the federal government has been collecting a personal income tax (PIT). The province of Ontario, as such, has never *collected* such a tax. Prior to 1936 PIT was collected in Ontario, to the limited and haphazard extent that it was collected, by the municipalities. From 1936 to the present day, the provincial PIT has been collected by the federal government: first, as the agent of the province; then, as the "tenant" that had rented the tax jurisdiction from the province; and, since 1962 again as the province's agent. (There were a few years near the end of the tax rental agreement, and before the inauguration of the tax collection agreements, when the PIT was not collected in Ontario.)

The first federal collection of PIT on behalf of the province was undertaken at the request of Premier Mitchell Hepburn who, in the midst of the Great Depression did not want to duplicate the costly federal collection apparatus and did not want to require Ontario taxpayers to complete two sets of tax returns.

Would-be demagogues were in vogue. Some may recall that this was the period when the decision to tear down the lieutenant-governor's residence in Toronto, Chorley Park, was a highly popular political move. It is not recorded whether the premier also anticipated with some relish the confusion that would be created in the minds of uninformed taxpayers concerning which government was actually imposing the provincial share of the PIT that Ottawa collected.

The present tax collection agreements, to which all provinces (plus the Yukon and Northwest Territories) except Quebec are signatories, were initiated in 1962 and evolved, as did federal equalization payments to the "have-not provinces," from the tax rental/tax sharing agreements that were in effect from 1940 to that date. It is not improbable that Premier Hepburn's request that Ottawa collect the Ontario PIT gave the federal government the idea that it could "rent" the provincial tax fields during the Second World War. It was from those rental agreements that the present complex federal-provincial fiscal arrangements have emerged with (inescapable) continuing federal-provincial conflict and complexity.

It has been said that federalism is a process rather than a structure. The existing tax collection agreements that have emerged from the process and their future modification should be viewed in terms of the evolution of the federation.

Since 1867 prolonged periods of intentional peace have coincided with the strengthening of the centrifugal forces of regionalism and tribalism that have threatened to destroy Canada. It was only during the First World War and the Second World War that centralist forces quickly gained the upper hand. Following each war, as peace continued, the power and authority of the federal government declined.

The present threat of Canadian disintegration follows the longest period of peace in Canada's history. With the collapse of the Soviet empire, a major international conflict is widely perceived to be unlikely for many years. If history repeats itself, there is thus a grave danger that Canada, without a common external enemy, will cease to exist in the next half-decade.

Ontario's participation in the federal-provincial tax collection agreements should be approached from this wider context, not from a narrow, technical tax perspective nor from a parochial one. In an effort to dissuade one or more provinces from establishing separate personal income tax systems, as Quebec did in 1954, the Government of Canada released a discussion paper entitled *Personal Income Tax Coordination: the Federal-Provincial Tax Collection Agreements* (hereinafter referred to as the discussion paper) in June 1991. This paper indicates a willingness on the part of the federal authorities to abandon, under certain conditions, their long-standing *stated* policy that the only type of PIT the Government of Canada would collect on behalf of a province under the tax collection agreements would be one that imposed a single, provincial rate of PIT on the taxpayers' "federal basic tax" as determined by the federal statute and regulations as administered by Revenue Canada, and, of course, as interpreted by the courts.

Federal Proposal

Although the "illustrative model" sketched in the federal discussion paper is presented "for the purpose of identifying issues and choices," not as a formal proposal, there seems no reason why, for the purposes of this discussion, it should not be treated as a federal proposal, albeit a tentative proposal.

In essence, what the federal authorities are proposing is that under amended tax collection agreements the federal government would collect, on behalf of signatory provinces, a provincial PIT that

- applied to each taxpayer's taxable income, defined in accordance with federal law, a schedule of provincially determined rates of tax; and
- provided federally defined non-refundable credits at provincially determined levels against this tax.

The federal proposal is not without irony. Despite its earlier stubborn refusal to back away from its "tax-on-tax" approach, in 1985, Ottawa acquiesced (presumably reluctantly) in collecting, on a "temporary and experimental basis", the imposition by Saskatchewan of a flat (single) rate of tax of 2 per cent applied to federally defined net income rather than to federal basic tax. In 1987 Ottawa agreed to levy similar flat-rate taxes in Manitoba and Alberta (in Alberta the rate is only 0.5 per cent and applies to taxable income).

Thus, for Saskatchewan and Manitoba – and to a lesser extent in Alberta – the federal authorities are, in a sense, inviting the provinces to "retreat" from a broader base, for which they fought successfully, to the federal taxable income base. In exchange, the federal authorities are willing to continue to collect provincial PITs that incorporate provincially determined schedules of rates and to apply provincially determined (but federally defined) non-refundable credits.

This federal quid pro quo probably will appear to federal critics as a package of concessions that are too little and too late. Given on-again-off-again federal intransigence in the past, many provinces, led by Ontario, have devised some ingenious PIT measures that have permitted them to modify provincial PITs without exercising influence, much less control, over the federal PIT base or rate structure.

Current Provincial Modifications

There are other ironies: under the aegis of the tax collection agreements, the federal government waged a continuing struggle with one or more provinces to maintain what federal tax officials might term the "integrity" of the personal tax. They resisted proposals for provincial PIT provisions that would create undue administrative difficulties for Revenue Canada and/or distort the allocation of productive resources (i.e., labour and capital). Ontario was the first province to persuade Ottawa that credits against Ontario PIT, even if made available to non-filers, could be administered relatively easily by Ottawa and, if adopted, would contribute to rather than detract from the equity of the income tax system.

In 1972 Ontario introduced, and Ottawa administered, the first such credit: it related to property taxes. In the following year, Ontario introduced, and Ottawa administered, a similar type of credit for retail sales taxes. Ontario now has four such credits. Other provinces have followed Ontario's lead, and, since then, there has been a plethora of these kinds of "social" tax credits enacted by most provinces.

More controversial, but now almost ubiquitous, are what might be called by their advocates "province-building" PIT investment credits or "beggar-my-neighbour" PIT investment provisions by their opponents. The federal-provincial battle began in 1978-79, when British Columbia attempted to introduce a dividend tax credit against provincial PIT liabilities for public corporations with headquarters in or managed from that province. The federal government of the day refused to implement this credit under the tax collection agreements and the Conservative government that came to power in 1979 stood by the earlier federal position that such provincial PIT provisions were inconsistent with the goal of a common market in Canada.

At about this time, Ottawa rejected a Saskatchewan attempt to introduce a provincial PIT credit that would offset certain types of capital gains; it accepted a modified Saskatchewan mortgage interest tax credit and persuaded Alberta to use expenditures rather than PIT credits to assist the construction of rental housing.

That Ottawa has lost many of these arguments with the provinces for special provincial PIT measures is attested to by the fact that five provinces (in addition to Quebec, which is not within the collection agreements) have in place investment incentive schemes administered by the federal government as part of the provincial PIT collection process. These incentives take the form of credits against provincial PITs for taxpayer participation in programs such as stock savings plans, or venture capital plans, or employee share ownership/venture capital plans.

Ontario Economic Council Study of 1982

Ontario, which heretofore has not had such a PIT investment incentive, has also been embroiled in the controversy with the federal tax authorities. In his budget of 1982, the then Ontario treasurer, Frank Miller, announced that he had asked the Ontario Economic Council (since disbanded) to investigate and report on the economic consequences of Ontario's withdrawal from the tax collection agreements and the institution of its own PIT. The council published in 1983 an official response entitled *A Separate Personal Income Tax for Ontario: An Ontario Economic Council Position Paper*. It later published two companion volumes, one an *Economic Analysis* (1983b), and the other *Background Studies* (Conklin 1984).

In *Economic Analysis* it was stated that "If the past is any indication of what the future portends, given the present and prospective general economic malaise, provincially, nationally and internationally, governments at all levels are now tempted and will no doubt be increasingly tempted to adopt short-sighted, 'beggar thy neighbour' policies.

It is vitally important that the Province of Ontario resist this temptation, for if it were to succumb it would almost certainly be quickly emulated by others, to the mutual detriment of us all"[1] (75).

Despite Ontario's adherence to this "self-denying ordinance," most provinces have now adopted, as indicated above, one or more of the investment credits that the Ontario Economic Council decried. This too is an important dimension of the context within which the federal discussion paper must be considered.

Changed Circumstances

Although the findings of the 1982 Ontario Economic Council's analysis of the pros and cons of a separate Ontario PIT remain valid, the several changes in relevant circumstances since that date make it useful to re-examine it and related issues. Among the most salient changes have been those listed below.

- The willingness of the federal government to consider continuing to collect provincial PITs when they involve the "tax on income" approach rather than the long-standing federal insistence that the signatory provinces accept a tax-on-tax approach. In 1982 there appeared to be an all-or-nothing choice: the federal way, or the separate Ontario PIT way.
- The proliferation of provincial provisions that seek to abide by the letter of the tax collection agreements while modifying the distribution of the PIT burden in their provinces through PIT reductions, surtaxes, and a variety of provincial PIT credits raises questions about possible avenues for PIT simplification in Ontario if the federal proposals were accepted.
- The quite extraordinary combination of progressive federal PIT rates and flat provincial rates now in place in Saskatchewan, Manitoba, and Alberta have led those provinces into inordinate complexity and taxpayer confusion. If they do not gain more control over their PIT structures within the tax collection agreements, they will have to institute their own collection agency. The desperation of these provinces is palpable, and their threats to "go it alone" consequently are credible. This threat probably accounts for the change in policy stance by the federal government.
- The proliferation, other than in Ontario, of economic development credits that provide incentives for resident investments in the shares of provincially based companies has made is increasingly difficult for the province to abstain from introducing similar provisions.

- Finally, but of even greater long-run importance, is the enormous uncertainty that overhangs the future of Canada as a result of the apparent increase in the demand for sovereignty in Quebec and the apparent increase in intransigence in the rest of Canada towards further recognition of Quebec's unique status. For Ontario to withdraw from the tax collection agreements now would be a highly symbolic act that could have implications that would go far beyond the confines of PIT collection in Ontario.

Some Political as Distinct from Partisan Considerations

The Ever-Present Quebec Model

Quebec introduced its separate but parallel PIT and CIT systems in 1954. When, in 1962, the federal-provincial tax rental agreements replaced the Tax Rental Agreements with the remaining provinces (and the Yukon and Northwest Territories) all of the signatories were aware that autonomous provincial PIT systems were, at least for the larger provinces (or conceivably groups of smaller provinces), politically, economically, and administratively feasible.

Unlike retail sales taxes, the constitutional right of the provinces to levy personal income taxes has never been in question. With Quebec as an ever-present "living example" of a separate PIT system, Ottawa has been at some apparent disadvantage in negotiating with the remaining provinces over the tax collection agreements. But the federal government has not been entirely without bargaining power.

Provincial Political Costs and Benefits

The provinces realize they can go it alone, but only at considerable political cost. The political cost arises from two considerations: a provincially separate PIT would make it transparent to uninformed taxpayers that a significant part of their PIT burden arises from a provincial levy; and it would also increase taxpayer compliance costs and be seen to increase, unnecessarily, provincial government overhead costs through the requisite expansion of the provincial tax collection machinery. The price exacted on the provinces for accepting federal collection has not been trivial.

Governments in office (and their finance ministers/treasurers) have to give the appearance of responding to voter demands that they "do something" about voter-perceived pressing problems. Under the original tax collection agreements *as strictly interpreted*, the PIT ceased to be an available provincial policy instrument. Yet provincial treasurers were certainly aware that rarely did a year go by without the federal minister of finance introducing one or more amendments to the PIT designed to please this or that interest group or make some contribution to the resolution of what was seen, at the time, as a pressing social or economic problem. Some of these federal PIT structural changes were, to some extent at least, symbolic. They sought to demonstrate the government's (and the minister's) awareness and concern, even though they may have been largely ineffectual (or worse).

Provincial treasurers face the same political problems. No doubt, they have resented being told by their senior officers that under the tax collection agreements they could not engage in the same practices as their federal counterpart without his (or potentially her) agreement, although they have the same constitutional authority. When the two elected officials are of different political parties, the irritation is, of course, intensified.

Another general reason for provincial restiveness under the tax collection agreements has been the failure of the federal tax authorities to give their provincial opposite numbers prior warning of, much less enter into prior consultations about, federal PIT changes, including those changes that had a major impact on provincial PIT revenues. Although there has been less of a problem in recent years, often in the past the federal minister of finance made unilateral PIT changes without warning that put provincial treasurers in awkward situations. Federal finance ministers have been known to be in receipt of praise from voters for a federally announced tax reduction while the provincial treasurers have been sent scurrying to make up the consequent revenue loss to the provinces in a way that would minimize voter disfavour.

This lack of consultation between the federal and provincial authorities on income tax matters has long been deplored by many observers. The parliamentary rules governing budget secrecy are the ostensible reason. In point of fact, the secrecy argument is less salient than federal apologists would like to admit. By first announcing in parliament an intention to consider certain tax structure changes, the federal minister of finance would then be free to consult with the treasurers of the provinces and other interested parties on the alternatives. The provincial tax authorities could then gauge from the federal reaction to their representations and other representations what PIT changes the federal minister of finance would be likely to announce in the next budget speech. Furthermore, many tax structure changes could be announced well in advance of their effective dates in order to give provincial treasurers ample opportunity to adjust their budgets in an orderly manner.

There is a suspicion that the fundamental reason for the heroic lack of federal-provincial consultation about (or even prior notification of) PIT amendments has been the love affair federal finance ministers have had with the limelight of budget night. Finance ministers are reluctant to give up one of the few rewards pertaining to that self-denying portfolio by agreeing to a procedure that reveals PIT changes in an undramatic manner.

Federal Political Costs and Benefits

One of the major political benefits to signatory provinces flowing from the tax collection agreements – the obfuscation of the locus of responsibility for provincial PIT levies – is a political cost to federal governments. The hostility that provincial treasures escape is visited on federal ministers of finance. What do they garner in return?

Federal finance ministers and their officials no doubt get some satisfaction from what has been their absolute control over the Canadian PIT structure (except for Quebec). Although exhausting on a day-to-day basis, it must be a source of personal gratification for the federal authorities to have provincial treasurers, interest group leaders, and particularly taxpayers making endless supplications for PIT change "favours."

The federal authorities should have, and presumably do have, a shared sense of martyrdom: they have fought valiantly, with little if any public support, to maintain the *integrity* of the Canadian PIT system. This stand can be translated into the federal tax authorities' mounting a perpetual defence against what they must perceive as the barbarians who would erode the *neutrality* of the Canadian PIT system. This defence, in turn, can be translated into the federal attempt to prevent the further erosion of the Canadian economic union through provincial adoption of PIT measures that distorted the allocation of productive resources within Canada with the economic efficiency (standard of living) losses this would entail.

Minimizing the losses in output that would occur through a provincially "balkanized" PIT system is a worthy goal. But it is not one that has substantial voter appeal. How many voters are grateful when they are told that had finance minister X not rejected provincial building initiative Y, *Canadians in general* would have had a slightly lower future standard of living? Selling the benefits of economic efficiency is somewhat akin to selling the hole in the doughnut: the benefits to the "buyer" are not immediately apparent.

Commentary on the Federal Argument

The discussion paper correctly recognizes that there is an inherent conflict between two positions. On one side is the federal insistence on the enormous importance of achieving tax "harmony" (uniformity) and simplicity. These objectives are best achieved when provincial PITs deviate as little as possible from the federal PIT, and the federal government collects the PIT for itself and the provinces. On the other side is the insistence of the provinces that their PIT regimes must differ from the federal PIT system, and from province to province in order to reflect adequately the differences in prevailing social values and the circumstances of their residents. The essence of the problem is expeditiously conveyed by first summarizing the federal position, as stated in the discussion paper, and then providing a commentary.

Coordination

Federal-provincial coordination with respect to income taxes requires the resolution of conflicts among four objectives.

Harmonization Objective

Federal Position. "Tax harmony provides consistency and uniformity in the tax base and structure. This means that tax measures of governments complement rather than contradict each other, thus helping to maintain a free flow of capital and labour across the federation" (Canada 1991b, 5).

Comment: It is understood that in a world where resource allocation is otherwise perfect, there is a need to avoid tax barriers or tax concessions that affect the allocation of labour and capital. What seems to be missing in the federal positions is recognition that *incentives* by way of actual expenditures, or tax expenditures, or regulatory loopholes (e.g., waiving of zoning restrictions) can equally distort the allocation of resources. Indeed, distortions can occur in the absence of government intervention. For example, distortions can occur where monopoly suppliers have the power to restrict output in order to raise prices, or where consumers are ill-informed about product or service quality (e.g., some licensed professional services), or where private provision of services will be necessarily inadequate because those who do not pay for the good or service cannot be excluded from enjoying the benefits (e.g., fire protection).

Some federal programs have as their explicit purpose the modification of the allocation of resources relative to the market allocation: unconditional equalization payments made to the "have-not" provinces and grants made under the regional economic development program are cases in point. Other federal expenditures, such as seasonal Unemployment Insurance benefits, allow persons to remain in localities that, in the absence of these payments, would force them to leave in search of year-round employment. The federal argument for provincial PITs that are neutral in their effects on the location of workers/taxpayers and on location of investment would be more persuasive if federal policies generally were also as geographically neutral as they are administratively feasible. This is far from the prevailing situation.

The adoption by the provinces of the same PIT base as the federal government (the Quebec base is not radically different from the federal base) is undeniably an important means of reducing taxpayer compliance costs and, through the use of a common collection agency, government collection costs. The federal position would seem to presuppose, however, that the common base is, in some sense, the "correct" PIT base.

All PIT bases fail, to some degree, the total neutrality test because some forms of income are not taxed, usually because of inherent valuation problems (e.g., benefits of owner-occupied housing and the benefits to husbands of wives who stay home and do the housekeeping) or because of liquidity problems (e.g., taxing unrealized capital gains).

The benefits of lower administrative/compliance costs of a common PIT base and a common collection agency are eroded as the degree of neutrality of that base is reduced. At what point to the costs of the distortions introduced by an extremely non-neutral tax base offset the benefits of a common collective agency?

The federal government is constantly making changes in its PIT base: the changing treatment of capital gains exemptions and retirement savings are cases in point. The discussion paper would seem to assume that all such federal changes are for the better (increase neutrality) and should therefore be accepted by the provinces without question. Why should the federal government be the sole arbiter of the "appropriate" degree and form of PIT neutrality/non-neutrality?

Flexibility Objective

Federal Position. "Differences in regional preferences and in economic and social structures mean that some differences [among provinces] in personal income taxation are inevitable and appropriate ... flexibility in pursuing their objectives enhances each jurisdiction's ability to provide the mix of tax and expenditure programs best suited to their individual circumstances" (ibid.).

Comment: The term "flexibility," as juxtaposed to the term "harmony," understates the depth of the conflict between the relevant objectives.

Canada adopted a federal system of government because it was decided that, in the absence of homogeneity in tastes, preferences, and the collective needs of people living in different parts of this vast country, differences could best be accommodated (i.e., the coercion of minorities by the majority minimized) by assigning certain powers and responsibilities to provincial governments. If the provinces were required to exercise these powers in complete harmony, there would be no rationale for having a federal rather than a unitary form of government.

The long-standing federal insistence on the tax-on-tax approach to provincial PITs implicitly denied that the provinces had a legitimate interest in modifying, for their own taxpayers, the progressivity that the federal government had injected into the PIT structure. Surely, interprovincial differences with respect to the desirable degree of income redistribution should be acknowledged in a federal country.

One might extend the argument in favour of provincial autonomy to cover not only differences in the degree of progressivity in provincial PITs but also all other aspects of tax fairness. Taxes are defined as equitable when there is "equal treatment of equals" and "appropriate differences in treatment" among taxpayers who are in difference circumstances. Clearly, the residents of different provinces could have materially different views about what constitute relevant similarities and differences in circumstances in defining the appropriate units to be subject to personal income taxation and the appropriate bases to which PIT rates should be applied. For example, with respect to the appropriate tax units, the majority of the residents of one province might wish to treat common-law marriages in the same way as traditional marriages, while the majority of the residents of another province might be unwilling to go beyond the socially sanctioned marriage. Similar differences could arise with respect to the appropriate recognition accorded in the PIT system to persons of the same sex who live together.

Similarly, there could be significant interprovincial differences in opinion concerning the appropriate definition of the PIT base: the residents of some provinces might wish generous allowances for retirement saving, while others might prefer a more restrictive approach; some would tax capital gains like other income, yet others would wish to accord such gains differential treatment in the belief (which may well be erroneous) that this would encourage entrepreneurship.

The discussion paper gives relatively little weight to the concern that the achievement of *fairness* may well be inconsistent with the achievement of interprovincial tax neutrality (harmony).

There is another type of conflict that is ignored in the discussion paper, although in practical terms it is of enormous importance – that is, interprovincial competition. Any and all interprovincial differences in the levels and composition of the taxes, expenditures, and regulations can potentially attract and repel labour and capital. In the long run, the limits imposed by the competition among provinces for skilled labour and capital are probably even more intractable than any limits arising from the constitutional division of powers and responsibilities between the federal and provincial orders of government or by federal-provincial agreements. The exercise of provincial autonomy is greatly circumscribed by the realities of interjurisdictional competition.

A provincial PIT that is completely "fair," in terms of the values of the residents of a province, may well be unattainable given the exigencies of creating and maintaining a vigorous provincial economy in the face of the competition offered by other provinces, and other countries, that have adopted what appear to be less equitable PIT regimes.

Simplicity Objective

Federal Position. The increasing complexity of modern economies, and greater use of the tax system as a government policy instrument mean it is increasingly difficult to design a tax system that is straightforward and that gives adequate recognition to varying economic and social conditions and differences in individual and family circumstances. Nevertheless, "simplicity minimizes the compliance costs and the administrative burden on tax filers, employers and government" (ibid., 6).

Comment: It is apparent to all that simplicity is desirable but elusive, particularly if adequate weight is given to the objective of tax fairness. A gain in simplicity often is associated with refusing to admit that some basic differences in taxpayer circumstances (e.g., differences in income, differences in family size, differences in non-money benefits, differences in the inflation rate) are relevant for tax purposes. Simplicity is also lost when attempts are made in tax legislation to create distinctions that have no objective tax bases. To purport to differentiate in PIT provisions between the gains from "speculation" and the gains from "investment" would lead to this kind of complexity.

Transparency Objective

Federal Position.   "Transparency ensures that each government's tax burden is clear to taxpayers, and the taxing governments can be held responsible for their actions (ibid.).

Comment: The term "transparent" is usually used as the antonym of "hidden". The federal collection of the Ontario PIT can hardly be described as the imposition of a "hidden" tax, at least in the sense that the now defunct Manufacturers' Sales Tax was hidden. What the present PIT collection arrangement does is reduce the *consciousness* of taxpayers that they are also bearing the burden of an Ontario PIT when they discharge their PIT liabilities to the federal government.

An argument can be made that income taxes gained in relative importance in the tax mix when the system of PIT deductions at source was introduced during the Second World War. The income tax was not made less transparent (i.e., it was not hidden) but the *consciousness* of PIT liabilities was reduced for many taxpayers relative to the previous system under which all taxpayers had to complete a return on an annual basis and make out a cheque to the government. If maximum tax *consciousness* is the goal, then PIT deductions at source should be prohibited, not required.

Do taxpayers who have PIT deductions made at source have the same antipathy to this tax as those, such as small businessmen, who must write out a cheque once a quarter? Would the apparent hostility to property taxes be as heavy as it is if they were paid automatically each month through withdrawals from the property owner's bank account? If tax consciousness generates tax hostility, which seems likely to be the case, there is a real possibility that governments will be led to impose a mix of taxes that does not reflect their merits in terms of fairness or economic efficiency but gives greatest weight to those taxes about which taxpayers are least aware.

Balance Conflicting Objectives

Federal Position. There are inherent conflicts between the goals of harmony and simplicity on the one hand, which are both best realized by a uniform tax system under a single administration, and flexibility and transparency on the other, which are probably both best realized by separate provincial personal income tax systems.

Comment: This position should be restated as follows: In order to recognize significant differences in the prevailing social/cultural values and economic circumstances among the provinces, the achievement of tax fairness within provinces requires a diversity of PIT regimes in Canada; but such diversity of PIT structures is antithetical to the realization of national tax neutrality (and a true common market) and the minimization of taxpayer compliance costs and government tax collection costs.

A compromise must be reached between the realization of greater fairness – which would necessitate higher compliance and collection costs – and the realization of provincial economic growth and prosperity in a global economic environment where crucial factors of production can shift to the uses and locations where the private returns on investments (including human capital) are highest without regard to the fairness of the tax regime. In short, the competition among tax jurisdictions, concern for the costs of taxpayer compliance, and government tax collection costs unfortunately, but inescapably, constrain the realization of fairness in the design of provincial PIT structures. The question to be addressed is not the *existence* of the constraint, but the appropriate *location* of that constraint with respect to particular provisions of the Ontario PIT system.

Tax Coordination in Canada

Federal Position. A tax collection agreement is an institutional framework that allows provinces to exercise their constitutional right to raise revenues through the personal income tax while accepting a high degree of federal tax policy harmonization and a single federally administered administrative process. "Thus, in entering tax collection agreements, governments accept some limitations on their flexibility to set tax policies independently in return for the economic and administrative benefits of harmonization" (ibid., 10).

Comment: Agreed. The question to be answered is: Does the sacrifice by Ontario of some fiscal independence with respect to the provincial PIT, *under current circumstances*, outweigh the benefits of "harmonization"? The effective degree of fiscal independence is restricted by interprovincial and international competition even more decisively than by federal-provincial tax collection agreements.

Federal Position.   Since the tax collection agreements were initiated in 1962, the federal government has been under pressure to amend the tax collection agreements so as to permit the federal government to administer a variety of provincial personal income tax systems that modified the earlier tax-on-tax restriction to encompass a variety of provincial, social, and economic objectives.

In 1981 the federal authorities introduced a set of guidelines concerning the provincial personal income tax measures it would administer under the agreement. In brief, provincial PIT measures would be administered by the federal government when they had the following characteristics: respected the common base; did not impede the free flow of capital, goods, services, and labour within Canada; and could be administered effectively.

Comment: As attested by the long list, provided in the discussion paper, of provincial PIT measures that the federal authorities agreed to administer, the guidelines have been interpreted with great, one could even say inordinate, leniency. The "flat taxes" of Saskatchewan and Manitoba are applied to net income, not taxable income (much less federal basic tax). The various provincial investment credits (stock saving plans, venture capital plans, and the like), if effective, alter the allocation of domestic saving/investment. Both are contrary to the guidelines.

Summary

Federal Position.   Some provinces are of the view that the limits of the present tax collection agreements have been reached in terms of the degree of complexity that has had to be introduced to approach the realization of provincial policy objectives. They are, therefore, considering the adoption of entirely separate provincial personal income tax systems. The report of finance ministers to the western provincial premiers released in August 1990 proposed a common separate personal income tax system for these provinces. Their May 1991 report welcomed the federal proposal to consult on this matter, but, warned that, in the absence of forward movement, they would be willing to undertake further study this year.

Comment: The complexity of which the finance ministers of the three western provinces complain is, to no small extent, the result of the imposition by these provinces of "flat taxes." These types of taxes have the short-term political advantage of imposing extremely low rates of tax that may delude the uninformed into the perception that such levies are inconsequential. But, because the flat tax base is seven to ten times the "old" tax-on-tax base, a one percentage point flat tax raises seven to ten times the revenue as a "traditional" provincial PIT tax increase of the same amount. In order to offset the unfair provisions of the flat tax, which ignores some relevant differences in tax filer characteristics, these provinces then were under pressure to introduce ameliorating provisions. These provisions were necessarily complex, and the purpose of tax filer calculations obscure.

Description of the Present PIT System

Before assessing the federal proposals, it is necessary to describe the main features of the present PIT system as it applies to Ontario and Quebec. The description needs to encompass the federal/Quebec PIT system not because it is some "ideal" towards which Ontario should move, but because it demonstrates the nature and extent of the deviations from the federal/Ontario system that *one* provincial government put in place when unconstrained by the federal restrictions imposed under the long-standing federal-provincial tax collection agreements.

Pro-Forma Federal Ontario and Federal/Quebec PIT Returns

Perhaps the best method of conveying in brief compass the essence of the Ontario PIT system is first to provide, for federal/Ontario and federal/Quebec, pro-forma income tax returns and then some illustrative calculations of the PIT taxes payable under certain assumptions. The inclusion of some figures showing the average rates of tax by income for single taxpayers, and for married taxpayers with two children under 16 years of age, makes it possible to derive some generalizations concerning the differences in PIT regimes among the three jurisdictions.

Simplified Pro-Forma Federal/Ontario PIT Return, 1990

To Calculate Federal Tax

ADD   Employment income
Pension income
Income from other sources (e.g., FA, UI benefits, rental, capital gains, registered pension plan income)
Self-employed income

= TOTAL INCOME

LESS   RPP contributions
RRSP premiums
Child-care expenses
Union dues
Employment expenses
Carrying charges and investment expenses
Alimony
Allowable business investment losses

= NET INCOME

LESS   Employee relocation loan deduction
Stock options
Partnership losses and other non-capital losses
Capital losses
Capital gains deductions
Northern residents deductions
Other deductions

= TAXABLE INCOME
x Federal PIT schedule of rates
= UNADJUSTED FEDERAL TAX

LESS   17 per cent of Total Non-Refundable Tax Credits
Personal amount
Married amount
Dependent children

Additional personal amounts
CPP/QPP contribution(s)
UI premiums
Pension income amount
Disability amounts
Tuition fees and deduction
Amounts transferred from spouse
Medical expenses
Charitable donations
Federal dividend tax credit
Minimum tax carry-over

= **BASIC FEDERAL TAX**
PLUS FEDERAL SURTAX
= **FEDERAL TAX**

LESS   Sale tax credit
CPP and UI overpayment
Investment tax credit

= **FEDERAL TAX LIABILITY**

To Calculate Ontario PIT (An Add-On to the Federal Return)

= **BASIC FEDERAL TAX × 53 PER CENT**
= **ONTARIO BASIC TAX**

PLUS   Ontario surtax

LESS   Ontario reduction

= **ONTARIO TAX**

LESS   Property tax credit
Sales tax credit
Ontario political contribution
Ontario Home Ownership Savings Plan Credit

= **PIT LIABILITY TO PROVINCE OF ONTARIO**

Simplified Pro-Forma Federal/Quebec PIT Returns, 1990

For expository convenience, the federal/Quebec returns are described
in terms of differences from the federal/Ontario returns.

To Calculate Federal Tax

Quebec has adopted a system of age-related federal Family Allowance payments. This difference, which is not related to differences in the PIT regimes as such, is reflected in the tax returns of Quebec residents. Ontario has not chosen this option.

The federal tax liability for a Quebec resident is calculated in the same way as it is for an Ontario resident *with one important exception*: the Quebec resident is eligible for an abatement (i.e., reduction) equal to 16.5 per cent of federal basic tax. This abatement is not available to an Ontario resident or the residents of other provinces. It forms part of the compensation received by the residents of Quebec because the province opted out of certain federal-provincial shared cost programs and thus has to forgo the federal transfers to the Government of Quebec that participation would have entailed.

To Calculate Quebec PIT (a Separate Return to the Government of Quebec)

ADD   Recovery of QSSP and PSSP deductions that exceed statutory limits.

These schemes have no counterpart in Ontario.

= TOTAL INCOME

LESS   Deduction for employment income (6 per cent up to $750)
         QPP and CPP deductions
         UI premiums
         Tuition fees
         Deduction for certain films
         Resource deduction
         Repayments to federal government for family allowance, UI benefits, and OAS pensions

The employment income deduction has no counterpart in the Ontario system. QPP/CPP deductions and UI premiums are included with non-refundable credits in the federal PIT system and, hence, in the Ontario system. The deduction for certain films and the resource deduction are economic incentives with no counterpart in Ontario. The deduction of the repayments to the federal government involves deducting from income, for Quebec tax purposes, the federal "clawback" of these social payments for high-income taxpayers. Without this Quebec deduction from income, the inclusion of such social benefits in income would constitute Quebec taxation of benefits that were not received. In short, Quebec taxes these amounts net of the clawback.

= NET INCOME

LESS   Allowable deductions with respect to strategic investments
Quebec Stock Saving Plan (QSSP)
SR & ED venture capital corporations
Savings and credit union permanent share purchase plan (PSSP)
Quebec business investment companies (QBICS)
Corporate investment plan (CIP)

Ontario does not have similar provisions. The plans themselves have no counterpart in Ontario and, if they did exist, the deduction from net income would not be possible under the federal requirement that provinces apply their PIT to federal basic tax.

= TAXABLE INCOME
x Quebec PIT schedule of rates
= UNADJUSTED QUEBEC TAX

LESS   20 per cent of total non-refundable tax credits

The federal equivalent is 17 per cent.
Does not include credits for CPP/QPP contributions, UI premiums, tuition, and child-care expenses that, as indicated above, in Quebec are allowed as deductions from total income.

   Tax reduction for families: Ontario has a similar, although less generous, tax reduction that is also available to persons without children. The Quebec reduction scheme is considerably more refined, and hence more complex, than the Ontario scheme.

   Tax credit for Fonds de solidarité des travailleurs du Québec: Ontario has no equivalent provision.

= QUEBEC TAX

LESS   Credit for taxi firms: No Ontario equivalent
Real estate tax refund: Ontario provisions not the same
Refundable Quebec sales tax credit: Ontario provisions not the same

= PIT LIABILITY TO PROVINCE OF QUEBEC

Salient Ontario and Quebec Differences

The salient differences between the federal/Ontario and federal/Quebec PIT systems may be summarized as follows:

- Quebec has a category of "strategic investments" designed to reduce the cost of capital to Quebec firms and thus encourage Quebec investment and entrepreneurship. Quebec residents may deduct the amounts of these investments (within stipulated limits) from net income to determine taxable income. The returns are taxable in the normal way as dividends, interest, or capital gains. Ontario taxpayers have no equivalent deduction. Many of the other provinces that have their PITs collected by the federal government do have similar investment incentive schemes, but these provincial PIT systems provide an incentive through a PIT credit against provincial tax liabilities rather than as a deduction from income. The Quebec deductions from income are more valuable, in a tax point context, to high-income taxpayers than to those with low or zero taxable income. The investment credits provided in other provinces are of the same absolute value to all taxpayers with provincial tax liabilities that can be offset.
- For Quebec residents CPP/QPP contributions, UI premiums, and tuition are also treated as deductions from total income rather than as non-refundable credits. This has the same consequence – for taxpayers in the higher-income brackets the tax "savings" are greater with respect to these items than for taxpayers in the lower-income brackets. The federal/Ontario non-refundable credit approach means that these items provide the same tax savings in absolute terms to all taxpayers regardless of income.
- Quebec has an automatic employment expense deduction. Federal/Ontario has no such deduction.
- Quebec taxpayers may deduct from income in calculating their Quebec PIT liability the federal clawback of UI, FA, and OAS benefits received by those above certain net income limits. Without this deduction, Quebec taxpayers would be taxed on benefits they did not retain. For whatever reason, Quebec has not instituted a similar clawback.

The significance of these differences between the Ontario and Quebec PIT regimes can be ascertained by examining some hypothetical examples. To that end, the calculations of federal, Ontario, and Quebec PIT tax liabilities are shown in the following three tables.

It is assumed in each case that the taxpayer is married with two children under the age of 16 and that the only source of income is from employment by one of the spouses. The examples assume employment income of $20,000, $40,000, and $60,000. The notes in the right-hand column of the tables refer to the notes given immediately above.

None of the tables takes into account provincial credits for property taxes or provincial sales taxes. The amounts of these credits are determined by factors that are too specific to be taken into account in these simple calculations. There are three figures for single taxpayers with no dependants, and three figures for married taxpayers with two children under 16 years of age.

As revealed by the average PIT rates shown in these figures, the salient differences between the federal/Ontario PIT system and the federal/Quebec PIT system are as follows:

For single persons: The combined PIT average rates are slightly lower in Quebec than in Ontario at low-income levels; for incomes above $12,500 they are significantly higher in Quebec.

For married persons with two children: The combined PIT average rates are likewise lower in Quebec for taxpayers below an income of $35,000, but for higher incomes they exceed those in Ontario by a widening margin.

There is a noticeable "jog" in the average rate for married taxpayers at an income from about $22,500 to $27,500. This is the result of the abrupt termination of the Ontario tax reduction.

The more generous treatment of low-income taxpayers in Quebec is primarily the result of the following factors:

- a combination of the federal PIT abatement for Quebec residents and the lower marginal rates in the first three Quebec tax brackets (as described below);
- the automatic deduction from income of 6 per cent of employment income; and
- the more generous family tax reduction provisions in Quebec.

The first two circumstances could not have been replicated by Ontario. Ontario residents were not entitled to the federal abatement (Ontario did not opt out of the major federal-provincial shared cost

TABLE 1
PIT Calculations Ontario and Quebec, 1991, Married Persons Two Children under
16, Employment Income: $20,000

Item	Ontario	Quebec	Comment
Employment income	20,000.00	20,000.00	–
Family allowance	814.32	748.32	Age related in Quebec
Net/taxable income	20,814.32	20,748.32	–
Unadjusted fed. tax	3,538.43	3,527.21	–
Tax credits	2,248.32	2,248.32	–
Basic fed. tax	1,290.11	1,278.89	–
Clawback FA	0.00	0.00	–
Federal sales tax credit	580.00	580.00	–
Federal child tax credit	1,170.00	1,170.00	–
Federal abatement	N/A	211.02	Quebec only
Federal PIT	(395.38)	(618.18)	Refundable
Provincial income	N/A	20,748.32	Quebec only
Additional deductions from income	N/A	1,646.00	
Taxable income	N/A	19,102.32	Quebec only
Provincial basic tax	683.76	3,521.49	All foregoing differences plus differences in PIT rates
Provincial reduction	683.76	970.00	Note difference
Provincial surtax	0.00	N/A	Quebec no surtax
Provincial tax credits	0.00	3,122.00	Property and sales tax credits not included
Provincial PIT	0.00	0.00	
Fed. + prov. combined PIT	0.00	0.00	

NOTE: CPP and UI are $391.00 and $505.00, respectively.

programs). Under the tax collection agreement, Ontario was not permitted its own PIT rate structure or the employment income deduction. On the other hand, the more generous family tax reduction could have been implemented had that been the province's wish.

To anticipate the later discussion of this study, it should be stated that if the federal proposals advanced in the discussion paper were accepted and put into effect, Ontario would not, of course, obtain the abatement except by withdrawing from several major shared-cost programs. And, if Ontario were to withdraw, it would have to raise Ontario taxes to compensate for the loss of the transfer from the federal government. Under the federal proposals, however, Ontario could adopt Quebec's lower PIT rates for those with low incomes by instituting both a credit against Ontario tax for a percentage of em-

TABLE 2
PIT Calculations Ontario and Quebec, 1991, Married Persons Two Children under
16, Employment Income: $40,000

Item	Ontario	Quebec	Comment
Employment income	40,000.00	40,000.00	–
Family allowance	814.32	748.32	Age related in Quebec
Net/taxable income	40,814.32	40,748.32	–
Unadjusted fed. tax	8,021.16	8,004.00	–
Tax credits	2,355.31	2,355.31	–
Basic fed. tax	5,665.86	5,648.70	–
Clawback FA	0.00	0.00	–
Federal sales tax credit	0.00	0.00	–
Federal child tax credit	390.03	393.33	–
Federal abatement	N/A	932.03	Quebec only
Federal PIT	5,559.11	4,605.76	–
Provincial income	N/A	40,748.32	Quebec only
Additional deductions from income	N/A	2,275.34	
Taxable income	N/A	38,472.98	Quebec only
Provincial basic tax	3,002.90	7,898.79	All foregoing differences plus different PIT rates
Provincial surtax	0.00	N/A	Quebec no surtax
Provincial reduction	0.00	506.36	Quebec more generous
Provincial tax credits	0.00	3,122.00	Property and sales tax credits not included
Provincial PIT	3,003.00	4,270.00	–
Fed. + Prov. Combined PIT	8,562.00	8,876.00	–

NOTE: CPP and UI are $632.50 and $892.84, respectively, in each province.

ployment income as well as a more generous system of family reductions.

As emphasized above, the federal government has acquiesced in
the collection of PITs for many provinces that provide for investment
incentive *credits* against provincial tax liabilities. Presumably, under
the existing tax collection agreements, the federal government could
not reject a request from Ontario that it do the same for this province.
However, the signatory provinces have not been able to provide this
incentive as a deduction from income rather than as a credit against
the provincial PIT. Adoption of the federal proposals, at least as they
stand, would not remove this constraint.

TABLE 3
PIT Calculations Ontario and Quebec, 1991, Married Persons Two Children under
16, Employment Income: $60,000

Item	Ontario	Quebec	Comment
Employment income	60,000.00	60,000.00	–
Family allowance	814.32	748.32	Age related in Quebec
Net/taxable income	60,814.32	60,748.32	–
Unadjusted fed. tax	13,082.43	13,082.43	–
Tax credits	2,355.31	2,355.31	–
Basic fed. tax	10,727.12	10,727.12	–
Federal surtax	536.36	536.36	–
Clawback FA	814.32	748.32	–
Federal sales tax credit	0.00	0.00	–
Federal child tax credit	0.00	0.00	–
Federal abatement	N/A	1,769.98	Quebec only
Federal PIT	12,077.89	10,241.82	–
Provincial income	N/A	60,748.32	Quebec only
Additional deductions from income	N/A	3,023.66	
Taxable income	N/A	57,724.66	Quebec only
Provincial basic tax	5,685.37	12,403.92	All foregoing differences plus differences in PIT rates
Provincial surtax	0.00	N/A	Quebec no surtax
Provincial reduction	0.00	0.00	–
Provincial tax credits	0.00	3,122.00	Property and sales tax credits not included
Provincial PIT	5,685.00	9,282.00	–
Fed. + prov. combined PIT	17,763.00	19,524.00	–

NOTE: CPP and UI are $632.50 and $892.84, respectively, in each province.

The Federal Government's "Proposal": The Illustrative Model

The discussion paper presents an "illustrative model" (hereinafter referred to as the IM) for the purpose of "identifying issues and choices – not to define a possible system of tax on income." It is put forward as an aid to resolving the conflict: the desire by the provinces for more flexibility, the federal concern for the maintenance of tax harmonization for economic reasons; and the taxpayer's concern for higher administration and compliance costs.

The principal features of the IM are as follows:

Figure 1: Federal Average Effective Tax Rates, 1991
Ontario and Quebec Single Persons

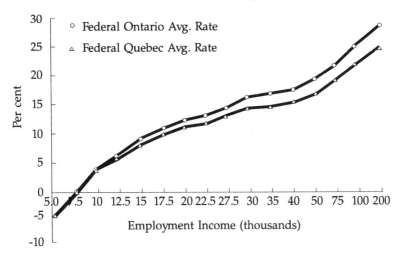

Figure 2: Ontario and Quebec Average Effective Tax
Rates, 1991 Single Persons

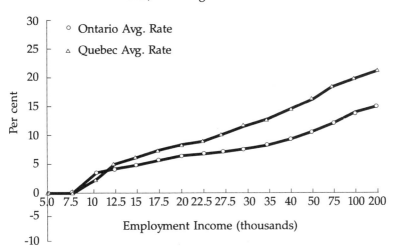

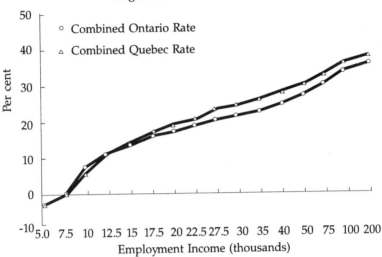

Figure 3: Combined 1991 PIT Ontario and Quebec,
Single Persons

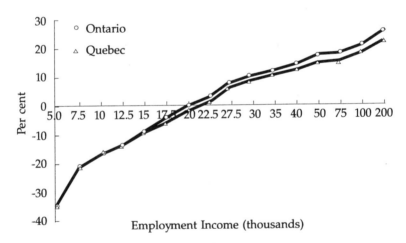

Figure 4: Ontario and Quebec PIT Married Persons,
Two Children under 16

Figure 5: Ontario and Quebec PIT Married Persons,
Two Children under 16

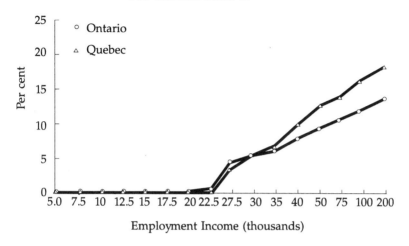

Figure 6: Combined PIT Ontario and Quebec,
Married, Two Children

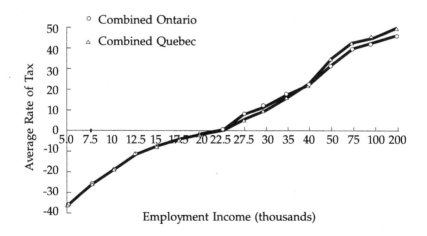

- the tax base for the provinces would be federally defined taxable income rather than federal basic tax;
- the provinces would be free to choose the income tax brackets and tax rates to apply to federally defined taxable income rather than be required to accept the tax brackets and rates determined by the federal government (in effect, the provincial rates now are a percentage – 53 per cent in the case of Ontario – of federal rates);
- the provinces would be free to chose the *levels* of the non-refundable credits that are deducted from provincial income tax to determine basic provincial tax rather than be required to accept the federally established levels; and
- the provinces would be free to change any and all of the foregoing from year to year.

The proposed constraints on provincial choices, as reflected in the IM, are stated as follows:

In the interest of avoiding undue complexity and maintaining a degree of consistency in the national tax system, provinces would adopt the federally defined block of non-refundable tax credits and the eligibility criteria for those credits:

- personal credits – basic, married or equivalent, child, disability, and age;
- expense credit – C/QPP contributions, Unemployment Insurance premiums, tuition fees, education expenses, medical expenses; and
- other credits – charitable donations, pension income (22).

The levels of these credits would be set by each province from time to time. However, it is stated in Annex A to the discussion paper entitled "Key Technical Issues" that certain limitations would be required. These limitations are

- establishment of a minimum value for each credit; and
- transfer of credits between related persons (33).

This annex also poses questions related to the appropriate treatment of the following items:

- dividend gross-up and credit;
- alternative minimum tax;
- measures with a carry-over provision; and

- multijurisdictional taxpayers.

The discussion paper suggests that the existing provincial income tax adjustments (low-income reductions, high-income surtaxes, and the net income tested social and economic credits) could remain, but that provinces might wish to reconsider them in the light of the greater flexibility that would be permitted with the adoption of some variant of the IM.

The present study does discuss the feasibility of achieving, through a new Ontario PIT rate structure, and a change in the amounts of the non-refundable credits, the same results as the present Ontario tax reduction, Ontario surtax, Ontario property tax credit, Ontario retail sales tax credit, Ontario home ownership savings plan credit, and the Ontario political contribution tax credit. As argued below, it seems unlikely that the adoption of the federal proposals would make it possible for the province to simplify the PIT returns for Ontario residents by incorporating these provisions in the rate structure, or in the present structure of non-refundable credits.

This study does not discuss how Ontario would cope with the dividend tax credit, minimum tax, carry-forward, and multijurisdictional issues that would be raised if the federal proposals were adopted and the province were to impose the tax on base rather than the tax-on-tax approach as at present. To simplify the discussion, these might be termed "jurisdictional allocation provisions". To launch into an exposition of the requisite provisions would be premature at this stage of the discussion.

Two points, however, can be made. Ontario would find it necessary to add provisions that would have the effect of allocating to Ontario the "appropriate" share of these measures or their equivalents. These provisions would increase materially the complexity of the provincial PIT for some Ontario residents. The proportion of all Ontario PIT filers affected would be small, but for the few, the additional record-keeping and calculations would be prodigious.

Consultation Process

The paper calls for a consultation process that would address the following questions:

Can the increased policy flexibility that provinces are seeking be accommodated under the tax collection agreements without seriously damaging their effectiveness?

If tax on income can be accommodated under the tax collection agreements, what constraints, if any, should be imposed on the new system in order to

- maintain the benefits of a national system;
- avoid undue complexity and minimize compliance costs for taxpayers and employers;
- ensure a single administration continues to be effective; and
- make governments more accountable for their tax policies?

Ontario's Options

Ontario faces three fundamental options with respect to the provincial PIT:

Option A: Accept the federal proposals with certain modifications and under certain conditions that are spelled out below.

Option B: Reject the federal proposals and adopt a separate PIT for Ontario.

Option C: Reject the federal proposals and remain with the status quo while pressing for certain conditions spelled out below.

The following sections of this study set forth an assessment of these options.

Assessment of Option A: Conditional Acceptance of the Federal Proposals

Fundamentally, the federal proposals boil down to this: the signatory provinces would impose their provincial PITs on federally defined taxable income and be free to impose their own PIT rates on this wider base. They would be required to adopt the federally defined non-refundable credits, but could vary (within limits) the amounts of the federal non-refundable credits. The provinces could retain, if they wished to do so, the existing or modified low-income reduction, the high-income surtax, provincial credits for property taxes, provincial sales taxes, home ownership savings, and political contributions.

Since the federal proposals would give Ontario slightly more future PIT flexibility than it now has *but would not require the province to change any feature of the existing provincial* PIT, it could be argued that the province would be foolish to favour the maintenance of the status quo. It could also be argued that, to the contrary, the adoption of the federal proposals would resolve few, if any, of the problems that Ontario has experienced under the tax collection agreements but would add to compliance costs and complexity.

Unlike Saskatchewan, Manitoba, and to a lesser extent Alberta, Ontario has not instituted a flat-rate PIT tax over and above the "tax on federal basic tax" provincial PIT. This is fortunate. There can be no doubt that flat taxes at low rates (e.g., 2 per cent) imposed on net income raise substantial revenue (about 25 per cent of provincial net PIT revenues), but they do so in a manner that is crude yet complex. As stated in the discussion paper, "[F]lat taxes in and of themselves have inherent weaknesses as major sources of revenue, particularly with respect to fairness and the loss of transparency due to the use of different tax bases" (19). The provinces that have introduced such flat taxes have been compelled also to introduce complex low-income reductions and high-income surtaxes in attempts to mitigate the fact that these taxes do not reflect ability to pay. As a consequence, a high proportion of Manitoba and Saskatchewan tax filers are unable to understand the logic behind the calculations required in completing the tax returns.

There seems little doubt that the pressure on the federal government from the western provinces for more PIT flexibility is largely a reflection of their need to correct at least some of the problems created by combining a provincial flat rate income tax and a federal progressive income tax. Had these provinces had the flexibility that the federal government now offers, presumably they would have adopted their own relatively flat PIT rates and thereby avoided the confusion and complexities that characterize their present PIT systems.

Because these are not problems shared by Ontario, the "solution" offered by the federal authorities provide few, if any, benefits for Ontario. Support for this contention is to be found in an examination of the advantages and disadvantages for Ontario of the greater flexibility that the federal proposals would accord.

Ontario Credits

Ontario currently has in place a property tax, a sales tax, a home ownership savings plan, political contribution tax credits, a tax elimination/reduction, and a surtax. Assuming that the government of the day wished to continue to give PIT reductions with respect to the same taxpayer outlays to which the present Ontario credits apply, there is no reason to suppose that the adoption of the federal proposals would lead to their abolition. The greater flexibility with respect to provincial PIT rates and the freedom to decide upon the magnitudes of Ontario's non-refundable credits would not affect the fact that special credits are required. The reasons are as follows:

- The property tax credit takes into account actual rents or actual property taxes paid and provides a low limit that makes the credit of greater relative significance to low-income tax filers rather than assume some arbitrary amount.
- The sales tax credit takes into account family composition and net income rather than assume some arbitrary amount.
- The Ontario political contribution takes into account actual amounts contributed rather than assume some arbitrary amount.
- The Ontario home ownership savings plan credit takes into account the income of taxpayer and spouse (if any) and actual contributions – including spousal contribution (if any) – rather than assume some arbitrary amount. To remove these credits and assert that they were being replaced by a general system of non-refundable credit, these "amounts" would eliminate the present incentives for political contributions and home ownership savings.

It is doubtful whether the property tax and provincial sales tax credits have any significant incentive effects. With the exception of those persons with no income (e.g., the homeless), virtually all low-income taxpayers pay either *some* rent or property tax, and *some* retail sales taxes. One could agree that these two credits are redundant if the province has control over its PIT rates. However, lowering PIT rates at the bottom of the income scale would be a poor substitute for the political "signals" of government awareness and concern about the property taxes and sales taxes paid by those with modest incomes.

The issue is not whether these two credits should be "wrapped into" the Ontario PIT rate structure or the Ontario determined levels of the federal system of non-refundable credits, but rather, the desirability of making some or all of them refundable. Those most in need of the property and retail sales tax credits probably do not have Ontario PIT liabilities that can be reduced by the present credits. They need cash to compensate them partly for the property and sales taxes they have paid, not relief for non-existent PIT liabilities.

Ontario Tax Reduction

The 1991 Ontario tax elimination/reduction is calculated as follows for a person with children under 16 years of age.
Add personal amounts of
  3 x $167 for each tax filer (married or unmarried)
  3 x $350 x number of children (or disabled dependants)
Less 2 x ONTARIO BASIC TAX = ONTARIO ELIMINATION/REDUCTION (for positive amounts only).

For a taxpayer with two children, the personal amounts equal $867. If the tax filer's Ontario tax (Ontario basic tax plus Ontario surtax less provincial foreign tax credit) is equal to or less than this personal amount, the Ontario PIT is forgiven. When neither the surtax nor the provincial foreign tax credit applies – the usual case – this Ontario tax forgiveness provision implies a federal basic tax of $1636 or less. For married tax filers whose spouses receive family allowance payments in respect of the two children, this provision, in turn, implies that no Ontario PIT is payable for such a taxpayer with employment income of $22,656 or less.

For tax filers with the same family obligations to Ontario basic tax of more than $1300 (federal basic tax of $2453), double the negative amounts exceeds three times the personal amounts and yields a zero tax reduction. Thus, a married taxpayer with two children, a non-working wife in receipt of family allowances, and employment income over $27,466 receives no Ontario reduction.

This form of PIT reduction has two advantages and one significant disadvantage. On the positive side, it is simple from a computational standpoint, and hence its purpose is readily understood. Another advantage is that the reduction is efficient in the sense that it gives Ontario PIT relief to low-income persons and families with no spillover of benefits to those with higher incomes. On the negative side, it results in high marginal rates of PIT for tax filers whose income increases by a relatively modest amount from the tax forgiveness level to the no reduction level. Although this subject is beyond the scope of this paper, it is important, too, to consider the combined disincentive effects not only of the rapid decline in the Ontario PIT reduction as income rises, but also the potential losses in other income-related benefits.

It is important to note that Quebec, although not inhibited by the federal limitations of the tax collection agreements, has in place provisions that are similar to, although certainly not identical with, the

Ontario provisions for political contributions, real estate tax refund, or sales credit. This fact strongly suggests that these measures have rationales that transcend the present federal restrictions.

The adoption of the federal proposals would not likely result in the replacement of these measures by an Ontario PIT rate structure or by establishing provincial amounts of the federally defined non-refundable credits. There may well be good reasons why the present Ontario measures should be revamped, but they are unrelated to the tax collection agreements provisions.

Ontario Surtax

The Ontario surtax, which in 1991 was 14 per cent of Ontario basic tax, applies only to Ontario basic tax in excess of $10,000. This means it applies only to those taxpayers with federal basic tax in excess of $18,868. Taxpayers with taxable incomes of less than $80,000–$90,000 were therefore not subject to the Ontario surtax in 1990.

The federal government presumably had four reasons for adopting a surtax: it raised additional revenues; it did not provide a windfall revenue gain to the provinces (other than Quebec) that would have occurred had it increased the top personal rate; the surtax applies only to income nearly twice as great as that to which the top federal rate applies; and the imposition of the surtax made a political statement.

The treasurer of Ontario presumably had some of these reasons for adopting the Ontario surtax. There is no doubt that, with an independent Ontario PIT rate structure with a top rate beginning at a taxable income of $80,000–$90,000, Ontario could have achieved the same revenue increase through an increase in its top marginal rate rather than through a surtax. It is moot, however, whether this would have been perceived as the political, as distinct from the financial, equivalent.

It should be noted that Quebec does not impose a PIT surtax and Quebec's top marginal rate, which applies to taxable income of $50,000 and over, was lowered in 1989 from 26 per cent to 24 per cent as a result of indexation. It would thus appear that the Ontario surtax *might* not have been imposed had Ontario been able to adjust the marginal rate in the highest income brackets of its own PIT rate structure – an adjustment that was precluded under the tax collection agreements.

Ontario's Own PIT Rate Structure

Because the Ontario Basic PIT is 53 per cent of federal basic tax, the Ontario PIT rate schedule is implicit: it is 53 per cent of the federal statutory rates.

For 1991, the unadjusted federal tax on federal taxable income is calculated in accordance with the following schedule of marginal rates.

Over	but less than	
$0	28,784	17 per cent
$28,785	57,567	26 per cent
$57,568	and over	29 per cent

The Ontario basic tax is therefore calculated in accordance with the following implicit schedule or marginal rates:

Over	but less than	
$0	28,784	9.0 per cent
$28,785	57,567	13.8 per cent
$57,568	and over	15.4 per cent

Because the brackets to which the federal rates apply are indexed each year in accordance with past changes in the Consumer Price Index, the Ontario PIT rate structure is similarly indexed. While bracket indexation is laudable in the sense that it reduces the PIT on purely inflationary gains in income, it is costly in revenue terms to the federal Treasury and to the Treasury of Ontario.

The Quebec PIT rate structure, which was reformed at the same time as the federal rate structure in 1988, differs significantly from the federal/Quebec rate structure in several significant respects.

- As previously stated, federal taxpayers resident in Quebec are subject to a federal PIT abatement of 16.5 per cent as partial compensation for that province's decision not to participate in several federal-provincial shared-cost programs. Quebec PIT rates should therefore be reduced by that percentage to obtain comparability with the implicit Ontario rates.
- Quebec has adopted a five-step PIT rate structure rather than the three-step structure of the federal plan.
- Quebec has not adopted automatic indexation, but in the last few

years it has adopted 4.5 per cent reductions in marginal rates to that end.
• When all PIT adjustments are made, the combined average PIT rates in Quebec are generally higher (for those with higher incomes) than they are in Ontario.

The Quebec PIT rate structure, after reducing the statutory rates by 16.5 per cent to take into account the federal abatement of that percentage, is as follows:

Over	but less than	
$0	7,000	13.4 per cent
$7,000	14,000	15.9 per cent
$14,000	23,000	17.5 per cent
$23,000	50,000	19.2 per cent
$50,000	and over	20.0 per cent

It can be seen that, roughly speaking, Quebec has subdivided the lower federal income bracket into three. This reduction permits a greater degree of "fine tuning"; but the lowest rate of 13.4 per cent applies only to those with taxable incomes of less than $7000. Although the Quebec structure has five brackets, the difference between the lowest and the highest rate is only 6.6 percentage points. The spread is about the same in Ontario.

This comparison and the previous discussion of the Ontario surtax would suggest that, should the federal proposal come into effect, Ontario might wish to adopt a six-bracket system in which the present federal low bracket was subdivided into three brackets, and the upper bracket was subdivided into at least two brackets. Alteratively, if the federal proposals were adopted, the province might wish to reduce the present degree of federal tuning achieved through a three-bracket structure and move in the opposite direction, namely, adopt a flat rate of provincial PIT with more generous credits. Under such an approach, some credits that are now non-refundable could be made refundable, so that the Ontario PIT would come closer to approximating what is commonly known as a "negative income tax."

TABLE 4
Federal Non-refundable Tax Credits, 1991: Basic Amounts, Federal Equivalent
Credit, Ontario Share

Type	Federal basic amount	Federal equivalent credit	Ontario share federal credit (53 per cent)
Basic	$6,280	$1,068	$566
Married or equivalent	5,233	890	472
First two dependent children under 19	406	69	37
Other dependent children under 19	812	138	72
Infirm dependants 19 and over	1,540	262	139
Over 65	3,387	576	305
Tax filer disability	4,118	700	371

Ontario's Values for Non-Refundable PIT Credits

Under the present system, 17 per cent of certain specified non-refundable tax credits are deducted from adjusted federal PIT. These
credits, in 1991, are shown in table 4.

The federal government substituted this form (the amounts are
escalated annually like the rate brackets) or non-refundable credit in
1988 as a major component of its tax reform package. Prior to that
change, these differences in the circumstances (ability to pay) of tax
filers were accommodated by a system of personal exemptions that
were subtracted from income before arriving at taxable income. The
non-refundable credits are deducted from the tax determined by applying the federal rates to taxable income.

As emphasized above, the non-refundable credits are of constant
value with respect to income levels. Assuming that the tax filer has
tax to offset, the non-refundable credits provide the same absolute
amount of tax relief to both the low-income and the high-income tax
filer. The former system of personal exemptions bestowed greater tax
reductions on those with high marginal rates (high incomes) than on
those with low marginal rates (low incomes).

Proponents of the credit system argue that it is more equitable to
assume that all tax filers have the same *non-discretionary* additional
expenses when they are married as when they are single, when they
have one child as when they have no children, and so on. They also
argue that it is only these non-discretionary expenditures that affect

the tax filer's ability to pay. Opponents of the credit system argue that the additional expenses for spouses and children rise at least as rapidly as income rises, and that tax offsets that also rise with income, as is accomplished by a system of personal exemptions, more appropriately reflect ability to pay.

There is another and more persuasive argument in favour of tax credits. If the ultimate purpose is to provide tax relief to those with the lowest incomes and the greatest obligations, a regime of tax credits provides substantially more *efficient* relief than exemptions for a given revenue forgone. Non-refundable tax credits accomplish the same result as adoption of a bundle of rate schedules each with a zero-rate bracket. The size of these zero-rate brackets would differ with respect to the same taxpayer characteristics as those for which there are credits: that is to say, there could be a separate rate schedule for single, no-dependants taxpayers, a schedule for married taxpayers with no dependants, and a schedule for married taxpayers with one child of a certain age, and so on, until all the differences in circumstances recognized by the non-refundable credits were also recognized by a separate schedule.

The first bracket in each such schedule would be subject to a zero rate of tax. The width of the zero-rate bracket in each unique schedule would correspond to the sum of one or more of the credit amounts specified in the foregoing table (assuming a lowest rate of 17 per cent). There is thus no mystery concerning the difference between exemptions versus the credit alternative. The former is equivalent to deducting income from the top, and the latter is equivalent to applying zero rates of tax to those amounts of income deemed to be necessary to meet non-discretionary expenditures.

Provision of Economic Incentives through PIT

Ontario has not yet adopted, as have most other provinces, economic incentives that provide provincial PIT reductions for those individuals who invest in provincial enterprises. This self-denial was probably attributable to the fact that during the 1980s Ontario was in the midst of an economic expansion that would have made any investment incentives redundant. But time has passed and economic circumstances have changed – Ontario has been hard hit by the current recession and by the adjustments that have occurred as a result of the Canada-United States Free Trade Agreement.

Should Ontario decide to adopt such "strategic investment incentives," to use the Quebec term, the federal government would presumably acquiesce in the collection of an Ontario PIT that provided investment tax credits, since the precedents established in other provinces would be impossible to deny. The federal proposals of the discussion paper would not, however, permit Ontario to adopt investment incentives in the form of deductions from income as does the province of Quebec.

Leaving aside the desirability of Ontario's establishing PIT investment incentives, a subject beyond the scope of this paper, how material would be the constraint that this incentive take the form of credits against Ontario PIT liabilities rather than deductions from income, as in Quebec?

Consider a hypothetical investment by an Ontario taxpayer of $2000 in year X that is exigible for an Ontario PIT incentive. Assume further that 20 per cent of certain "amounts" were treated as non-refundable credits against Ontario tax. If the $2000 were treated as such an "amount" the tax credit would be $400 in year X – the cost of the shares would be lowered to the taxpayer by 20 per cent. If, on the other hand, Ontario had the same "flexibility" as the province of Quebec, this investment could be deducted from income. Because the top Quebec marginal rate is also 20 per cent the federal abatement having been taken into account, the tax saving would be the same as with the credit approach.

Even if the federal abatement is ignored, for an incentive "amount" of $2000, the difference between a 20 per cent credit and a deduction at the top Quebec marginal rate of 24 per cent in 1991 is only $80. Ontario could make any economic incentive equally attractive to upper-income tax filers, as is done in Quebec, by establishing the credit at 24 per cent of the appropriate "amount." The Ontario credit on the amount would then exceed the Ontario tax base on the same amount because the Ontario top marginal rate is only 15.4 per cent. In short, Ontario can match the generosity of the Quebec economic incentives provided through the deduction of certain limited annual amounts from income by the adoption of a set of allowable annual amounts and percentage credits. As is the case with "social" credits, providing the incentive in the form of credits rather than as deductions would make such investments particularly attractive to Ontario residents with low taxable incomes.

Assessment of Option B: A Separate PIT for Ontario

The foregoing assessment of Option A, the federal proposal, implicitly constitutes part of the assessment of the more dramatic alternative – the establishment of a separate PIT by Ontario.

Generally speaking, tax credits are a more efficient method of providing tax relief for those with low income and/or bearing particularly onerous obligations; tax credits can be used to provide investment incentives that can match or surpass in generosity the deduction from income of allowable amounts. If this argument is accepted, the only substantive constraints arise from differences of opinion concerning the appropriate composition of the PIT base and the appropriate structure of PIT rates.

Disagreements are certainly possible between the federal and the Ontario tax authorities concerning matters such as the appropriate deduction for the expenses of earning income, the appropriate exemption for capital gains, the appropriate deduction for retirement savings, and the appropriate treatment of capital and business losses, to name only a few. In the past, decisions about these contentious issues essentially have been treated as entirely within the federal prerogative. There is nothing in the constitution that would warrant such a federal stance. But until such questions have been the subject of federal-provincial negotiations over a number of years, it would seem premature to assume that agreements on the PIT structure cannot be reached and that a separate PIT for Ontario is therefore warranted if Ontario is to secure the requisite degree of autonomy.

A substantive constraint of the present system also arises from the difficulties faced by provinces that wish to substitute a flat rate of tax on income for a progressive rate of tax. The three prairie provinces have placed themselves in an incongruous position by trying to combine the two, because they have not, up to now, been able to cut themselves loose from the progressive federal PIT rate structure.

Until such time as Ontario decides that a flat rate of tax is essential to the achievement of an equitable distribution of the provincial PIT burden, or that a flat tax with refundable credits would provide the best means of integrating the positive and negative income taxes, or for some other explicit reason, it would seem premature to abandon the present system with all the costs involved in adopting Options A or B, for the freedom to do something that is unlikely to be done. In short, if it is assumed that the federal government and the provinces (Quebec formally excepted) can arrive at a mutually acceptable definition of taxable income, the benefits from a separate Ontario PIT are most unlikely to outweigh the costs.

This conclusion is based on the following eight considerations.

- Administrative costs: The Ontario Economic Council's 1982 investigation, which was carried out by John Thomson, a partner in Coopers & Lybrand, is summarized in the volume entitled *A Separate Personal Income Tax for Ontario* in the following terms: "Because of the nature of the present Canadian personal income tax, the system would require a duplication of most of the administrative machinery that is already being used by the federal government in collecting the same tax from the same taxpayers. The cost of the additional Ontario administration would be in the order of $75–100 million annually, aside from start-up costs and a capital investment in buildings of some $60 million. There would be no noticeable decline in the costs of administering the federal personal income tax system" (192). Given that prices have roughly doubled over the past decade, the estimated additional administrative costs to the Ontario taxpayer would be about $100 per year.
- The same accountant in the same document estimated that a separate Ontario PIT would entail additional compliance costs for 1982 as follows (215):

  – for individuals $ 75–225 million per year
  – for employers $ 30–60 million per year
  _____
  Total $105–285 million per year

  Taking into account the doubling of prices over the past decade, the additional compliance costs would be roughly $200 million per year.
- A separate Ontario PIT would therefore involve an estimated increase in administrative and compliance costs of about $300 million per year.
- Although the transformation of the MST into the GST was entirely a federal matter, it would be foolhardy to suppose that taxpayers generally, and small businessmen particularly, have accepted, much less forgotten, a tax change that imposed a substantial increase in compliance costs upon them.
- For the province of Ontario to assume an additional administrative burden of something in the order of $100 million per year, which would result from a separate Ontario PIT in a period of fiscal aus-

terity, would be difficult to justify, unless there were some resulting obvious, immediate, and material benefits to taxpayers. This is unlikely to be the case.

- "Transparency" is a virtue, but the present Ontario PIT is certainly not a hidden tax. Adoption of a separate Ontario PIT would be bound to create more hostility towards this form of taxation, a hostility that would be sadly misplaced given the fairness of the levy compared with the obvious alternatives. Requiring employers to report separately on T4 slips the amounts of federal and Ontario PIT deductions would go a long way towards raising taxpayers awareness of the Ontario PIT with a relatively small additional compliance cost.
- A separate PIT for Ontario would not permit great simplifications in the sense that the present credits for property taxes, sales taxes, home ownership savings, political contributions, and tax reductions could be eliminated. Quebec, which has a separate PIT, has the counterpart of each of these measures. Income deductions would not be an adequate substitute for the existing Ontario credits. Even with a separate Ontario rate structure and some control over the magnitude of non-refundable credits, these measures are likely to remain.

  Some of the Quebec income deductions for expenses, such as employment expenses, child care, and tuition are probably better dealt with by the present system of non-refundable credits. The Quebec incentive provided by the deduction of limited amounts for taxpayer investments in provincial enterprises from income could be matched, although not precisely replicated, through a system of credits. It is a matter of establishing the appropriate annual limits for the allowable amounts and the percentage of the allowable amounts that could be subtracted from provincial tax in the light of the top provincial marginal rate.
- A symbolic concern overwhelms all of the foregoing negative considerations. As we all are aware, the Canadian federation is in grave danger of collapse. For Ontario to decide to adopt a separate provincial PIT at this point in Canada's history would be taken by all Canadians as a further sign of national disintegration. Historically, the residents of Ontario have played a dominant role in Canadian development. Now is the time for Ontario to support the federal government's recent emphasis on improving the economic union. Insisting on a separate Ontario PIT would be taken, rightly or wrongly, as a move in the opposite direction.

Recommended Conditions for Ontario's Acceptance of the Federal Proposal

- It would greatly increase tax filer compliance costs and federal collection costs of eligibility for the non-refundable credit "amounts" differed from province to province. (The Quebec definitions do not appear to differ significantly from the federal.)

  This is not to say that the present federal definitions with respect to qualifications are satisfactory. The federal definition of a married tax filer excludes common-law marriages. This limitation poses problems when one partner has a child from an earlier marriage. If they marry, the parent, if working, cannot obtain the married equivalent credit. When gay or lesbian persons live together with only one working, the earner is not eligible for a married amount. If Ontario is to abide by the federal eligibility rules, it must insist on having a voice in determining those rules.
- Limitations on the provincial amounts of these credits would seem to be unnecessary. It is true that if they differ from province to province, tax filers with the same characteristics will be taxed as difference average rates in different provinces. But that result will obtain if provincial PIT rates differ. They have differed in the past; they will not doubt differ in the future.

  The discussion paper shows that in 1990 the average effective PIT rate in Saskatchewan was 64.1 (the highest) and in Alberta it was 49.5 (the lowest). This disparity arose because of the flat tax on net income imposed in Saskatchewan. Giving the provinces complete latitude in setting the size of the credits is unlikely to bring about disparities that approach this magnitude.
- Ontario should insist that the federal government undertake prior consultation on all significant PIT changes. This consultation should involve not only the provinces but all interested parties. To ensure that such a commitment is honoured, the consultation requirement should form part of the amended tax collection agreements.
- The discussion paper rightly emphasizes the importance of achieving tax neutrality in Canada. The more recent federal paper entitled *Canadian Federalism and Economic Union: Partnership for Prosperity* also stresses the need to remove the impediments to a full economic union. There is no doubt that some provincial policies have adversely affected the allocation of resources; it is equally obvious that some federal measures have also impeded factor mobility within Canada. The commission recommends that Ontario require that the

federal government undertake a full independent investigation of
all impediments to factor mobility, both federal and provincial. This
study would attempt to estimate the quantitative importance of each
such impediment with the analysis of provincial PIT differences
forming part of the investigation.

After the results of this investigation have been published and
considered by all orders of government, a conference should be
held in which each government would disclose its plan for removing the barriers for which it is responsible within a stated time
frame. A federal commitment to such an investigation and conference should be a condition of Ontario's acceptance of the federal
proposals advanced in the discussion paper.

Assessment of Option C: Maintaining the Status Quo

There are several features of the present Ontario PIT that should be
re-examined; among them are the following:

- The tax reduction – under some circumstances forgiveness – might
  be designed to provide relief only for parents with one or more
  dependants rather than including single persons without dependants. The decline in the reduction is too rapid, with the result that
  the marginal rates faced by tax filers with low taxable incomes are
  relatively high. The method adopted for the surtax, namely applying a reduction of X per cent to all Ontario tax less than Y dollars,
  and a reduction of $2X$ per cent to all Ontario tax less than one-half
  Y dollars might provide a superior alternative.
- Although mindful of the revenue cost, there would be merit in
  considering the conversion of the present property tax and sales
  tax credits to refundable credits.
- Consciousness of the Ontario PIT could be enhanced by employers
  to show separately on the T4 slips issued to their employees the
  amounts of federal and Ontario PIT deducted at source.
- Should Ontario decide to introduce an investment incentive into
  the provincial PIT, it should be done by providing a credit against
  provincial tax. The appropriate limit(s) of creditable investments
  and the percentage rate of credit are beyond the scope of this paper,
  but there is no reason why these credits could not be made as
  generous as required by interprovincial competition.

All of these changes could be made within the context of the present
tax collection agreement provisions.

The fundamental weakness of the federal proposals, from the point of view of Ontario, is that they do not address the issues in contention between the province and the federal government with respect to the present PIT arrangements. Among the problems that need to be addressed, but are not addressed by the federal proposals, are the following:

- There have been many clarion calls for greater federal-provincial consultation with respect to the federal PIT structure. The latest of these calls can be found in the Department of Finance's document prepared for the constitutional debate entitled *Canadian Federalism and Economic Union: Partnership for Prosperity* released on 26 September 1991. Although the emphasis in this document is upon greater federal-provincial coordination with respect to macroeconomic policy, the same case can be made for PIT structure matters. Such expressions of good intent carry little weight after so many earlier promises have been broken.
- The present arrangements encourage each order of government to avoid PIT measures that would have the effect of transferring funds from one treasury to another through the PIT system. Thus, provinces try to avoid transfer payments, or tax relief, or investment incentives that would be taxable by the federal government – and conversely. The point is not that PIT benefits provided by one government should not be taxed by the other government, but that the revenues derived from taxing them by another order of government should be returned to the government that bore the initial cost. Without such federal-provincial cooperation, PIT provisions will be unduly complex, and hence incomprehensible to the average tax filer, because their design will reflect interjurisdictional rivalries as much as or more than the stated objectives.
- When the federal government cuts its expenditures for PIT administration, thereby reducing the effectiveness of its audits, the interests of the provinces for which it collects the tax are adversely affected. Admittedly, the provinces do not reimburse the federal government for the additional cost of provincial PIT collection. But the federal government has assumed an obligation. The interests of the provinces in adequate enforcement need to be explicitly recognized by the federal government. The present basis of unilateral federal determination of the appropriate degree of enforcement is not satisfactory.
- The discussion paper and the more recent federal constitutional paper entitled *Canadian Federalism and Economic Union* make much

of the virtues of tax harmonization as a necessary condition for the achievement of a more complete Canadian economic union. What both papers fail to clarify are the criteria that should be applied in determining which policies, by either order of government, are inconsistent with the more complete realization of the Canadian economist union. Provincial contracting/purchasing policies that give preferences to goods produced in the province are clearly beyond the pale. The same is true of provincial professional licensing provisions that are designed to exclude qualified practitioners from outside the province from practising in the province.

But there are a host of provincial and federal policies that are non-neutral in their effects geographically. Are federal regional development subsidies acceptable but similar provincial schemes unacceptable? What about seasonal unemployment insurance benefits provided by the federal government that principally benefit Atlantic fishermen? Can provincial liquor-store purchasing policies that favour local products over imported products continue? Can provinces sell electric power to their own producers below the costs imposed on other purchasers? There is great merit in having a neutral PIT system in Canada, but the same neutrality criteria should be applied to all policy instruments deployed by all orders of government.

The Ontario Fair Tax Commission recommends that the Government of Ontario accept the federal proposals advanced in the discussion paper with the following conditions:

- The federal government must agree to consult with the provinces concerning possible changes in the definition of the eligibility requirements for non-refundable credits, and these requirements should be jointly reviewed on a regular basis.
- The federal government must agree to introduce an open consultative process with regard to all significant changes in the federal PIT base, and this process should be entrenched in the tax collection agreement.
- The federal government must abandon any attempt to limit the amounts of provincial non-refundable credits.
- The federal government must initiate an independent investigation of *all* government measures that distort the allocation of productive resources and attempt to provide quantitative estimates of their perverse effects. When this information has been circulated and studied, a conference should be held to which government rep-

resentatives would be invited and at which they would unveil their target dates for removing these impediments to a strong economic union. Provincial differences in PIT structures would be one of the matters investigated and reported upon.

Within the context of a continuing PIT collection arrangement with the federal government, the commission believes that Ontario should assess its current provisions for surtaxes, tax reductions, and Ontario credits. A comparison of the measures adopted by other provinces, especially Quebec, should form part of this investigation.

Conclusions

Unless the province of Ontario decides that is wishes to impose a flat-rate PIT, the federal proposals do not seem to offer sufficient benefits to the province relative to the status quo to warrant the higher compliance costs that would be incurred by some tax filers if the proposals were adopted. Even if the province had control over the provincial PIT rate structure and the amounts of provincial non-refundable credits, it would not be able to abandon its present provisions for tax reductions and property tax, sales tax, home ownership savings, and political contributions and achieve the same results by simpler means.

It is true that under the proposal the Government of Ontario would be seen by its tax filers as forgoing revenues with respect to the provision of Ontario non-refundable credits – a perception that is not now shared by a high proportion of Ontario residents who file PIT returns. The province would also be seen by poorly informed tax filers to be imposing a PIT, a perception that also is not now shared by a high proportion of Ontario residents. From Ontario's standpoint, there are many serious flaws in the present PIT system, but none of them would be corrected by the adoption of the federal proposals. These proposals seem to have been designed to satisfy the western provinces that, probably unwisely, have adopted flat-rate PIT provisions.

Before abandoning the present PIT arrangements and adopting a separate PIT for Ontario, with the substantial increase in compliance and collection costs that doing so would entail, the federal government should be given an opportunity to correct the flaws in the existing system. This action would require that the federal government consult with the provinces that are signatories of the tax collection agreements with respect to all significant changes in the PIT base and rates and in the administration of PIT collection. The consultation must be more than a formality – it must give the provinces a significant voice in PIT decisions.

An agreement must be reached concerning the general principles that will guide the PIT treatment by one order of government of the benefits provided to (or conceivably the burdens inflicted upon) tax filers by another order of government. Such agreement is necessary to avoid policies of the different orders of government negating one another, in whole or in part, or leading to the adoption of complex measures that are contrived largely in an attempt to foil the enjoyment of benefits by the other, or the inflicting of costs on the other. If provincial "flexibility" with respect to their PITs is to have any meaning, Ottawa must not, in whole or in part, capture benefits intended for Ontario residents through legitimate provincial measures.

There is an urgent need to arrive at a mutually acceptable set of standards that will differentiate between those federal and provincial measures that will be accepted as legitimate and those measures that will be rejected as unacceptable. These standards should reflect three sets of considerations:

• constitutional requirements;
• economic union requirements that would prohibit barriers to the mobility of goods, services, people, and capital; and
• economic neutrality requirements that would prohibit "tilting the playing field" in favour of some locations rather than others.

Although the constitutional requirements are absolute in a legal sense, there is no prohibition against agreements by which one order of government would assign powers and responsibilities to the other, presumably for a consideration. The second and third requirements are not absolute in even a legal sense. Geography itself is a barrier to mobility, and perfect neutrality is not attainable if different jurisdictions are to have different public sectors.

Nevertheless, it would not seem beyond human wit to differentiate broad classes of policies that are acceptable from those that are unacceptable. For example, generous benefits provided to low-income families by tax relief or by transfers of cash or by subsidized housing would, of course, attract such families to jurisdictions that offered them. But, if the benefits were offered to all resident families with low incomes (without a long waiting period), one would expect that prudence exercised by provincial and municipal governments would ensure that the disparities in the benefits offered would not differ greatly from jurisdiction to jurisdiction. Greater difficulties arise with respect to industry-specific policies when, as is often the case in Canada, the industries are tied to natural resources that are fixed in location. When dealing with such industries as farming, fishing, forestry, and mining, it is difficult to determine what constitutes a neutral, tax-expenditure-regulatory policy, because each has unique features.

Even more intractable are the problems posed by so-called "depressed" or "slow-growth" regions – whether consisting of contiguous parts of more than one province (e.g., the Atlantic provinces) or one or more parts of one province (e.g., northern and eastern Ontario). A rule that places federal measures inside the bounds and provincial measures outside the bounds should not be acceptable.

The existence of mutually acceptable criteria for differentiating between acceptable and unacceptable policies by all orders of government would place the consideration of PIT measures within the appropriate context – the PIT is one of many policy instruments. PIT provisions should be judged by the same general criteria as are applied to other policy instrumentalities deployed by all Canadian governments.

In summary, three important areas of federal-provincial agreement are essential if, in the long run, the interests of the residents of Ontario are to be served by remaining within the tax collection agreements: participation in future decisions about potential PIT changes; the development of rules about the measures that may be adopted by Ontario without having a significant portion of the benefits captured by the federal government; and the development by all orders of government of mutually acceptable criteria to differentiate between the policies that are consistent with certain national standards and those that are unacceptable. These standards must meet the requirements of the constitutional division of powers, the Canadian economic union, and geographic economic neutrality. PIT provisions, whether adopted by the federal government or by the province, should meet these standards, as should all policy measures by all Canadian governments.

It would be naïve to expect that these agreements would be easily reached or that, with the agreements in hand, all sources of federal-provincial conflict would be removed. But the agreements would narrow the focus of the areas in dispute and thereby reduce the likelihood that emotion would overwhelm common sense.

painful fact that the future of the Canadian federation is now in jeopardy. For the Government of Ontario to abandon the tax collection agreements at this time and adopt a separate Ontario PIT would be taken as yet another symbol of national disintegration. This is reason enough to reject that option. If the future of the nation were not in peril, the additional compliance and administrative costs would weigh heavily against it, as would the temptation it would present for the adoption of beggar-my-neighbour PIT policies by Ontario and other provinces.

Annex: Personal Income Tax, 1991, Federal, Ontario, and Quebec, by Employment Income Levels

List of Annex Tables

Single No Dependants: Federal, Ontario, Quebec, and Federal + Provincial Combined
Table A1.: Comparison of 1991 PIT : in Dollars
Table A2.: Comparison of 1991 Average PIT Rates in Per Cent
Table A3.: Comparison of 1991 Marginal PIT Rates in Per Cent

Married with Two Children under 16: Federal, Ontario, Quebec, and Federal + Provincial Combined
Table A4.: Comparison of 1991 PIT : in Dollars
Table A5.: Comparison of 1991 Average PIT Rates in Per Cent
Table A6.: Comparison of 1991 Marginal PIT Rates in Per Cent

TABLE A1
Comparison of 1991 PIT: Federal, Ontario, Quebec, and Federal + Province, Single Taxpayer with No Dependants, in Dollars

Income	Federal Ontario	Federal Quebec	Ontario	Quebec	Combined Ontario	Combined Quebec
5,000	−190	−190	0	0	−190	−190
7,500	−25	−51	0	0	−25	−51
10,000	400	307	297	195	697	502
12,500	825	665	512	618	1,337	1,283
15,000	1,249	1,023	727	1,070	1,976	2,093
17,500	1,674	1,381	941	1,562	2,615	2,943
20,000	2,099	1,739	1,155	2,061	3,254	3,800
22,500	2,523	2,097	1,370	2,561	3,893	4,658
27,500	3,508	2,948	1,798	3,610	5,306	6,558
30,000	4,102	3,458	2,071	4,157	6,173	7,615

TABLE A1 – *cont'd.*

Income	Federal Ontario	Federal Quebec	Ontario	Quebec	Combined Ontario	Combined Quebec
30,000	4,102	3,458	2,071	4,157	6,173	7,615
35,000	5,443	4,588	2,747	5,275	8,190	9,863
40,000	6,806	5,737	3,436	6,423	10,242	12,160
50,000	9,536	8,038	4,814	8,723	14,350	16,761
75,000	17,091	14,433	8,535	14,701	25,626	29,134
100,000	25,066	21,212	12,663	20,701	37,729	41,913
200,000	56,966	48,327	29,878	44,701	86,844	93,028

SOURCE: Data supplied by David B. Perry, Canadian Tax Foundation, using the foundation's PIT model (1991).

TABLE A2
Comparison of 1991 PIT Average Rates: Federal, Ontario, Quebec, and Federal + Province, Single Taxpayer with No Dependants, in Dollars

Income	Federal Ontario Av. Rate	Federal Quebec Av. Rate	Ontario Av. Rate	Quebec Av. Rate	Combined Ontario Av. Rate	Combined Quebec Av. Rate
5,000	−3.80	−3.80	0.00	0.00	−3.80	−3.80
7,500	−0.33	−0.68	0.00	0.00	−0.33	−0.68
10,000	4.00	3.07	2.97	1.95	6.97	5.02
12,500	6.60	5.32	4.10	4.94	10.70	10.26
15,000	8.33	6.82	4.85	7.13	13.17	13.95
17,500	9.57	7.89	5.38	8.93	14.94	16.82
20,000	10.50	8.70	5.78	10.31	16.27	19.00
22,500	11.21	9.32	6.09	11.38	17.30	20.70
27,500	12.76	10.72	6.54	13.13	19.29	23.85
30,000	13.67	11.53	6.90	13.86	20.58	25.38
35,000	15.55	13.11	7.85	15.07	23.40	28.18
40,000	17.02	14.34	8.59	16.06	25.61	30.40
50,000	19.07	16.08	9.63	17.45	28.70	33.52
75,000	22.79	19.24	11.38	19.60	34.17	38.85
100,000	25.07	21.21	12.66	20.70	37.73	41.91
200,000	28.48	24.16	14.94	22.35	43.42	46.51

SOURCE: See table 1.

134   Douglas G. Hartle

TABLE A3
Comparison of 1991 PIT Marginal Rates: Federal, Ontario, Quebec, and Federal + Province, Single Taxpayer with No Dependants, in Dollars

Income	Federal Ontario M. Rate	Federal Quebec M. Rate	Ontario M. Rate	Quebec M. Rate	Combined Ontario M. Rate	Combined Quebec M. Rate
5,000						
7,500	6.60	5.56	0.00	0.00	6.60	5.56
10,000	17.00	14.32	11.88	7.80	28.88	22.12
12,500	17.00	14.32	8.60	16.92	25.60	31.24
15,000	16.96	14.32	8.60	18.08	25.56	32.40
17,500	17.00	14.32	8.56	19.68	25.56	34.00
20,000	17.00	14.32	8.56	19.96	25.56	34.28
22,500	16.96	14.32	8.60	20.00	25.56	34.32
27,500	19.70	17.02	8.56	20.98	28.26	38.00
30,000	23.76	20.40	10.92	21.88	34.68	42.28
35,000	26.82	22.60	13.52	22.36	40.34	44.96
40,000	27.26	22.98	13.78	22.96	41.04	45.94
50,000	27.30	23.01	13.78	23.00	41.08	46.01
75,000	30.22	25.58	14.88	23.91	45.10	49.49
100,000	31.90	27.12	16.51	24.00	48.41	51.12
200,000	31.90	27.12	17.22	24.00	49.12	51.12

SOURCE: See table 1.

TABLE A4
Comparison of 1991 PIT: Federal, Ontario, Quebec, and Federal + Province, Married Taxpayer with Two Children under 16

Income	Federal Ontario	Federal Quebec	Ontario	Quebec	Combined Ontario	Combined Quebec
5,000	−1,750	−1,750	0	0	−1,750	−1,750
7,500	−1,750	−1,750	0	0	−1,750	−1,750
10,000	−1,750	−1,750	0	0	−1,750	−1,750
12,500	−1,670	−1,692	0	0	−1,670	−1,692
15,000	−1,245	−1,334	0	0	−1,245	−1,334
17,500	−820	−976	0	0	−820	−976
20,000	−395	−618	0	0	−395	−618
22,500	29	−260	94	0	123	−260
27,500	1,209	780	1,327	993	2,536	1,773
30,000	2,076	1,544	1,638	1,610	3,714	3,154
35,000	3,916	3,174	2,315	2,923	6,231	6,097
40,000	5,559	4,606	3,003	4,270	8,562	8,876
50,000	8,679	7,300	4,381	6,971	13,060	14,271
75,000	16,774	14,220	7,991	12,882	24,765	27,102
100,000	24,749	20,999	12,054	18,882	36,803	39,881
200,000	56,649	48,114	29,268	42,882	85,917	90,996

SOURCE: See table 1.

TABLE A5
Comparison of 1991 PIT Average Rates: Federal, Ontario, Quebec, and Federal +
Province, Married Taxpayer with Two Children under 16

Income	Federal Ontario Av. Rate	Federal Quebec Av. Rate	Ontario Av. Rate	Quebec Av. Rate	Combined Ontario Av. Rate	Combined Quebec Av. Rate
5,000	−35.00	−35.00	0.00	0.00	−35.00	−35.00
7,500	−23.33	−23.33	0.00	0.00	−23.33	−23.33
10,000	−17.50	−17.50	0.00	0.00	−17.50	−17.50
12,500	−13.36	−13.54	0.00	0.00	−13.36	−13.54
15,000	−8.30	−8.89	0.00	0.00	−8.30	−8.89
17,500	−4.69	−5.58	0.00	0.00	−4.69	−5.58
20,000	−1.98	−3.09	0.00	0.00	−1.98	−3.09
22,500	0.13	−1.16	0.42	0.00	0.55	−1.16
27,500	4.40	2.84	4.83	3.61	9.22	6.45
30,000	6.92	5.15	5.46	5.37	12.38	10.51
35,000	11.19	9.07	6.61	8.35	17.80	17.42
40,000	13.90	11.52	7.51	10.68	21.41	22.19
50,000	17.36	14.60	8.76	13.94	26.12	28.54
75,000	22.37	18.96	10.65	17.18	33.02	36.14
100,000	24.75	21.00	12.05	18.88	36.80	39.88
200,000	28.32	24.06	14.63	21.44	42.96	45.50

SOURCE: See table 1.

TABLE A6
Comparison of 1991 PIT Marginal Rates: Federal, Ontario, Quebec, and Federal +
Province, Married Taxpayer with Two Children under 16

Income	Federal Ontario M. Rate	Federal Quebec M. Rate	Ontario M. Rate	Quebec M. Rate	Combined Ontario M. Rate	Combined Quebec M. Rate
5,000						
7,500	0.00	0.00	0.00	0.00	0.00	0.00
10,000	0.00	0.00	0.00	0.00	0.00	0.00
12,500	3.20	2.32	0.00	0.00	3.20	2.32
15,000	17.00	14.32	0.00	0.00	17.00	14.32
17,500	17.00	14.32	0.00	0.00	17.00	14.32
20,000	17.00	14.32	0.00	0.00	17.00	14.32
22,500	16.96	14.32	3.76	0.00	20.72	14.32
27,500	23.60	20.80	24.66	19.86	48.26	40.66
30,000	34.68	30.56	12.44	24.68	47.12	55.24
35,000	36.80	32.60	13.54	26.26	50.34	58.86
40,000	32.86	28.64	13.76	26.94	46.62	55.58
50,000	31.20	26.94	13.78	27.01	44.98	53.95
75,000	32.38	27.68	14.44	23.64	46.82	51.32
100,000	31.90	27.12	16.25	24.00	48.15	51.12
200,000	31.90	27.12	17.21	24.00	49.11	51.12

SOURCE: See table 1.

Note

The first draft of this paper was prepared for the Ontario Fair Tax Comission and was completed in November 1991. The data shown in tables 1, 2, 3, and A1 – A6 were supplied by David B. Perry, Research Staff, Canadian Tax Foundation. They were derived using the Foundation's PIT model. The assistance of Mr Perry is acknowledged with gratitude.

Bibliography

Canada. 1991a. *Canadian Federalism and Economic Union: Partnership for Prosperity.* Quebec: Supply and Services Canada
– 1991b. *Personal Income Tax Coordination: the Federal-Provincial Tax Collection Agreements.* Discussion Paper. Ontario: CCH
Conklin, David W., ed. 1984. *A Separate Personal Income Tax for Ontario: Background Studies.* Toronto: Ontario Economic Council
Ontario Economic Council. 1983a. *A Separate Personal Income Tax for Ontario: An Ontario Economic Council Position Paper.* Toronto: Ontario Economic Council
– 1983b. Hartle, D.G., ed. *A Separate Personal Income Tax for Ontario: An Economic Analysis.* Toronto: Ontario Economic Council

4 The Compliance Costs of a Separate Personal Income Tax System for Ontario

Simulations for 1991

BRIAN ERARD and FRANÇOIS VAILLANCOURT

Introduction

The purpose of this study is to assess the likely compliance costs of a separate personal income tax (PIT) system for Ontario. This topic is addressed below in five major sections and one appendix. The first section provides a discussion of the conceptual issues relating to the definition and measurement of compliance costs. In the second section, a survey of the existing literature on taxpayer compliance costs is presented and discussed. The third section provides an overview of the existing Canadian provincial and U.S. state personal income tax systems. In the fourth section, the compliance costs of a separate Ontario PIT system are estimated using alternative assumptions about the degree of provincial harmonization with federal tax rules and collection procedures. The estimation methodology, which is first introduced in that section, is described in greater detail in the appendix. The fifth section provides a discussion of policy implications and conclusions.

Conceptual Issues

Compliance costs may be defined as those costs experienced by taxpayers and third parties (such as unpaid tax preparers, employers, and financial institutions) in the process of reporting, collecting, and paying taxes that are in excess of the amount of tax paid. For filers of personal income tax returns, these costs include the value of the taxpayer's own time in learning about the tax laws; identifying and

documenting deductions, credits, and exemptions; planning transactions; preparing and filing returns; and responding to inquiries from
the tax agency. To this amount should be added the time value of
tax assistance from friends or family members, the financial expenses
of taxpayers for paid tax assistance and for tax preparation materials,
and the costs incurred by employers and financial institutions in complying with withholding, and information reporting requirements. In
addition, some taxpayers may experience "psychic" or "mental" costs
due to the anxiety and frustration associated with complying with the
tax laws. Although there is no Canadian evidence on their size, evidence for Great Britain indicates that these costs can be substantial,
and that they tend to "fall disproportionately on certain classes of
individuals, in particular, the poorer pensioners, widows, and divorced or separated women" (Sandford, Godwin, and Hardwick 1989,
193; see also Pope and Fayle 1990, 3). These costs could lead taxpayers
to seek tax assistance. It is therefore interesting to note that in Canada
self-preparation of PIT returns is less common among women (29.8
per cent) than men (36.8 per cent); less common among elderly taxpayers (28 per cent for taxpayers aged 60 and over) than young taxpayers (37.4 per cent for taxpayers 18 to 29); and less common among
married taxpayers (32.0 per cent) and separated, divorced, or wid-
owed taxpayers (29.9 per cent) than single taxpayers (40.7 per cent)
(Vaillancourt 1989, 102).

Start-Up Costs vs. Long-Run Costs

Certain compliance costs are of a non-recurring nature. For example,
an employer may incur a fixed cost for the installation of a computer
system to keep track of employee accounts for withholding purposes.
Another example is a taxpayer who invests time in learning about
how the tax laws apply to a particular income item. If the taxpayer
retains knowledge of this information, he or she will not need to
make the investment again (at least until the reporting requirements
change). In contrast, some costs are incurred by taxpayers on an annual basis. For example, taxpayers must spend time each year maintaining records for tax purposes. It is important to distinguish between
start-up costs and long-run or steady-state costs when assessing the
compliance cost implications of a change in existing tax laws or the
introduction of a new tax system. Frequent changes in the tax laws,
even when associated with long-run reductions in compliance burdens, can exact a high toll from taxpayers in the form of start-up costs.

Separate estimates are provided in this report of the start-up costs and the change in steady-state compliance costs associated with the introduction of a separate Ontario PIT system.

Marginal Costs vs. Total Costs

Another important distinction should be made between marginal compliance costs and total compliance costs. With reference to the Canadian PIT system, total compliance costs may be defined as the total cost associated with complying with federal and provincial income tax laws. Marginal compliance costs may be defined as the change in total compliance costs associated with a change in the federal-provincial income tax structure. The estimates provided in this report reflect the marginal compliance costs associated with the introduction of a separate Ontario PIT system.

Valuation of Time

Although monetary costs, such as payments for professional tax assistance are straightforward to measure, other costs, such as the value of time spent by taxpayers (and their unpaid assistants) in return preparation, are more difficult to quantify. The cost to a taxpayer of spending time preparing an income tax return, which economists call the taxpayer's "opportunity cost," is represented by the value of his or her next-best alternative use for that time. For example, if, in the absence of tax return preparation, the taxpayer would have enjoyed a leisure activity, the cost of return preparation time is the value of forgone leisure. Alternatively, if the taxpayer would have spent the additional time working, the cost of return preparation time is the forgone employment income. Typically, the value of forgone leisure is measured by the after-tax wage rate, while the value of forgone work is measured by the gross wage rate.[1] In this study, the latter measure is employed; the gross wage rate represents the approximate social value of output that could have been produced if a taxpayer were able to devote an hour of time to work rather than to tax compliance.

Excluded Expenses

In measuring compliance costs, those costs that would be incurred, even in the absence of a tax, should be excluded. For example, in the case of employers who withhold income taxes, costs for keeping accounting records that would be maintained even in the absence of withholding requirements should be excluded. Similarly, for self-employed taxpayers, accounting and auditing procedures that would be used, even in the absence of taxation, should be excluded. In practice, however, it is sometimes difficult to separate compliance costs from ordinary operating expenses.

Time Period

The natural time period for a compliance cost study would appear to be one full taxation cycle – that is, the period during which all activities (data gathering, planning, statement preparation, calculation, reporting, and so forth) associated with collecting, withholding, and remitting taxes are carried out at least once. In many cases, this period will naturally correspond to a calendar year or fiscal year. In cases where a full taxation cycle covers a shorter tax period, such as a quarter, seasonal fluctuations in tax collection and withholding activities nevertheless may often make it appropriate to consider a one-year period.

   If the objective of the study is to measure steady-state compliance costs, it is important to select a "typical" tax year for the analysis. Cyclical fluctuations in economic activity (business cycles) can influence the level and distribution of compliance costs, which makes it desirable to avoid selecting years characterized by business-cycle peaks or troughs. Moreover, years in which substantial new tax legislation is introduced also should be avoided, because new tax rules are generally associated with significant start-up compliance costs, which can confound the analysis.

Literature Survey

The literature on the compliance costs of taxation begins in 1935; the early studies are of little relevance to the present analysis, however, because of their overly general focus – all taxes – and their methodological shortcomings (see Vaillancourt 1987 for a discussion of these studies). The literature surveyed here consists of 12 independent studies that were performed since 1960 for five countries with a similar tradition of taxation: Australia, Canada, New Zealand, the United Kingdom, and the United States. These studies were identified through discussions with C. Sandford, J. Slemrod, and J. Pope, prominent researchers in the field, and a literature search (see Sanford 1989 for a recent survey of the literature). Together, these studies provide evidence on the costs to individuals of complying with income tax laws, and the costs to employers of complying with income and payroll tax withholding requirements. The primary features of these studies are summarized in table 1, and the key findings are presented in table 2.

As table 1 reveals, the studies performed since 1970 tend to be based on larger survey samples than those performed in the 1960s. In our opinion, the increase over time in sample size has been accompanied by improvements in sample quality, questionnaire design, survey administration, and data analysis (including a greater use of multivariate techniques). Thus, greater weight should be given to the results of these more recent studies.

Turning to table 2, we find it useful to consider the key findings for taxpayers separately from those for employers. In the case of individuals, compliance costs range from 1.8 per cent (United Kingdom) to 10.8 per cent (Australia) of tax revenue. The relatively low estimate for taxpayer compliance costs in the United Kingdom reflects a lower reliance on taxpayer self-assessment in that country. Administrative costs in the United Kingdom tend to be relatively high for the same reason. The estimated compliance cost for taxpayers in Australia is unusually large in relation to the findings for other countries. A sensitivity analysis conducted by the authors of the Australian study yields compliance cost estimates ranging from 4.3 per cent to 10.8 per cent. After examining the results of this analysis, we have concluded that their figure of 7.9 per cent is the most reasonable estimate (see Pope and Fayle 1990, 36). This figure is much more in line with the results of the other studies. In all of the studies, compliance costs are significantly higher for self-employed taxpayers than for other taxpayers. Relatively high compliance costs also are experienced by taxpayers with investment income and by individuals who file supplementary forms and schedules (such as the U.S. schedule for itemizing deductions). None of these studies provides direct evidence on the change in taxpayer compliance costs associated with a change in the federal-provincial or federal-state income tax structure. However, the results do provide some indication of overall taxpayer compliance costs and the factors that influence them.

In the case of employers, withholding cost estimates for Canada range from 0.68 per cent to 3.5 per cent of taxes withheld. For the other countries studied, the estimates fall in the 1–2 per cent range.

TABLE 1
Main Characteristics of Studies of Compliance Costs of PIT, Individuals and Employers

Tax(es) Studied	Author/Year Published	Method and Year of Data	Area Studied	Universe Size	Sample Size	Usable Answers	Response Rate (Per Cent)	Comments	Costs Included
PIT	M.H. Bryden (1961)	Mail survey (1960)	Canada	107,387[a]	500 businesses	125	25	The sample is made up of corporate supporters of the Canadian Tax Foundation.	Wages and salaries, direct costs, share of overhead and outside fees are included.
State income tax	J.H. Wicks (1965)	Handout to students (1965)	Montana	240,000[b]	318 individuals[c]	106	33.3	50 non-respondents were phoned and had lower costs than respondents; results were adjusted accordingly.	Time costs were calculated using survey data on hours spent keeping records and preparing income tax returns. Dollar value of time was computed from estimates of hourly earned income from survey data on taxes paid. Money costs include amounts paid for record keeping and return preparation work.
Federal income tax	J.H. Wicks (1966)	Handout to students/mail return (1964)	Montan	237,000[d]	380 individuals	118	31.1	75 non-respondents were phoned and had lower costs than respondents; results were adjusted accordingly.	Time costs were calculated using survey data on hours spent keeping records and parparing income tax returns. Dollar value of time was computed from estimates of hourly earned income from survey data on taxes paid. Money costs include amounts paid for record keeping and tax return preparation work.

Income tax	C.T. Sandford (1973)	Face to face (1971)	Great Britain	Unknown	3,555 individuals	2,773	78	In some calculations, only respondents from England and Wales (2,472) are used.	Time costs were calculated using survey data on time spent attending to "personal tax affairs." The value of time was chosen to be less than wages, yet high enough to represent the disutility associated with tax work. The work of unpaid advisers is also included.
*		Mail survey (high cost taxpayers) (1971)		Unknown	335 individuals	116	34.6	30 non-respondents were interviewed; the sample may have a disproportionate share of self-employed taxpayers who use tax advisers.	Money costs were obtained from survey data on fees to tax advisers, corrected for sampling biases and under-billing and miscellaneous expenses incurred by high-cost taxpayers.
Federal and state income tax	J. Slemrod N. Sorum (1984)	Mail survey (1982)	Minnesota, U.S.A.	1,713,000e	2,000 individuals	600	30	The sample weights were adjusted to account for undersampling of low-income households.	Time costs were calculated using survey data on time spent learning about tax rules, keeping records, reading tax tables, preparing returns, and providing information to tax advisers. The value of time was computed from survey data or imputed data (when information was missing) on the after-tax wage rate. Money costs include fees to tax advisers and miscellaneous expenses.

TABLE 1 – *cont'd.*

Tax(es) Studied	Author/Year Published	Method and Year of Data	Area Studied	Universe Size	Sample Size	Usable Answers	Response Rate (Per Cent)	Comments	Costs Included
Federal income tax	Arthur D. Little (1988)	Diary study (1983)	U.S.A.	Unknown	700 individuals	700	100	The sampling frame was the universe of all individual tax filers living in housing units in the continental U.S.A.	The results of this study were used to adjust the survey results for recall response bias.
		Mail survey (1983)	U.S.A.	96,143,473	6,212 individuals	3,831	65.2	The sample weights were adjusted on the basis of a telephone follow-up of a sub-sample of non-respondents.	This study contains detailed data on taxpayer form and line-item usage as a result of a computer match of survey and tax return data.
Income tax	C.T. Sandford M. Godwin P. Hardwick (1989)	Mail survey (1984)	Great Britain	24,700,000	4,241 individuals	1,776	41.9		Time costs were calculated using responses to "the hourly value of this time to me" question. Only total time was requested.
PAYE and NI		Mail survey (1982)		1,013,000	3,039 employees	783	25.8	A pilot was carried out in 1981. Seventeen respondents were interviewed face to face.	Hours were multiplied by the average hourly cost to get wage costs. Other costs also are collected.
PIT and payroll taxes	F. Vaillancourt (1989)								
Individuals		Face to face (1986)	Canada	15,926,804	2,040 individuals	2,040	100	The sampling procedure guaranteed the desired sample size through replacement of non-respondents.	Time costs were calculated using gross wages or imputed gross wages. Specific use of time were examined.

Employers		Mail survey (1987)		54,273	4,196 employers	385	9.2	The universe employed for sampling was the number of Dun and Bradstreet registered firms, not the full universe of employers.	Wages and salaries and overhead costs were collected.
PIT	J. Pope R. Fayle M. Duncanson (1990)	Mail survey (1989)	Australia	8,362,400	7,000 individuals	1,098	15.7	Pilot of 100 in 1987	Time costs were calculated using responses to "the approximate value per hour of this time to me" question. Total preparation time was requested.
PIT	M. Blumenthal J. Slemrod (1992)	Mail survey (1990)	Minnesota, U.S.A.	1,990,443f	2,000 individuals	708	43.4	Very similar to 1982 study by Slemrod and Sorum	Time costs were computed using the after-tax wage rate. Seven time uses are recorded.
PAYE and other withholding taxes	C.T. Sandford J. Hasseldine (1992)	Mail survey (1991)	New Zealand	140,076	4,743 employers	1,887	39.8	Sample was selected from the Inland Revenue file of employers (1/27).	Time costs of employers and all costs of agent/adviser are included. Overhead costs are specifically excluded.
PAYE	J. Pope R. Fayle D. Chen (1992)	Mail survey (1991)	Australia	519,008	3,084 employers	745	24.2	Pilot of 100 in western Australia carried out in 1991.	–

a Taxation Statistics, 1962, Revenue Canada, Section III, Table I, p. 110; all corporations except inactive ones

b Statistical Abstract of the United States 1968, Table 554, Number of returns for 1965, Federal income tax

c Estimate based on Wicks's statement that "The 106 represented approximately one-third of those to whom questionnaires were submitted"

d Statistical Abstract of the United States 1967, Table 555, Number of returns for 1964, Federal income tax

e Statistical Abstract of the United States 1985, Table 517, Number of returns, Federal individual income tax

f Internal Revenue Service, Annual Report 1990, Table 7, Number of returns filed

TABLE 2
Key Findings of Studies of Compliance Costs of the Personal Income Tax

Author/Year Published	Compliance Cost as Percentage of Tax	Key Fact
M.H. Bryden (1961) Employers	0.684 per cent[a]	– Cost of collecting the PIT is higher in Québec (1.06 per cent) than for all Canada.
J.H. Wicks (1965) Individuals	7 per cent[b]	– "Costs tend to be especially high for those who are self-employed." (41) – "For the typical taxpayer, the state cost is only about 11 per cent of the federal." (41)
J.H. Wicks (1966) Individuals	3 per cent[b]	– "The self-employed bore the highest costs." (20) – "Probably no significant correlation between cost and income." (21) – [Itemizer] "had higher average costs ... all the self-employed itemized." (21)
C.T. Sandford (1973) Individuals	1.87–3.39–7.32 per cent Estimates from table 3.8 (44) vary depending on value of fees, own time and miscellaneous expenses.	– "Compliance costs tend to fall with disproportionate weight ... (on) the self-employed and to a lesser extent on the executive and professional classes." (146) – "Compliance costs have little relationship to income." (146) – A cost in the 3–5 per cent range would appear reasonable to the author.
J. Slemrod and N. Sorum (1984) Individuals	7 per cent (federal and state income tax)	– [Everything else equal] "The self-employed have $400 more in total resource cost than ... employees." (27) – "The lowest income class is associated with relatively high compliance cost, as is being in the highest income class." (27)
Arthur D. Little (1988) Individuals	No estimate given	Average time burden is 26.4 hours. Time burden varies with the numbrer of line items and forms completed.
Sandford et al. (1989) PIT Individuals	3.6 per cent	– "The most important factors ... were size of income and category of employment." (79)

TABLE 2 – *cont'd.*

Author/Year Published	Compliance Cost as Percentage of Tax	Key Fact
PAYE and NI	1.0 per cent	– "Compliance costs showed a regressive pattern (for the self-employed)." (79) – "Factors associated with high compliance cost may include ... the number of different types of income the allowances claimed." (234) – "Capital gains increase compliance costs." (237) – "Firms using standard IR documents reported higher cost: yield ratios than firms using substitute document." (86) – "The impact of compliance costs was regressive." (95)
F. Vaillancourt (1989) Individuals	2.5 per cent	– "Self-employment increase costs as does the receipt of investment income." (44)
Employers	3.5 per cent	– "Compliance costs are regressive." (53)
J. Pope et al. (1990) Individuals	4.3–10.8 per cent	– "Taxpayers with business/investment income have higher costs." (56) – "Compliance costs as a percentage of income tend to follow a u-shaped curve." (48)
M. Blumenthal and J. Slemrod (1992) Individual.	Similar to 1984 study	– "Self-employed ... spend significantly more ... on compliance." (14) – Itemizers have higher costs.
C.T. Sandford and J. Hasseldine (1992) PAYE	1.92 per cent	– "Compliance costs were exceptionally regressive in their incidence." (48)
J. Pope, R. Fayle and D. Chen (1992) PAYE	1.4 per cent	– "Compliance Costs as a percentage of tax tend to be regressive." (62)

[a] Respondents were specifically asked to exclude the costs of the unemployment system.

[b] These are the median values of the costs distribution. They were used rather than mean values of 32 per cent and 11.5 per cent, since Wicks favours using median values.

The difference between the two Canadian estimates reflects the cost of withholding unemployment insurance, which was included only in the study providing the higher estimate. Since the withholding of unemployment insurance accounts for approximately one-half of all withholding compliance costs, a more reasonable estimate of the withholding compliance costs associated with the PIT is 1.8 per cent (see Vaillancourt 1989, 51 for discussion of this adjustment). This figure is comparable to the results of the other studies. The principal finding across studies is that employer compliance costs tend to decrease as employer size increases. For example, in Vaillancourt (1989, 54) employer compliance costs as a percentage of business income are computed to be 3.36 per cent for firms in the lowest business income tiertile, 0.722 per cent for firms in the second business income tiertile, and only 0.0637 per cent for those in the highest business income tiertile.

Description of Provincial and State PIT Systems

In this section, the primary characteristics of the Canadian provincial and U.S. state PIT systems are described.

Ontario PIT System

Under the existing federal-provincial tax collection agreements, Ontario levies its personal income tax as a percentage of the basic federal tax, and the federal government collects the tax for the province. Taxpayers file only a single tax return, and employers are required to make only one deduction from a taxpayer's source income to meet PIT withholding requirements. Under this arrangement, the federal and Ontario PIT systems are closely integrated. However, the computation of federal tax payable takes into account certain tax credits for items such as federal political contributions, investment, labour-sponsored funds; dependent children, and the GST, not accounted for in the computation of provincial income tax. Similarly, certain provincial tax credits for items such as property (or rental payment) tax, sales tax, Ontario political contributions, home ownership savings, investment, worker ownership, and small business development corporations are not accounted for in the computation of federal income tax. Moreover, in addition to these provincial credits, there also exists a provincial tax reduction for low-income taxpayers.

With the exception of Quebec, whose PIT system is described below, the remaining provinces have similar tax collection agreements with the federal government (see Courchene and Stewart 1991 for more detailed discussion of these agreements). In general, the high degree of federal-provincial PIT harmonization together with the federal administration of the Ontario PIT are beneficial in terms of administrative and compliance costs; the requirement to base provincial taxes on the basic federal tax, however, as well as the federal government's restrictions on the types of provincial tax credits it has been willing to administer, has limited Ontario's freedom to use the PIT to accomplish its own policy objectives. In June 1991 the federal government issued a discussion paper on possible changes to the tax collection agreements (Canada 1991). One possibility that was explored in this paper was changing the provincial tax base to federal taxable income. This switch would provide each province with the opportunity to impose its own tax rate schedule and system of nonrefundable tax credits. The compliance cost implications of an Ontario PIT system based on federal taxable income is explored below in the compliance cost estimates section.

Quebec PIT System

Since 1954 Quebec has administered its own PIT system. Although the general structure of the Quebec PIT system is fairly similar to the structure of the federal PIT system, some important differences do exist. Under the Quebec system, the basic personal credits and child dependant credits are higher, the rate structure is somewhat more progressive, child-care-expense provisions are more liberal, and automobile expenses are subject to rather different limitations. Quebec also offers certain provincial deductions and credits that are unavailable at the federal level, such as the various deductions for strategic investments (QSSP, venture capital corporation, QBIC, CIP, PSSP) and employment expenses; the credits for political contributions, research and development, sales tax, and property tax; and the family tax reduction. Moreover, whereas credits exist for unemployment insurance, CPP and QPP contributions, tuition fees, and charitable donations on the federal return, these items are treated as deductions on the Quebec return.

In addition to the above differences, the Quebec and federal PIT regulations have diverged in a number of other ways over time, including the treatment of deductions for capital gains and interest, the rules for RHOSP contributions, and indexing provisions. Moreover, even in cases where the provincial and federal regulations have been the same, the provincial and federal interpretations of these regulations have not always been consistent. Nor does Quebec automatically maintain conformance with amendments to the federal PIT system. (See Foreget 1984 and Thompson 1984 for discussion of additional differences existing previously between the two systems.)

For tax year 1991 the Ontario portion of the federal-provincial income tax booklet consisted of two pages of forms and four pages of instructions (including the forms and instructions for Ontario tax credits and the Ontario tax reduction). In contrast, the long-form version of the 1991 Quebec income tax return contained 28 pages of forms, attachments, and work charts, and 36 pages of instructions; even the short-form version contained 10 pages of forms and attachments and 20 pages of instructions. The initial effort to read and understand the instructions for the Quebec income tax return represents a substantial time investment for taxpayers who prepare their own returns; for taxpayers with relatively uncomplicated tax circumstances, however, the actual record-keeping and reporting requirements are fairly modest. For these taxpayers, the start-up costs from learning about the Quebec tax laws may be substantial, but the long-run or steady-state provincial compliance costs tend to be fairly low. In contrast, for taxpayers with more complicated tax affairs, both the start-up costs and the steady-state costs of compliance can be substantial. Employers and financial institutions also experience additional start-up and steady-state costs from complying with separate federal and provincial withholding and reporting requirements. Unfortunately, no study was performed at the time the Quebec PIT was introduced to measure the start-up compliance costs associated with the tax.

State PIT Systems in the United States

Currently 43 states, plus the District of Columbia, in the United States administer their own personal income tax systems. In response to concerns over administrative and compliance costs, the PIT regulations in many states have evolved over time to conform in significant measure to the federal Internal Revenue Code (IRC). Like the Canadian provinces (excluding Quebec), North Dakota, Rhode Island, and Vermont define state tax liability as a percentage of federal tax liability. In these three states, the degree of harmonization to the federal tax code is extremely high. Twenty-five states, plus the District of Columbia, use federal adjusted gross income (AGI) as the starting point for computing state income taxes; eight states use federal taxable income as the starting point; two states tax only interest and dividend income; and the remaining five states impose income taxes that are not based on federal income or tax concepts.[2] These results are illustrated in table 3.

As states using federal tax liability as a tax base do, those states using federal taxable income as a starting point tend to harmonize their rules fairly closely with federal personal exemption and deduction concepts. In contrast, the degree of harmonization with these concepts varies considerably among the remaining states. Many states also impose their own tax credit provisions, which in many cases differ substantially from the menu of credits offered at the federal level.

Table 3 indicates that the states choose between two different methods of defining their conformity to the federal tax code. The first method, employed by 21 states, conforms on a current basis to the federal IRC. Unless deliberate state action is taken to the contrary, the tax regulations in these states are automatically adopted to changes enacted in the federal code. The remaining states (and the District of Columbia) define conformance to the federal code as of a particular date. In these states, legislation must be enacted to incorporate subsequent federal tax law changes. Although these states commonly adopt federal tax law changes on an annual basis, it is evident from the dates provided in table 3 that this is not always the case.

The existence of separate state PIT systems has negative consequences for employers who must withhold taxes for both the state and the federal government. Eleven states have withholding requirements corresponding to federal withholding rules and/or payment dates, which tends to ease the burden for employers in these states (this information from Federation of Tax Administrators 1992, 2).

As is evident from the diversity of state PIT systems, self-administration of the income tax provides states with the freedom to use the PIT to accomplish policy objectives; however, these benefits are not achieved without cost. Taxpayers face additional burdens from the need to comply with separate state and federal income tax provisions. Furthermore, variations in income tax regulations across states impose additional hardships on taxpayers who have income from more than one state. This issue might become important in Canada should more provinces choose to implement their own PIT systems. Aggregate tax system operating expenses in the United States also tend to be relatively high, owing to the need for separate tax admin-

TABLE 3
State Personal Income Taxes: Federal Starting Points

State	Relation to Internal Revenue Code	Tax Base
Alabama	–	–
Alaska	No state income tax	
Arizona	1 Jan. 1991	Federal adjusted gross income
Arkansas	–	–
California	1 Jan. 1991	Federal adjusted gross income
Colorado	Current	Federal taxable income
Connecticut	Current	Federal adjusted gross income
Delaware	Current	Federal adjusted gross income
Florida	No state income tax	
Georgia	1 Jan. 1991	Federal adjusted gross income
Hawaii	31 Dec. 1990	Federal taxable income
Idaho	1 Jan. 1991	Federal taxable income
Illinois	Current	Federal adjusted gross income
Indiana	1 Jan. 1991	Federal adjusted gross income
Iowa	1 Jan. 1991	Federal adjusted gross income
Kansas	Current	Federal adjusted gross income
Kentucky	1 Dec. 1989	Federal adjusted gross income
Louisiana	Current	Federal adjusted gross income
Maine	Current	Federal adjusted gross income
Maryland	Current	Federal adjusted gross income
Massachusetts	1 Jan. 1988	Federal adjusted gross income
Michigan	Current	Federal adjusted gross income
Minnesota	31 Dec. 1990	Federal taxable income
Mississippi	–	–
Missouri	Current	Federal adjusted gross income
Montana	Current	Federal adjusted gross income
Nebraska	Current	Federal adjusted gross income
Nevada	No state income tax	
New Hampshire	Interest and dividends only	
New Jersey	–	–
New Mexico	Current	Federal adjusted gross income
New York	Current	Federal adjusted gross income
North Carolina	1 Jan. 1991	Federal taxable income
North Dakota	Current	Federal liability[a]
Ohio	Current	Federal adjusted gross income
Oklahoma	Current	Federal adjusted gross income
Oregon	1 Jan. 1991	Federal taxable income
Pennsylvania	–	–
Rhode Island	Current	Federal liability
South Carolina	31 Dec. 1990	Federal taxable income

TABLE 3 – *cont'd.*

State	Relation to Internal Revenue Code	Tax Base
South Dakota	No state income tax	
Tennessee	Interst and dividends only	
Texas	No state income tax	
Utah	Current	Federal taxable income
Vermont	Current	Federal liability
Virginia	Current	Federal adjusted gross income
Washington	No state income tax	
West Virginia	1 Jan. 1991	Federal adjusted gross income
Wisconsin	31 Dec. 1990	Federal adjusted gross income
Wyoming	No state income tax	
District of Columbia	5 Nov. 1991	Federal adjusted gross income

SOURCE: Federation of Tax Administrators (1992, table 1).

a Or federal taxable income based on current IRC; taxpayer's option

– State does not employ a federal starting point. Current indicates state has adopted IRC as currently in effect. Date indicates state has adopted IRC as amended to that date.

istration, collection, and enforcement operations at the state and federal levels. It is likely that the administrative and compliance burdens associated with state income tax systems are lowest among those states that have chosen to (1) base their taxes on federal income or tax concepts; (2) maintain conformance with the federal tax code on a current basis; and (3) harmonize their withholding requirements with the federal requirements.

Compliance Cost Estimates

In this section, estimates of the compliance cost changes for taxpayers, employers, and financial institutions associated with the introduction of a separate PIT system for Ontario are provided. Two alternative scenarios are considered. In the first, Ontario introduces a PIT system similar in structure and complexity to the Quebec PIT system. In our opinion, Ontario is unlikely to implement a PIT system that deviates more from the federal PIT system than does the Quebec PIT system. In this sense, the compliance cost change associated with the first scenario represents an upper bound on the likely compliance cost change associated with the introduction of a separate PIT system for Ontario. This first scenario also was considered in the Ontario Economic Council background study by A.E. John Thompson (1984). In the second scenario, the federal definition of taxable income is used as the base for computing provincial tax liability, and Ontario imposes its own tax rate schedule and system of tax credits. A scenario similar to this was considered in the June 1991 federal discussion paper (Canada 1991) on changes to the federal-provincial tax collection agreements. For this second scenario, the alternative possibilities of provincial administration (Case 1) and federal administration (Case 2) of the Ontario PIT are considered.

Estimation Approach for Taxpayers

To estimate the marginal change in taxpayer compliance costs associated with a change in the federal-provincial tax structure, it is necessary to have a means of disaggregating federal and provincial compliance costs. Unfortunately, compliance cost studies generally provide only joint estimates of federal and provincial (or federal and state) compliance costs. An exception is the study by John Wicks (1965) in which taxpayers were asked to identify the additional time it took them to complete their Montana personal income tax returns for tax year 1955. The 1955 Montana tax return was quite similar to the federal tax return for that year. The major differences were the inclusion of interest on state, county, or municipal bonds in the state tax base and the exclusion from the base of interest from federal government obligations and dividends from national banks in Montana. Montana also had special provisions for income earned outside the state. The results of this study indicate that state compliance costs were about 11 per cent of federal compliance costs for the "typical" Montana taxpayer. Unfortunately, the results of this study are based on a small and somewhat unrepresentative sample. In addition, it is not clear how the findings could be used to explore the compliance cost implications of alternative tax structures.

In an Ontario Economic Council study of the compliance costs associated with a separate Ontario PIT system, Thompson (1984) considered the possibility that the Ontario PIT system would be similar in structure and complexity to the existing Quebec PIT system, a possibility that corresponds to the first scenario analysed in this study. Thompson assumed that the cost of preparing a Quebec tax return was approximately 25 per cent of the total federal and provincial tax preparation costs. He also made assumptions about the proportion of professionally prepared returns in Ontario in 1979, the fees for professional assistance, and the opportunity cost for taxpayers who prepared their own returns. These assumptions were applied to 1979 federal tax statistics on Ontario taxpayers to generate the compliance cost estimates. Thompson's conclusion was as follows: "This very rough estimate indicates a cost of preparing returns on the order of $75 million to $225 million. On the basis of this quick and crude analysis, the cost of preparing returns could therefore be on the order of $150 million a year" (232). Thompson's figure of $150 million implies an average provincial tax compliance cost of approximately $42 per taxpayer (in 1984 dollars).[3]

In this study, an alternative procedure is employed to estimate taxpayer compliance costs. This approach is based on the finding of Arthur D. Little's (1988) study of U.S. taxpayers in which the total record keeping, learning, preparation, and sending time associated with filing individual tax forms and schedules are highly correlated with the number of line items present. An analysis was performed of the number of line items present on the 1985 federal-Ontario income tax return, including all of the major forms and schedules. Usage rates for these forms and schedules also were obtained both from *Taxation Statistics* (Revenue Canada Taxation 1987) and from conversations with Revenue Canada and Ontario Ministry of Treasury and Economics (Communications Branch) officials. These results were combined with survey findings on the average total compliance time burden from Franois Vaillancourt's (1989) study of 1985 tax year Canadian taxpayers to derive a time estimate of the average compliance burden per line item for taxpayers who prepared their own tax returns. This figure was converted into a dollar estimate of the compliance burden per line item for these taxpayers using the average gross hourly wage rate for Ontario workers. An adjustment to this estimate was made to make the figure representative of the general Ontario taxpayer population, which includes taxpayers who use paid or unpaid tax assistance. The adjusted measure then was used to estimate the marginal steady-state compliance costs associated with the introduction of alternative Ontario PIT systems based on assumptions about the probable number of line items and the form usage rates that apply to each alternative. These estimates represent the predicted net change in federal-provincial compliance costs from replacing the existing Ontario PIT system with each alternative system. The estimation procedure is described more fully in the appendix.

The First Scenario

In the first scenario, the new Ontario PIT system is similar in structure to the 1991 Quebec PIT system. Under this scenario, the shift to a new provincial PIT system is predicted to result in an increase in the provincial share of federal-provincial taxpayer compliance costs from the present estimated level of $5.46 per taxpayer to a new level of $28.50 (1991 dollars). The latter figure represents approximately 30 per cent of the estimated total federal-Ontario taxpayer compliance burden under the existing system, which is comparable to the finding of the Thompson study. The former figure represents 5.8 per cent of the total federal-Ontario taxpayer compliance burden. When these average figures are multiplied by the projected number of Ontario tax filers for tax year 1991, the result is a predicted net increase in aggregate federal-provincial taxpayer compliance costs of $167.8 million, or $23.04 per taxpayer. An important reason for this large estimated net increase in taxpayer compliance costs is that a federal starting point is not used in the computation of the Quebec income tax. Some line items on the Quebec return merely duplicate line items on the federal return. In developing our estimates, we assume that the duplication of federal line items on the provincial return entails less additional compliance effort than the completion of entirely new items. None the less, this duplication does require some additional effort on the part of taxpayers. More importantly, there are significant differences in form design, line-item definition, and record-keeping requirements associated with the Quebec return, which add significantly to taxpayer compliance costs.

The above compliance burden estimate represents the long-run or steady-state level of compliance costs. Unfortunately, there is no direct Canadian evidence on start-up taxpayer compliance costs. The Little (1988, III-5) study of U.S. taxpayers, however, indicates that learning time alone accounts for approximately 15 per cent of total compliance costs. In the same study (V-29, V-41), the presence of new forms and schedules is found to have a substantial positive influence on learning time. Presumably, the presence of new forms and schedules also influences preparation and record-keeping time, although this possibility apparently was not explored in the study. We conclude that a reasonable estimate of start-up compliance costs might be on the order of 25 to 50 per cent of steady-state compliance costs. We estimate start-up taxpayer compliance costs of $72.6 million or $9.98

per taxpayer, based on the assumption that start-up costs are 35 per cent of total steady-state costs.

The Second Scenario

In the second scenario, the federal definition of taxable income is used as the base for computing provincial tax liability, and Ontario defines its own tax rate structure and system of tax credits. The new menu of credits is assumed to be more extensive than the current menu. Specifically, it is assumed that the new system of credits is similar in design to the Quebec system of credits and deductions for strategic investments. The Quebec deductions are assumed to take the form of credits under the new Ontario PIT system, however, so that the tax base is unaffected. Under this scenario, the average tax-payer compliance cost associated with the provincial PIT system is predicted to double from the present estimated level of $5.46 to $10.92 per taxpayer. This represents an aggregate increase of $39.8 million in steady-state taxpayer compliance costs or $5.46 per taxpayer. Again, an initial start-up cost of 25 to 50 per cent of steady-state compliance costs can be expected. We estimate that start-up taxpayer compliance costs are $27.8 million or $3.82 per taxpayer, based on the assumption that start-up costs are 35 per cent of total steady-state compliance costs.

In principle, it makes relatively little difference for taxpayer compliance costs under this scenario whether the provincial PIT system is administered by the federal government or the Ontario government. In either case, taxpayers would complete approximately the same number of line items for the provincial tax computation. A small cost savings, however, might result from federal administration, owing to a reduction in the costs associated with obtaining documents, mailing returns, responding to tax inquiries, and appealing tax judgements. We therefore assume that, under this scenario, both steady-state and start-up taxpayer compliance costs are 5 per cent lower under federal administration of the Ontario PIT system. An important practical concern is that there may exist a greater potential for provincial tax policy to deviate from federal policy over time under provincial PIT administration, owing to political pressures. An example is the increasing divergence between the federal and Quebec PIT systems during the 1980s. Taxpayer compliance costs may be adversely affected by such deviations. As discussed below, federal administration of the provincial tax also would tend to be associated with lower compliance burdens for employers and financial institutions.

The Distribution of Taxpayer Compliance Burdens

A lesson from the existing literature on taxpayer compliance burdens is that compliance costs tend to be skewed towards certain taxpayers. Under the first scenario, those taxpayers taking advantage of available tax credits and deductions modelled after the Quebec PIT provisions would tend to experience disproportionately high marginal compliance costs associated with the provincial system. Under the second scenario, taxpayers claiming credits fashioned after the Quebec system of credits and deductions for strategic investments would tend to experience disproportionately high marginal compliance costs associated with the provincial system. Presumably, under each scenario those taxpayers who experienced disproportionately high marginal compliance costs also would be receiving substantial benefits; otherwise, they simply could choose not to claim the relevant credits or deductions and thus would avoid these costs. Estimates of the steady-state compliance burden from particular credit and deduction provisions of the Quebec PIT system provide an indication of the potential compliance burden associated with the introduction of new credit or deduction provisions into the Ontario PIT system. An estimated steady-state compliance burden of $2.56 is associated with claiming dependant credits on Attachment A of the Quebec return. In contrast, the estimated steady-state burden from completing the child-care deduction on Attachment C is $12.35, and the estimated steady-state burden from completing the tax reduction, the sales tax credit, or real estate tax refund on Attachment B is $16.62. The estimated steady-state compliance burden associated with the QSSP deduction claimed on Schedule F is $11.87. Start-up compliance costs associated with these provisions may be on the order of 25 to 50 per cent of steady-state compliance costs. In general, the following rule may be used to estimate the additional compliance burden associated with a "typical" new tax provision. The steady-state burden per taxpayer may be estimated by multiplying the number of line items it takes to administer the provision by 47.5 cents (1991 dollars). The range of possible start-up costs per taxpayer may be estimated as 25 to 50 per cent of the estimated steady-state burden. An estimate of the aggregate compliance burden associated with the new provision may be computed by multiplying these figures by the expected number of taxpayers who will complete the portion of the tax return associated with the provision. These estimates should be adjusted downwards for provincial tax provisions that largely duplicate federal tax provisions and adjusted upwards for particularly complex provisions or provisions that are likely to promote substantial tax planning activity. For example, the Little (1988, v-29–v-30) study indicates that provisions associated with lengthy instructions that heavily reference the tax code as well as provisions that are associated with substantial record-keeping requirements impose relatively large compliance burdens on taxpayers. The study by Vaillancourt (1989, 32) indicates that both the proportion of taxpayers spending money on tax planning and the average tax planning costs are significantly higher in Quebec than in other provinces, presumably because of the various investment incentives offered under the Quebec PIT system.

Estimation Approach for Employers: All Scenarios

The additional compliance burden for employers from the introduction of a separate personal income tax system for Ontario is estimated, based on Vaillancourt's findings (1989, 83) in which the average total compliance cost to employers amounts to approximately $104 per T4 slip or $173 per taxpayer (in 1986 dollars). However, he estimates (51) that 50 per cent of this amount represents compliance costs associated with unemployment insurance and public pension systems, which leaves a remainder of $86.50 per taxpayer in PIT-related compliance costs. Adjusted to 1991 dollars, the latter figure amounts to $110.37 per taxpayer.[4] It is assumed that the additional employer cost of complying with the new provincial requirements would be 25 per cent of the current compliance cost, or $27.59 per taxpayer. This assumption is consistent with the evidence presented in the study by Thompson (1984, 242) that (at least for relatively small firms in Quebec) 25 per cent of payroll costs are attributable to the Quebec PIT collection system. Aggregated over all 1991 Ontario taxpayers, the above estimate implies an increase in aggregate steady-state employer compliance costs of $200.9 million. A similar amount might be required for initial adjustment costs. If the modified Ontario PIT system were administered by the federal government, the increase in steady-state compliance costs would be negligible. Start-up costs under federal administration of the new provincial PIT system presumably also would be lower, because employers would continue to receive withholding instructions from only one source, the federal government, with whom they have had prior experience relating to withholding requirements. We assume that start-up costs under federal administration of the new provincial PIT system would be one-half as large as start-up costs under provincial administration.

Estimation Approach for Financial Institutions: All Scenarios

The additional compliance burden for financial institutions from the introduction of a separate personal income tax system for Ontario is estimated, based on the findings of Vaillancourt's study (1989). He finds (83) that the average cost to financial institutions from preparing T5 and T600 slips is approximately $1 per slip, or $1.65 per taxpayer (in 1986 dollars). Adjusted to 1991 dollars, the latter figure amounts to $2.11 per taxpayer. It is assumed that the additional cost of preparing slips for the Ontario government would be 25 per cent of the current compliance cost, or 0.53 cents per taxpayer. Aggregated over all 1991 Ontario taxpayers, this figure implies an increase in aggregate steady-state financial institution compliance costs of approximately $3.8 million. A similar amount might be required for start-up costs. If the modified Ontario PIT system were administered by the federal government, the increase in steady-state compliance costs would be avoided entirely and the start-up costs would be reduced substantially. We assume that the start-up costs under federal administration of the new Ontario PIT would be only one-half as large as start-up costs under provincial administration.

Total Compliance Cost Increase

Table 4 summarizes the findings for changes in compliance costs for taxpayers, employers, and financial institutions under the alternative scenarios. Combining the above figures for the first scenario, an Ontario PIT system similar in structure and complexity to the current Quebec PIT system, the total estimated increase in net steady-state compliance costs for taxpayers, employers, and financial institutions is estimated at $372.5 million, or $51.16 per taxpayer. The former figure represents approximately 3.1 per cent of provincial income tax payable.[5] In addition, start-up costs for these groups are estimated at $277.4 million, or $38.10 per taxpayer. With provincial administration of the new Ontario PIT system under the second scenario (Case 1) – a provincial PIT system based on the federal definition of taxable income – the total estimated increase in net steady-state compliance

TABLE 4
Summary of Estimated Change in Compliance Costs

	Scenario 1: Ontario PIT System Similar in Structure and Complexity to Quebec PIT System	Scenario 2, Case 1: Ontario PIT System with Federal Taxable Income Base; Ontario Administration of Provincial PIT System	Scenario 2, Case 2: Ontario PIT System with Federal Taxable Income Base; Federal Administration of Provincial PIT System
Steady-state compliance cost change: taxpayers			
Average change per taxpayer	$23.04	$5.46	$5.19
Total change	$167.8 million	$39.8 million	$37.8 million
Steady-state compliance cost change: employers			
Average change per taxpayer	$27.59	27.59	$0.00
Total change	$200.9 million	$200.9 million	$0.00
Steady-state compliance cost change: financial institutions			
Average change per taxpayer	$0.53	$0.53	$0.00
Total change	$3.8 million	$3.8 million	$0.00
Steady state compliance cost change: all groups			
Average change per taxpayer	$51.16	$33.58	$5.19
Total change	**$372.5 million**	**$244.5 million**	**$37.8 million**
Total start-up costs: all groups			
Average start-up cost per taxpayer	$38.10	$31.94	$17.69
Total start-up costs	**$277.4 million**	**$232.6 million**	**$128.8 million**

costs amounts to $244.5 million, or $33.58 per taxpayer. The former figure represents approximately 2.0 per cent of provincial income tax payable. Start-up costs for this case are estimated at $232.6 million or $31.94 per taxpayer. With federal administration of the new Ontario PIT system (Case 2) under the second scenario, the total estimated increase in net steady-state compliance costs is $37.8 million, or $5.19

per taxpayer. This figure reflects the absence of a change in the steady-state employer and financial institution compliance burdens under federal administration of the new Ontario PIT system as well as a slightly lower taxpayer compliance burden under federal administration. The former figure represents only approximately 0.3 per cent of provincial tax payable. Initial start-up costs for this case are estimated at $128.8 million or $17.69 per taxpayer.

Although the above estimates are somewhat speculative, given the absence of firm data on the provincial share of total federal-provincial PIT system compliance costs, we believe that they provide a reasonable description of the possible compliance cost implications of a change to a separate Ontario PIT system. In interpreting the aggregate compliance cost changes, it is important to note that the number of Ontario taxpayers implicitly has been assumed to remain constant under the alternative tax scenarios. If there was reason to expect a change in the number of filers resulting from the imposition of a separate Ontario tax system, the aggregate figures would have to be adjusted to take this fact into account.

Policy Issues and Conclusions

If Ontario were to administer its own separate PIT system, there are several lessons from previous studies concerning ways to reduce compliance burdens. First, the use of a federal starting point for the computation of provincial tax liability is associated with much lower taxpayer compliance costs. Second, harmonization with federal withholding requirements helps to reduce employer compliance costs. Third, maintaining automatic conformance with federal tax law changes reduces burdens for both taxpayers and their employers. Frequent changes in the tax laws should be avoided, because they tend to be associated with high start-up costs. Moreover, these changes can have a negative impact on taxpayer morale. A reasonably high level of voluntary taxpayer support for the provincial tax system is vital for its efficient operation. Programs to assist taxpayers in complying with their obligations can be beneficial in developing taxpayer support.

It is important to recognize that a trade-off frequently exists between the reduction of compliance costs and other policy objectives. For example, although the repeal of the child tax credit would reduce compliance costs for those who currently claim the credit, its repeal may run counter to equity objectives. Alternatively, the taxation of capital gains on an accrual basis might be favoured for economic efficiency, but it may be associated with relatively high administrative and compliance costs. Similarly, many tax incentives, such as the investment tax credit, are associated with additional compliance burdens. Ideally, the tax structure should be designed to attain the various policy objectives up to the point that the additional social benefit from a change in the tax structure is equal to the additional administrative, compliance, and distortionary costs associated with that change.[6]

Another trade-off exists between various types of compliance and administrative costs. For example, the repeal of employer withholding requirements would reduce employer-related compliance costs, but it would increase administrative costs and employee-related compliance costs. It is important to distinguish between policies that result in a change in the total level of social costs associated with taxation and those that result in a change in the mix of social costs (see Sandford, Godwin, and Hardwick 1989, 203, for further discussion).

The estimates in this study provide a measure of the additional compliance burden that would be experienced by taxpayers, employers, and financial institutions if Ontario were to administer a separate PIT system. These costs are an important consideration, but they should not be evaluated independent of other factors. In evaluating the costs of a change in the tax structure, changes in federal and provincial administrative burdens also should be considered, as well as any changes in economic distortions. The expected overall net benefits of this change in the tax structure should be compared with the expected net benefits of alternative changes in provincial fiscal policy, such as the introduction of new expenditure programs.

Appendix: Methodology for Estimating Compliance Costs

The taxpayer compliance burden estimates that are presented in this paper were derived from estimates of line-item taxpayer compliance burden. Line-item counts were made for the major forms and schedules on the 1985 federal-Ontario tax return. These counts were then weighted by estimates of 1985 Ontario taxpayer form and schedule usage rates, which were obtained from Revenue Canada Taxation (1987) as well as from conversations with Revenue Canada and Ontario Ministry of Treasury and Economics (Communications Branch) officials. For example, Schedule 10 (the child tax credit) was determined to contain the equivalent of ten line items in tax year 1985.[7]

Approximately 13.3 per cent of all Ontario filers claimed a 1985 child
tax credit, so the weighted average number of line items for this
schedule was computed as 10 x 0.133 = 1.33 items. Similar compu-
tations were made for the other major forms and schedules. The
weighted average line-item counts were then added together to obtain
a weighted average total line-item count, which was determined to
equal 200 items.

Vaillancourt (1989, 36) estimates that the total time spent by Canadian taxpayers who prepared their own returns in complying with
the personal income tax laws averaged 6.3 hours in tax year 1985.[8]
This figure was adjusted upwards to 6.5 hours to account for the out-
of-pocket expenses of these taxpayers. Based on the above weighted
average total line-item count of 200 items, an average compliance
time burden of 1.95 minutes per line item is implied.[9] The Vaillancourt
study (103) indicates that approximately 33.3 per cent of all 1985
taxpayers prepared their own tax returns. The study also indicates
that average total compliance costs for taxpayers using paid or unpaid
tax assistance amounted to 96 per cent of the average total compliance
costs for taxpayers who prepared their own returns. Based on these
results, the average compliance burden for all taxpayers was taken
to be 97.3 per cent of the estimated average burden for taxpayers
who prepared their own returns.[10]

To determine the share of aggregate federal-provincial taxpayer
compliance costs associated with the existing 1991 Ontario personal
income tax system, the weighted average total line-item count for the
1991 Ontario tax and credit forms and the Ontario tax items on the
federal-provincial tax form were computed. The average taxpayer
compliance cost was calculated, based on the above estimate from
tax year 1985 returns that each line item takes 1.95 minutes to complete. The average value of time for all Ontario taxpayers was computed using 97.3 per cent of the 1991 average hourly wage rate of
$15.02 for Ontario taxpayers, which was obtained from Statistics Can-
ada (1992). The total compliance cost for all Ontario taxpayers was
computed by multiplying the average compliance cost by the projected number of Ontario tax returns filed in tax year 1991.[11]

In summary, the estimated taxpayer compliance time burden was
computed, based on an analysis of 1985 tax returns. This estimate
was applied to the weighted average line-item count of 1991 Ontario
tax forms and schedules to get an average taxpayer compliance time
estimate for the 1991 Ontario PIT system. This average time estimate
was converted into dollar amounts using 97.3 per cent of the 1991

average hourly wage rate for Ontario taxpayers. Finally, the average compliance cost per taxpayer was converted into a total compliance cost figure by multiplying it by the projected number of Ontario tax returns in tax year 1991.

It was necessary to make some additional assumptions to predict the taxpayer compliance cost changes that would be associated with a switch to a provincial tax system similar in structure and complexity to the 1991 Quebec PIT system. Many of the items on the Quebec tax forms and schedules are quite similar to items on the federal return. The marginal cost of completing these items presumably is relatively low after similar items on the federal return are completed. For the 65 items on the main 1991 Quebec return that directly corresponded to federal tax return items, it was assumed that average total completion time was ten minutes. Of the fifty-four tax items on the main return that did not correspond directly to tax items on the federal return, one-half were simply computational items. The Little (1988) study indicates that actual return preparation accounts for about 30 per cent of all learning, record keeping, preparation time, and sending. Based on this result, the line-item counts for the purely computational items were reduced by 70 per cent. The same reduction was applied to the line-item counts relating to the amount for dependants and transfers of amounts (Attachment A), the reporting of rental income (Attachment D), the reporting of investment income (Attachment E), and the reporting of capital income (Attachments G and H). The reporting of these tax items is closely related to the reporting of similar items on the federal return. A somewhat weaker link exists between the Quebec and federal treatments of child care and motor vehicle expenses. The line-item counts for the computation of child care expenses (Attachment C) and motor vehicle expenses (Attachment I) on the Quebec return were reduced by one-third to account for the reporting and record-keeping overlap with the federal provisions. Usage rates for Quebec return forms and attachments were obtained from *Portrait de la Fiscalité des Particuliers au Québec* (Revenue Québec 1991) for tax year 1988. It is assumed that usage rates for Ontario taxpayers would be similar to those experienced in Quebec in tax year 1988.

Notes

The first draft of this paper was prepared for the Ontario Fair Tax Commission and completed in November 1992. The authors wish to thank Allan Maslove, director of research, Fair Tax Commission, and an anonymous reviewer for their comments on the preliminary draft of this paper.

1 Technically, these measures are strictly valid only if labour markets are competitive and no market imperfections exist, such as rules limiting the number of hours an individual may work. In addition, the measures are premised on the assumption that taxpayers derive no benefits, such as improved accounting skills or a better understanding of their financial circumstances, from tax preparation activity.

2 Federal-adjusted gross income and taxable income are both based on total income, which includes wages and salaries; tips; taxable interest, dividend, alimony, business, and farm income; capital gains; taxable pensions, annuities, and individual retirement account (IRA) income; unemployment compensation; taxable social security income; and certain other items. Total income is adjusted for items such as IRA contributions, Keogh contributions, and alimony payments to arrive at adjusted gross income. Federal taxable income is then determined by deduction of personal exemptions and standard or itemized deductions from adjusted gross income.

3 This figure was computed based on the estimate provided in Thompson's study that there were 3.573 million Ontario taxpayers in tax year 1979.

4 Here, and throughout the study, the adjustment to 1991 dollars is based on the 1991 average consumer price index for Ontario of 127.6 (1986 = 100), which was computed by Statistics Canada.

5 Here and below, the total compliance costs as are proportion of provincial tax payable is computed based on the average provincial income tax payable per return for tax year 1988, which was obtained from Revenue Canada (1990).

6 Tax systems tend to distort relative prices, which can adversely affect economic efficiency. For example, an income tax, which makes work less valuable relative to leisure, may influence the number of hours taxpayers choose to work. The distortionary costs associated with a tax are often called "deadweight loss."

7 No official counts of line items on federal tax forms exist. The counts used in this study are based on a careful examination of the relevant tax forms, schedules, and attachments.

8 The national average compliance time burden for taxpayers who pre-

pare their own returns is used, because the Vaillancourt study does not provide a disaggregated figure for Ontario taxpayers who prepare their own returns. An examination of the overall average compliance time burden estimates for both Ontario and Canada as a whole (given in table 2.1, 26–28), however, indicates that the average compliance time burden for Ontario taxpayers does not differ substantially from the national average. If anything, the use of a national average may slightly overstate the compliance time burden of Ontario taxpayers.

9 This figure was computed as follows: 6.5 hours, or 390 minutes, divided by 200 line items yields 1.95 minutes per line item.

10 The figure 97.3 per cent was determined as follows. If the average wage for the 66.7 per cent of all taxpayers who use paid or unpaid tax assistance was 96 per cent of the average wage for the 33.3 per cent of all taxpayers who prepare their own returns, then the average wage for all taxpayers combined must be 97.3 per cent of the average wage for taxpayers who prepare their own returns. The proportion of Ontario taxpayers who prepared their own 1986 tax returns (36.1 per cent) was somewhat higher than the national average. Presumably, fewer Ontario taxpayers would prepare their own returns if a separate Ontario PIT system were introduced. For example, the proportion of Quebec taxpayers who prepare their own returns is only 27.8 per cent.

11 Based on an analysis of the number of Ontario returns filed in previous years, the number of Ontario personal income tax returns for tax year 1991 was projected to be 7,280,696.

Bibliography

Armour, Travis. 1992. "The Costs of Complying with the Tax System: A Review." Preliminary draft. Toronto: Fair Tax Commission

Bakija, Jon, and Eugene Steuerle. 1991. "Individual Income Taxation Since 1948." National Tax Journal, 44: 451–75

Bird, Richard M. 1986. Federal Finance in Comparative Perspective. Toronto: Canadian Tax Foundation

Bird, Richard. 1982. "The Cost of Collecting Taxes: Preliminary Reflections on the Uses and Limits of Cost Studies." Canadian Tax Journal, 30: 860–65

Blumenthal, Marsha, and Joel Slemrod. 1992. "The Compliance Cost of the U.S. Individual Income Tax System: A Second Look After Tax Reform." National Tax Journal, 45: 185–202

Bradford, David F. 1986. *Untangling the Income Tax*. Cambridge, MA: Harvard University Press

Bryden, Marion H. 1961. *The Costs of Tax Compliance*. Toronto: Canadian Tax Foundation

Canada. 1991. Department of Finance. *Federal-Provincial Tax Collection Agreements*. Discussion Paper, 25 June 25. Ottawa: Queen's Printer

Canadian Tax Foundation. 1992. *The National Finances 1991*. Toronto: Canadian Tax Foundation

Conklin, David W., and France St-Hilaire. 1990. *Provincial Tax Reforms: Options and Opportunities*. Halifax: Institute for Research on Public Policy

Courchene, Thomas J., and Arthur E. Stewart. 1991. "Provincial Income Taxation and the Future of the Tax Collection Agreements." In *Provincial Public Finances: Plaudits, Problems, and Prospects*, ed. Melville McMillan, 2 vols, 2: 266–300. Toronto: Canadian Tax Foundation

Erard, Brian. 1993. Forthcoming. "Taxation With Representation: An Analysis of the Role of Tax Practitioners in Tax Compliance." *Journal of Public Economics*

Federation of Tax Administrators. 1992. "Impact of Federal Tax Changes on State Tax Systems." Monograph. Washington DC: Federation of Tax Administrators

Forget, Claude E. 1984. "Quebec's Experience with the Personal Income Tax." In *A Separate Personal Income Tax for Ontario: Background Studies*, ed. D.W. Conklin, 187–212. Toronto: Ontario Economic Council

Hartle, Douglas G., et al., eds. 1983. *A Separate Personal Income Tax for Ontario: An Economic Analysis*. Toronto: Ontario Economic Council

Little, Arthur D. 1988. *Development of Methodology for Estimating the Taxpayer Paperwork Burden*. Final Report to Department of Treasury, Internal Revenue Service, IRS Contract no. Tir 83–234

Ontario Economic Council. 1983. *A Separate Personal Income Tax for Ontario: An Ontario Economic Council Position Paper*. Toronto: Ontario Economic Council

Pechman, Joseph A. 1987. *Federal Tax Policy*. 5th ed. Washington, DC: Brookings Institution

Penniman, Clara. 1980. *State Income Taxation*. Baltimore: Johns Hopkins University Press

Penniman, Clara, and Walter W. Heller. 1964. *State Income Tax Administration*. Chicago: Public Administration Service

Pope, Jeff, and D.L. Chen. 1992. "The Compliance Costs of Employment-Related Taxation in Australia Interim Report." Perth: ERC-UWO

Pope, Jeff, and M. Duncanson. 1990. *The Compliance Costs of Personal In-*

come Taxation in Australia 1986/87. Sidney: Australian Tax Research Foundation

Pope, Jeff, and Richard Fayle. 1990. "The Compliance Costs of Personal Income Taxation in Australia 1986/87: Empirical Results." *Australian Tax Forum*, 7: 85–126

Revenue Canada Taxation. 1987. *Taxation Statistics, 1987 Edition*. Ottawa: Revenue Canada Taxation

– 1990. *Taxation Statistics, 1990 Edition*. Ottawa: Revenue Canada Taxation

– 1992. *1992–93 Estimates, Part III*. Ottawa: Revenue Canada Taxation

Revenue Québec. 1991. *Portrait de la Fiscalité des Particuliers au Québec, Statistiques 1988*. Government de Québec

Sandford, Cedric. 1973. *Hidden Costs of Taxation*. Bath: Institute for Fiscal Studies

– 1986. "The Costs of Paying Tax." *Accountancy*, June: 108–11

– 1989. "Le coût de la perception de l'impôt à charge de l'administration et des contribuables." In *Cahiers de Droît Fiscal International* 74b (Administrative and Compliance Costs of Taxation): 41–66

Sandford, Cedric, M. Godwin, and P. Hardwick. 1989. *Administrative and Compliance Costs of Taxation*. Bath: Fiscal Publications

Sandford, Cedric, and J. Hasseldine. 1992. *The Compliance Costs of Business Taxes in New Zealand*. Wellington: Wellington Institute of Policy Studies

Sherbaniuk, D.J. 1988. "Tax Simplification – Can Anything Be Done About It?" In *Report of the Proceedings of the Fortieth Tax Conference*, 28–30, November 3: 1–3: 21. Toronto: Canadian Tax Foundation

Slemrod, Joel. 1989. "The Return to Tax Simplification: An Econometric Analysis." *Public Finance Quarterly*, 17: 3–28

– 1992. "Did the Tax Reform Act of 1986 Simplify Tax Matters?" *Journal of Economic Perspectives*, 6: 45–57

Slemrod, Joel, and Nikki Sorum. 1984. "The Compliance Cost of the U.S. Individual Income Tax System." *National Tax Journal*, 37: 461–74

Statistics Canada. 1992. *Employment Earnings and Hours*, April

Thompson, A.E. John. 1984. "Costs of Taxpayer and Employer Compliance under a Separate Ontario Personal Income Tax System." In *A Separate Personal Income Tax for Ontario: Background Studies*, ed. D.W. Conklin, 225–53. Toronto: Ontario Economic Council

Vaillancourt, Franois. 1987. "The Compliance Costs of Taxes on Businesses and Individuals: A Review of the Evidence." *Public Finance*, 42: 395–414

– 1989. *The Administrative and Compliance Costs of the Personal Income and Payroll Tax System in Canada, 1986*. Toronto: Canadian Tax Foundation

Wicks, John H. 1965. "Taxpayer Compliance Costs from the Montana Personal Income Tax." *Montana Business Quarterly*, Fall: 37–42

– 1966. "Taxpayer Compliance Costs from Personal Income Taxation." *Iowa Business Digest*, August 16–21

Wicks, John H., and Michael N. Killworth. 1967. "Administrative and Compliance Costs of Taxes." *National Tax Journal*, 20: 309–315

5 Evaluating the Options for Fiscal Stabilization Policy at the Provincial Level

D.A.L. AULD

Introduction

The genesis of fiscal stabilization policy is usually attributable to John Maynard Keynes and his ground-breaking work on macroeconomic theory in the 1930s. Fiscal stabilization policy is defined as the deliberate use of fiscal instruments such as tax rates and expenditure levels to bring about a change in the rate of increase/decrease in aggregate demand, employment, or prices. Changes in the overall level of aggregate demand in any part of the economy can certainly impact on employment and prices, but fiscal instruments can be used directly to change prices or the level of employment in the economy.

Why should the government deliberately change tax rates, levels of transfer payments, or expenditures to effect a change in aggregate demand and, in doing so, produce a deficit or surplus in the budget? In addition to having to manage a debt or surplus within the context of the domestic and international monetary system, a deliberate short-term change in the budget balance likely will interfere with the longer-term goals of providing for public goods (if the policy instrument is public expenditures) and ensuring the equitable distribution of wealth in the economy (if the policy instrument is taxation).

These problems were recognized clearly, but the idea of being able to slow an overheated, rapidly inflating economy or of preventing another Great Depression was too attractive to set aside.

Keynes's prescriptions for managing the economy at the macro level were never administered in the 1930s because of the eruption of the Second World War (although the United States did introduce large scale public works programs to offset the devastating effect the depression was having on employment). Following the war, and the immediate period of reconstruction and relaxation of wartime price and quantity controls, western economies found themselves face to face with either inflation or excess unemployment. Not all countries were quick to adopt Keynesian policies to meet these problems, although Australia did follow counter-cyclical demand management policies in the late 1940s and into the 1950s with some success (Auld 1969). While the federal government's White Paper on Employment in 1945 did embrace Keynesian principles, Canada did not put Keynesian ideas into action until the 1950s, especially during the 1957–58 recession. The Americans were a little more sceptical, but by the 1960s Keynesian economic policy was viewed by some as the only way to provide long-term growth with low unemployment and low inflation.

Fiscal policy had its detractors. First, there were those who argued that by the time the government recognizes persistent inflation or unemployment levels and enacts legislation to alter one or more fiscal instruments and allows time for these fiscal changes to impact on aggregate demand, the problem may have corrected itself, and the government-induced fiscal changes then will exacerbate the business cycle. This concern led to a considerable research effort to measure the length of these time lags in the context of the business cycle. Second, stabilization policies in times of a recession that expanded government spending in the name of job creation would lead to permanent increases in public expenditure simply because politicians would find it difficult to reduce expenditure once the economy was back on a full-employment path. The third concern had to do with debt management: if the government opts for a deficit, it must be financed by drawing down government cash reserves, selling bonds to the public, increasing the money supply, or a combination of these policies. Any or all of these options will impact on the monetary sector of the economy. If deficits are financed by the sale of bonds, which in turn drives up the interest rate, the effect of higher interest rates on investment and consumer spending could thwart the success of the counter-cyclical policy. Finally, in the case of an economy that is highly integrated with the economies of the rest of the world in terms of trade and capital flows, fiscal policy can have undesirable effects on the balance of payments and the exchange rate (see Mundell 1961, 1963 for an excellent review and detailed discussion; see also McKinnon and Oates 1966).

The 1970s were marked by a period of "stagflation" – less than full employment, slow economic growth, and unacceptable inflation. Both fiscal and monetary policy were not well suited to attacking the twin evils of inflation and unemployment simultaneously and, in place of such intervention, more direct controls in the form of incomes policies or wage and price controls emerged. By the end of the 1970s the combination of large accumulated deficits and the ineffectiveness of traditional stabilization policies, in particular fiscal policy, led to a decline in the popularity of Keynesian economics and the call for a much less interventionist role for government. Stabilization policy, when absolutely necessary, would be exercised by the central bank through the management of the money supply and interest rates.

Stagflation alone did not, however, spell the end for fiscal stabilization policy. There were other issues as well, and it is important to review them because they are not unique to fiscal policy at only the federal level; there are clear ramifications for regional or provincial stabilization policy as well.

Current Concerns Regarding the Efficacy of Fiscal Policy

Rational Expectations

In the 1960s and 1970s there was widespread acceptance of the trade-off between inflation and unemployment. To lower inflation through fiscal policy there would have to be an increase in unemployment, and to reduce unemployment inflation would have to rise. The "doctrine" of rational expectations challenged this assumption, holding the view that there was a so called "natural rate" of unemployment that was fixed, in the short run at least, and therefore inflation could be reduced without incurring more unemployment. And, of course, it implied that the government had no real control over the level of aggregate output and employment.

Supply-Side Economics

The school of thought that has advocated supply management in place of demand management argues that policies should impact on the aggregate supply/cost side of the economy, not the demand side. Supply management, in the form of wage and price controls, is more certain than demand management, and the lags are likely to be much shorter and, hence, not pro-cyclical.

Tax-Push Inflation

If it is assumed that employees bargain in terms of their net, after-tax wage, an increase in personal income tax rates (as an anti-inflationary policy) drives a wedge between the gross and take-home wage, and to restore the take-home wage, unions and workers bargain for a higher gross wage, thus intensifying wage inflation. In a period of excess demand in the economy, employees will have considerable bargaining strength, and it may take some time before the reduction in aggregate demand creates sufficient unemployment to dampen the rate of increase in gross wage rates. (See Auld and Wilton 1988 for empirical estimate of the extent to which higher income taxes have contributed to wage inflation.)

As far as indirect taxes are concerned, higher sales and excise rates can sustain an inflationary cycle (Brennan and Auld 1968). The federal government's goods and services tax (GST) is a case in point. After one year, the effect of this tax on prices is still evident, although diminishing, and only the existence of persistently high unemployment has limited the effect of this tax on inflation. Higher taxes in the traditional model of fiscal policy would reduce aggregate demand and, hence, inflation. An economy characterized by long-term contracts, rigidities in terms of adjustments, and strong wage and price-making power has called into question the effectiveness of this traditional policy.

Ricardian Equivalence Theory

An operating budget deficit must be financed by expanding the money supply, drawing down government cash balances, or selling bonds. If the deficit is induced by a reduction in personal taxes, for example, and is financed by issuing long-term bonds, households have more disposable income now, but they will have to repay the debt, plus interest, in the future. Suppose households, recognizing this fact, use the additional disposable income to purchase the government bonds, they will then receive the interest, and eventually the principal, to pay for the higher future taxes when the bonds are redeemed. The result is no change in wealth or aggregate demand, and fiscal policy is ineffective in combating unemployment. Whether or not households in general behave in this fashion is an empirical issue, but the possibility of such behaviour is one more reason for the decline in the popularity of fiscal policy.

Crowding Out

The term "crowding out" has more than one meaning in the macro-economic literature, but the common denominator in all the definitions is the notion that the debt-management strategies to finance government deficits translate into higher interest rates. Higher interest rates reduce private spending, and the increase in government spending is simply a substitute for private expenditure. This possibility was recognized in the nineteenth century when Ricardo (1951) argued that, while it was acceptable for government to borrow for projects such as roads and canals, such borrowing should not occur if the sale of government securities drove up interest rates and deterred private investment. A voluminous literature exists on the subject (and it continues to grow) but there is no discernible consensus on the issue. Notwithstanding, the distinct possibility that crowding out will occur, in total or in part, as a consequence of fiscal-policy-induced deficits, has created suspicion about the efficacy of stabilization policy.[1]

The Natural Rate of Unemployment

Much of the belief in the good of fiscal policy was based on knowledge about the trade-off between unemployment and inflation.[2] Reducing the unemployment rate would put upward pressure on prices, but in the late 1950s and 1960s the "price" one would have to pay for lower unemployment in terms of inflation was deemed small. In the late 1960s the concept of the natural rate of unemployment emerged; the rate of unemployment at which the rate of change in prices is neither accelerating nor decelerating. This level of unemployment is determined by factors such as labour productivity, unemployment compensation, technical change, and skills development. An observed change in unemployment could be precipitated, then, by either a deficiency in demand, in which case a fiscal stimulus could possibly reduce unemployment without inflation, or the observed change in unemployment could be the result of other factors' impacting upon the "natural rate." In the latter case, a fiscal stimulus may do little more than raise the level of inflation, making the natural-rate theory a powerful weapon in the debate against the use of fiscal policy.

The factors listed above would appear to all but condemn fiscal policy to future texts on economic history (see Auld 1991 for more detailed assessment and references). While these arguments cannot be ignored, the large accumulated federal public debts in both the United States and Canada have also contributed to fiscal policy's unpopularity. Imagine if, in the early stages of the 1990–91 recession, the federal government's budget were in balance. It is hard to imagine that Ottawa would not have proposed tax reductions or expenditure increases to offset the rapid rise in unemployment. At the more esoteric level of economic theory, the gap between those who advocate fiscal intervention (the Keynesians) and those who are opposed to such action (the monetarists) has narrowed. Several important empirical studies in the 1982–87 period concluded that bond-financed tax reductions produce a clear stimulus to the economy, (Boskin 1987; Eisner 1986; Feldstein 1982; Modigliani and Sterling 1986). In 1973 Alan Blinder and Robert Solow published a paper entitled "Does Fiscal Policy Matter?" The answer would appear to be a cautious and qualified "yes." Crucial to the success of any fiscal action would be solid understanding of the economic climate at the time action is being taken and the ability to engage in policies that have very short implementation and action lags.

The Regional Dimensions of Fiscal Policy: An Overview

The standard treatment of fiscal policy relates to a central/federal government's changing fiscal instruments that reduce unacceptable levels of unemployment or inflation in the national economy. What is the role of fiscal policy if there are one or more other levels of government, each with its own taxation and expenditure powers? What special problems confront policy makers when the "national" problem of inflation or unemployment is considerably more severe in one part of the country than in another? How does a federal government respond when a state, or provincial, or local/municipal government decides to exercise fiscal policy independent of the central government? These are important dimensions of fiscal policy in a federal country, and, before they are examined in detail, a brief overview of the three major issues seems worthwhile.

Fiscal Perversity

Almost half a century ago, researchers recognized the fact that the budgetary decisions of non-federal[3] levels of government may thwart the fiscal policy of the central government (Hansen and Perloff 1944). In an economic downturn, local governments would experience a decline in revenues, and since they were required (often by law) to balance their budgets, they were faced with the choice of raising taxes or reducing public expenditures, further exacerbating the downturn. Inflation and buoyant economic times produced a rapid growth in revenue, and since there was no advantage in having a surplus, expenditures were increased or taxes were reduced, actions that were pro-cyclical and that had a "perverse" impact on economic activity.

Regionally Directed Federal Fiscal Policy

Most business-cycle fluctuations do not impact evenly in every region of a country, no matter how large or small the country. The uneven effects of a recession or inflation are likely to be more pronounced, however, if the country is geographically large, with a diverse economic base, and a population that is not randomly distributed across the regions – a country like Canada. The "blunt" instruments of fiscal policy such as changes to income tax rates or accelerated depreciation do not always focus on where the fiscal action would be most desirable. Changes in public expenditure can be targeted to a greater degree. This suggests that the federal government should, if it employs fiscal policy, direct the instruments to the regions where they are most needed. There are three difficulties with such an approach. One is political: for example, a personal income tax reduction in Ontario to stimulate the Ontario economy is not likely to win the prime minister any accolades in British Columbia or New Brunswick. Second, under current tax laws, such a move would likely precipitate a challenge in the Supreme Court. The third difficulty has to do with expenditure "leakages" or "spillovers" – the extent to which an increase in spending in Ontario spills over into another province, creating the jobs where the need is less acute. A later section of this report evaluates the importance of these expenditure leakages in Canada.

Provincial or State Fiscal Policy

Clarence Barber, in a study of provincial fiscal policy for the Ontario Tax Committee, wrote: "In their discussions of fiscal policy economists have usually had the central government of the country in mind. Yet it is not entirely clear why state and provincial governments should not pursue a conscious fiscal policy" (Barber 1966, 47). He identified several key issues that must be addressed before the implied question could be answered, and they will be examined in detail below. The following is a brief summary of the key issues. The *differences* between the federal and a provincial or state government (pertaining to fiscal policy) are

- control over the supply of money;
- control over the exchange rate of the economy;
- the size of expenditure leakages; and
- borrowing capacity and debt service ability.

While these differences are important, Barber concluded that they were a matter of degree and did not preclude the use of provincial fiscal policy.

Notwithstanding the ability of non-federal governments to exercise fiscal policy, is there any *need* for a non-federal jurisdiction to follow an independent counter-cyclical policy?

The answer is "yes," given that there are significant variations in economic activity across the regions of a country.[4] A national policy to write off depreciation at accelerated rates to encourage capital spending could well be pro-cyclical in some provinces. A second reason, in support of provincial fiscal policy, is related to the fiscal instruments themselves and the ability of a provincial government to change the necessary instrument more quickly and effectively than the federal government can. Barber argues that provincial governments are responsible for a wide variety of public capital expenditures involving education, health, transportation, water, and sewage facilities. The ability to accelerate or reduce the rate of expenditure in these areas is, potentially, a powerful fiscal instrument.

Fiscal Perversity and Budget Sensitivity to the Business Cycle

Numerous studies since the Great Depression have examined the cyclical sensitivity of provincial/state and local government revenues and expenditures. The pioneering work by Hansen and Perloff (1944, 199) concluded that "states and localities have in fact *followed* the swings of the cycle and have thereby *intensified* the violence of economic fluctuations ... unless their fiscal systems are planned in relation to the federal stabilization program, they are likely to nullify, in large measure, the national counter-cyclical activities" – a sobering conclusion, but one that was soon challenged. Several subsequent studies questioned both the interpretations of Hansen and Perloff's results, which concentrated on the 1930s, and the obsolescence of their findings in relation to the 1950s (Newcomer 1954; Brown 1956; Maxwell 1958; Sharp 1958; and Baratz and Farr 1959).

The reasoning underlying the "perversity hypothesis" is based on the following points:

• local government revenue sources are, in the short run, inelastic; that is, they do not respond quickly to the business cycle;
• rapid economic expansion frequently involves increased demand for goods and services at the state/provincial and local level;
• non-federal governments do not have access to a central bank to finance deficits; and
• a reduction in taxes or rise in expenditure at the local or provincial/ state level would result in a considerable amount of the "stimulus" leaving the area, owing to the openness of local economies. In short, local or regional expenditure multipliers would be small.

While these are factors that *may* produce fiscal perversity, they do not guarantee that non-federal budgets will change in a pro-cyclical or perverse fashion. Furthermore, not all the factors noted above apply consistently across levels of government. Robert Rafuse, Jr (1965) undertook the first major study that did not set out to question the conceptual foundation of the perversity hypothesis. Instead, he did an exhaustive statistical analysis of state-local finance in the United States. Thereafter, he concluded that, for the 1948–64 period the hypothesis was on shaky ground: "The behaviour of total state and local receipts was stabilizing during every expansion and perverse during every contraction. Expenditures on the other hand, were stabilizing during all four contractions and destabilizing during every expansion" (117). Over the entire period, the author discovered that revenues were becoming increasingly stabilized and expenditures had become *less* perverse. In terms of the overall budget (the change in the surplus or the deficit), the study concluded: "These governments, [state and local] have been a significant factor in moderating the seriousness of the postwar recessions and in promoting recovery" (118).

In the late 1970s a major study of state-local budgets by the Advisory Commission on Intergovernmental Relations (ACIR 1978) reached the conclusions that

• in every downswing since World War II, state and local budgets were counter-cyclical, and

- state and local budgets have not been a major cause of inflation (ACIR 1979).

A discussion on Canada's Royal Commission on Taxation on fiscal stabilization policy in a federal setting was held, and while the idea of regional fiscal policy was rejected in the report of the commission, it was not because of the commission's belief that provincial local finance was cyclically perverse.[5] Barber (1966) examined the aggregate provincial/municipal budget balance during the four economic expansions and three recessions that occurred between 1950 and 1963. He concluded that there was overall a "mildly counter-cyclical pattern with revenues increasing more rapidly than expenditures in periods of expansion and expenditures rising more rapidly than revenues in periods of contraction" (47).

The first definitive work on the perversity hypothesis and its relevance to Canada was published shortly after the Royal Commission on Taxation *Report* (Robinson and Courchene 1969). In the first part of their research, the authors estimate government surplus equations (for all governments and for the federal and provincial/local sectors separately) where the budget result (surplus or deficit) is a function of the rate of unemployment or the ratio of actual to full employment GNP. The authors discovered that for the non-federal budgets, "there is a definite statistical relationship between the surplus and the utilization variable ... and [it] is of a stabilizing nature" (169). In short, the evidence for the postwar period in Canada is that the "perversity hypothesis may not describe, at least in the aggregate, the Canadian case."

The second part of the paper provides a model to estimate the short-run and the long-run responses of government revenues and expenditures to changes in national income. The model is designed to test the stabilizing influences of government revenues and expenditures at the federal and the non-federal levels. If a revenue source is stabilizing, revenues ought to decline as the economy worsens – that is, as the ratio of actual to full employment GNP declines – and revenues should rise rapidly in a period of inflation. On the expenditure side, a stabilizing influence would be recorded when expenditures increased as the economy worsened and decreased in periods of inflation.

The model was tested for the postwar period covering the early 1950s to 1965, during which there were periods of both economic expansion and contraction. The results led the authors to conclude the following:

- the local government sector played a negligible role in terms of its sensitivity to the business cycle;
- total federal expenditures were strongly stabilizing;
- total provincial expenditures were destabilizing, but not sufficiently so as to outweigh the federal influence;
- budgets of the non-federal governments collectively were stabilizing, but the influence was considerably less than the impact of the federal budget; and
- provincial revenue was stabilizing.

In their conclusion, Robinson and Courchene emphasize that the perversity hypothesis must be viewed in terms of two components: the automatic, and the discretionary impact of the budget. While the overall result suggests that fiscal perversity exists with respect only to provincial expenditures, the result does not inform us if non-federal governments made decisions about taxation and expenditures that were pro-cyclical.[6]

In the late 1970s Winer (1979) examined the cyclical sensitivity of Canadian government budgets in the context of an open-economy, general macroeconomic model that allowed for an examination of stabilization policy under both fixed and flexible exchange-rate regimes. The model also allows for the interaction between each government budget equation (one for the federal government and one for the provincial/local government sector). Unlike earlier studies in both Canada and the United States, the financing implications of non-federal deficits are examined in Winer's model.[7] The author emphasizes that because non-federal debt is held to a larger extent by non-residents, "the foreign sector repercussions may be more important in determining the total effects on demand of a change in B(NF) [non-federal budgets] than of the same change in B(F) [federal budget]" (14).

The major conclusion from Winer's study that is of relevance here is that while the domestic monetary base had the greatest impact on money income in Canada during the 1947–74 period, non-federal purchases of goods and services seem to have been at least as important as a determinant of income. Furthermore, there is no evidence to suggest that non-federal fiscal policy is perverse.

A third detailed study of non-federal budget results and their impact on the business cycle became available early in 1981 (Lynch and Selody 1981). In this study, the authors develop an econometric model to examine how fiscal policy responded to nominal and real changes in national income and changes in the price level. The period under scrutiny was 1957 to 1979, extending the Robinson and Courchene work by almost 15 years. While different in approach and structure, the results of this study are comparable to those obtained in the earlier study. The main conclusions are as follows:

- short-run fluctuations in nominal income induce pro-cyclical move-ments in total government expenditures and are therefore desta-bilizing;
- in the short run, that is, over the business cycle, federal and non-federal revenues behave in a counter-cyclical or stabilizing manner;
- provincial revenues tend to exhibit a *larger* stabilizing influence than federal revenues; and
- over the short run, all revenues respond positively to an acceler-ation in price inflation, thereby exhibiting a stabilizing effect. Over the long-run period, all revenues are pro-cyclical with respect to deviations in the price level from long-term trends.

The overall conclusion regarding fiscal perversity is that there is "no evidence that provincial/municipal fiscal policy is less responsive to economic cycles than federal policy" (28).

The conclusion from our examination of the above studies and research suggests that, with the exception of provincial expenditure in some instances, changes in the budget result of the non-federal government sector in the aggregate have not been destabilizing, at least in the postwar period up to 1980. In fact, there is evidence to suggest that the overall effect has been a stabilizing one. Whether this is true for individual provinces, the extent to which the local and provincial sectors differ, and the nature of the impact of the budget result in Ontario is unknown. The latter issue will, be addressed in a subsequent section.

Regional Targets for Fiscal Stabilization Policy

The amplitude and timing of the business cycle in Canada is not identical across all regions. In fact, history has shown that the country can simultaneously experience supply bottlenecks and excess demand in one region and unacceptably high unemployment in another region. Furthermore, in a general recession, deficient demand and the severity of the downturn display unique regional/provincial patterns. When this configuration occurs, does it make sense for the federal government – assuming for the moment that it possesses complete control over discretionary fiscal policy – to pinpoint its policy measures in its attempt to alleviate the recession?

As noted earlier, there is the obvious and perhaps overriding factor of politics. The federal government would generate very little sympathy in Ontario if, because the Ontario economy was "overheating," Ottawa applied a dose of anti-inflationary policies in Ontario and nowhere else. To a significant degree, Canada has accepted the idea of regionally differentiated fiscal policies to combat chronic unemployment, but it might be a different matter if this were done on a cyclical basis and applied to periods of expansion as well as contraction.

The situation has been somewhat different in the United States. In 1977 Congress passed the Intergovernmental Anti-Recession Act, a program that "selectively distributes emergency assistance in the form of unrestricted grants to state and local governments which have been adversely affected by sustained periods of high unemployment" (Advisory Commission on Intergovernmental Affairs 1978, 16). While the ACIA concluded that the programs were "well targeted," the overall effectiveness was yet to be determined.

From a purely economic viewpoint, the most crucial issue is that of regional multipliers and "leakages." In simple terms, these concepts are related to the likelihood that any increase or decrease in demand in one region of a country will have spillover effects in other regions. If, for example, the marginal propensity to import consumer goods *from other parts of Canada* is 0.3, then a general tax reduction of $1.00 in Ontario will raise demand for consumer goods in other regions by $0.30. Assuming that there is no foreign spending, the existence of this marginal propensity to import from other regions reduces the value of the expenditure multiplier in Ontario. Furthermore, it stimulates the economy in other regions, a result that may not be desirable. Obviously, the size and pattern of these regional leakages are important to any discussion about regionally targeted federal fiscal policy.

Two of the first major studies of the regional aspects of fiscal policy were published by Stanley Engerman (1965) and Alan T. Peacock (1965). Engerman constructed a two-region model of the economy where "one particular region is posed against another which repre-

sents the rest of the nation" (34). Using this model, Engerman sim-
ulates a series of policy experiments. In one the interest of the policy
maker is on maximizing national income and it is not important where
the stimulus is applied. In another the target is one region with no
concern for the effects outside the region. The third examines the
spillover effects of a fiscal action in one region. By using a variety of
values for the marginal propensity to consume and the marginal propensity to import (from the other region), the magnitude of the effects
of various policies can be measured. The author notes that national
input-output statistics based on regional flows of raw, intermediate,
and final goods would be of considerable help in evaluating the
regional dimensions of stabilization policy.

Engerman concludes that "regionally pinpointed stabilization
measures increase the efficiency of stabilization policy." He further
adds that this conclusion does not point to the need for fiscal policy
conducted by regional authorities because "the origins of differential
rates of regional unemployment are largely national in character" (53).

Peacock (1965) also employs a two-region, macroeconomic model
policy that is slightly more complex than Engerman's, allowing for
two sources of income to drive the consumption function and the
incorporation of a production account to demonstrate the interregional goods flows. Peacock examines hypothetical situations where
the national government could take action in one region but not in
another, owing to different levels of unemployment or inflation. He
draws no specific conclusions regarding these simulations, but he does
point out the political problem of trying to tax one region of the
country but not another in a period of regionally specific excess demand.

As Peacock (1965), Engerman (1965), and others have pointed out,
the effectiveness of a fiscal policy involving regional "targets" depends considerably on the size of the import leakages from one re-
gion/province to another. The most thorough empirical work for
Canada has been done by Miller (1980; 1987; 1988) and Miller and
Wallace (1983). In the first paper by Miller (1980), the author con-
structs a model involving a set of structural equations explaining income, consumption, taxes, investment, imports, and exports to and
from each province. The subsequent paper by Miller and Wallace
(1983) employs a similar model, except that consumption spending
is a function of present and lagged disposable income, and investment
expenditure depends on a distributed lag of past levels of provincial
income. These changes allow the authors to examine the repercus-

sions of exogenous policy changes over time, rather than in the static framework implied by the model in the earlier paper.

Using the results of the model, the authors calculate the multipliers associated with changes in government expenditure or taxation in each province. While there are obvious "leakages" from one province to others, they are not sufficiently large to render regional fiscal policy inoperative. In fact, the authors argue that the selective use of expenditure policies, targeted to the regions where an expansion or contraction was most desirable, would be more effective than general, nationwide policies. Tax changes would also work, but the effect is not as pronounced, and there is the obvious difficulty of raising the tax rate in one province but not in another. Overall, the authors conclude that "these results confirm our previous conclusion that regionally differentiated expenditure policies can be used successfully to secure regional stabilization" (274).[8]

In a wider context, Pierre Fortin (1982a) has examined also the subject of regional multipliers and expenditure "leakages." Based on the data available at the time concerning interregional trade flows, Fortin (1966) concludes that the differences in multipliers (the national versus the regional ones) were not that great. For example, he found that if the federal government injected $1.00 in the Atlantic provinces and an injection proportional to provincial GDP elsewhere, the expenditure multiplier was 1.185. An injection of $1.00 into the Atlantic provinces, and nothing elsewhere, resulted in a multiplier of 1.027. Examining all five regions of Canada, he discovered that the ratio of the regional to national multiplier varied between 76 and 89 per cent. These regional multipliers are probably higher because a considerable portion of the total public investment expenditure is in the labour-intensive construction area, and most of this expenditure occurs at the provincial level. Fortin also points out that "the larger the cyclical disturbance ... and the larger the provincial budget's share of the consolidated public sector ... the more it is possible and desirable for the provinces to contribute actively to the compensation for these disturbances" (16).[9]

The extent to which a provincial government expenditure is "local" is a critical issue. In Wallace Oates's model of decentralized fiscal policy, there is a crucial assumption that increases in government expenditure at the margin reflect the same import content as total private expenditure (Oates 1968). This assumption leads to a small local expenditure multiplier and provides substance for the conclusion in Oates's paper that "the case for the central government to assume primary responsibility for the stabilization function appears to rest on a firm economic foundation" (44). Auld (1978) found, in a reworked version of the model, that, "not surprisingly ... in the balanced budget case, expansion will occur provided the public sector spends less, at the margin, on foreign produced goods than does the private sector" (273). In a later paper, the author argues that provincial fiscal policy will be much more successful if the expenditures are directed towards activity in the province or region (Auld 1978). Hiring the unemployed to expand public works projects implies a high rate of consumption and a minimum increase in import expenditure. Furthermore, to minimize provincial leakages, expenditure can be directed towards the purchase of supplies and materials from local producers.

Monetary and Exchange Rate Aspects of Regional Fiscal Policy

This issue has already been alluded to above, but it is of considerable importance and deserves to be examined in some detail. Wilson (1977) emphasizes the need to analyse provincial fiscal policy in the context of the exchange-rate regime and monetary framework within which stabilization policy is operating. If conditions are such that the debt financing operations of a deficit render fiscal policy ineffective, then "the *national* impact of provincial fiscal policy is also zero. Provincial fiscal policies may nevertheless be effective in influencing economic activity within the province. However, in the pure monetarist case, this must be at the expense of economic activity in other provinces" (126). For example, if Ontario runs a $10 billion deficit and finances it by borrowing domestically, the borrowing, given the nature of capital markets, is done nationally. If higher interest rates ensue and crowd out $10 billion of private investment then, nationally, the impact of the fiscal action has been zero. Only part of that $10 billion reduction in private investment likely has taken place in Ontario, however, while there has been an injection of $10 billion (less any import leakage) into the province.

In terms of the exchange-rate regime, Wilson points out that "the difference ... is perhaps more meaningful, precisely because the province does *not* control the money supply and hence cannot engineer particular monetary/fiscal combinations under a floating exchange rate" (126). Under a fixed exchange rate, domestic expansion initiated by Ontario will lead to increased imports and an increase in the demand for Canadian dollars, which the federal government, by way of the central bank, will have to offset through the money supply. Under a floating exchange rate, no federal action would be required, although the rise in the exchange rate may not be welcome in other parts of the country.[10]

In terms of provincial fiscal policy involving deficit financing, the one option *not* available to the province is the monetization of the debt – provinces must borrow, even if it is from their own pension funds, to finance a deficit. How the deficit is financed is important not only for the immediate period, but for the long run as well. We have already noted that if the bonds are sold in Canada, higher interest rates could "crowd out" private investment across Canada, with some of that effect occurring in the deficit-financing province. When the debt is serviced each year, at least some of the income will flow to non-residents of the province, and similarly, when the debt is finally redeemed, provincial revenues will be transferred elsewhere. If the deficit is financed by bonds sold to foreigners, the "crowding-out" possibility is eliminated, but repayment and servicing of the debt require a transfer of income to non-residents of the province and country. It was this likely outcome that led Wallace Oates (1972) to conclude that local governments must treat this debt with considerably greater concern than need the central government, since its eventual repayment, including interest charges, will represent a transfer of income to non-residents. Given the size of the current deficit in the province at this time, and the expected deficit over the next three to four years, this "concern" must be taken seriously.

Finally, if the deficit is financed by the sale of provincial bonds to provincial agencies like as employee pension funds or crown corporations that have cash reserves, the assets remain in the province as do the debt-servicing expenditures and eventual redemption of the bonds. While convenient for the government, this course of action may not necessarily be in the best interests of the pension funds or crown corporations.

According to Barber (1966), the ability of a province to carry out its own expansionary fiscal policy depends to a considerable degree on the province's borrowing capacity. He argues that, compared with the 1930s and 1940s – at least in 1965 – most provinces were in a relatively strong credit position because of the substantial reduction in overall debt and the greatly diversified revenue base. He even argues that a province's credit rating could improve if there was "moderate" increase in borrowing: "If there were a larger volume of Ontario government securities available and a wider range of maturities, a more active market might develop" (28). In addition, he also assumes that the types of cyclical fluctuations likely to be experienced in the near future would be slow-downs in the rate of growth or worse, a small and short-lived decline in gross provincial product, fluctuations that would not require significant increases in debt.[11]

Several suggestions have been advanced to assist provincial governments with deficits *and* surpluses induced by the business cycle. The *Carter Report* (1966) recommended that the federal government offset the loss in provincial revenue due to a provincial economy's deviating from a full employment growth path. When provincial revenue receipts were above the full employment level, the "surplus" would be deposited in a special federal fund. Wilson (1977) suggested that this practice be extended to local governments as well. In 1971, the idea of a regional stabilization fund was put forward by André Reynauld (1971). There would be a financial institution that would issue its own securities, guaranteed by the federal government, and that would make the proceeds available to the provinces. The interest rate on the loan would be negotiated or set by Ottawa, and up to a limit of borrowing, the interest would be forgiven and assumed by the central government. A variation on the *Carter Report* idea was proposed by Yves Rabeau and Robert Lacroix (1979). Their stabilization fund would involve increased transfers to the provinces during periods of recession but would be targeted for the creation of new public sector infrastructure.

Evaluating Ontario's Counter-Cyclical Fiscal Policy

A number of studies have examined the overall performance of non-federal fiscal policy, but only five have focused on the province of Ontario. The first of these was by Auld (1975), who evaluated the discretionary fiscal policies of the Ontario government during the recessionary/recovery period of 1960 to 1967. By calculating the change in the weighted budget result from year to year and desegregating the revenue components into changes due to automatic responses in the budget and discretionary tax changes, Auld concluded that "it would appear that the Ontario provincial budget is capable of exerting counter-cyclical changes on aggregate demand" (181).[12]

In 1977, using the concept of the full employment budget surplus (FEBS), the performance of Ontario's fiscal policy for the 1970–77 period was evaluated (Ontario, Treasury and Economics 1977).[13] An increase in the FEBS from one year to the next indicates a restrictive discretionary fiscal policy, while a decline in the FEBS is indicative of an expansionary fiscal policy. The change in the FEBS for 1971–76 and the economic conditions at the time are shown as follows:

In 1970–71 the Canadian economy, Ontario included, was in a recession, although inflation remained above the 4 per cent per annum level. The action taken in 1971 by the Ontario government was clearly stabilizing. As unemployment fell, the stimulus was moderated, becoming slightly restrictive in 1973. Budget policy in the next year was clearly stimulating and, with prices rapidly rising through 1973 and 1974, this action may well have contributed to the rate of inflation. By 1975–76, the economy of Ontario was caught in a period of "stagflation" – high unemployment and high rates of inflation – and while the stimulating budget policies of 1975 clearly reduced the severity of unemployment, they also appear to have been inflationary. However, given the consensus that much of the inflation was the result of supply-side shocks, notably the oil crisis, the stimulation did not, most likely, add to the inflationary pressures. In fact, one specific policy, that of eliminating the sales tax on automobiles, may have provided a temporary reprieve from the inflationary push.

The 1975 automobile tax rebate was the subject of a thorough study by the Conference Board (Gusen 1978). To stimulate the economy by increasing automobile sales, the government announced that the 5 per cent tax on automobiles would be rebated on all vehicles purchased between 7 July and 31 December 1975. Using a regression model to explain sales in the industry, Gusen concluded that the tax rebate did stimulate sales substantially but at a cost of lower sales the following year: the measure simply rearranged the time profile of automobile sales and production and, as such, produced no overall increase in employment over the two years, 1975–76.

Auld (1984), employing the FEBS technique, provides an evaluation of Ontario's discretionary fiscal policy performance for the period 1969 to 1982. As a broad measure of fiscal performance, the author plots the annual *change* in the FEBS against the *change* in the difference between actual and full employment gross provincial product (GPP). During the 13 years, there appears to have been only one year, 1977, when discretionary fiscal policy was significantly pro-cyclical. After two years of historically large deficits, the province took action to reduce the rapidly expanding public debt, and with high interest rates at the time, the debt servicing cost was of some concern. On one other occasion, when the gap between actual and potential GPP was closing, discretionary expansionary policies were introduced. Auld

TABLE 1
Change in Ontario's FEBS and Economic Conditions

	1971	1972	1973	1974	1975	1976
Change in FEBS	−346	−82	+45	−341	−605	+212
Economic Conditions		Per Cent				
Inflation	+4.1	+4.9	+7.9	+10.5	+10.7	+7.3
Unemployment Rate	5.4	5.0	4.3	4.4	6.3	6.2

SOURCES: *Quarterly Economic Review*, Department of Finance, Ottawa, 1989; Jones et al. (1977)

concludes: "On balance, discretionary policies over this period appear to have been counter-cyclical" (93).

Finally, in a more recent paper, Auld (1987) details the specific discretionary fiscal policies of the Ontario government in the 1970s, noting that in the budget speech of 1978, the minister all but abandoned the notion of an active Ontario discretionary fiscal policy in the future: "One reluctantly comes to the conclusion that the taxpayers of Ontario would see only marginal returns to the Provincial Treasury when government stimulates the economy through *general measures*" (McKeough 1978, 4; italics are mine).

The minister was prepared to use selective fiscal instruments in a limited manner to stimulate particular sectors, but the growing provincial debt was clearly a priority for the government.

Summary and Conclusion

Major Concerns

In the 1970s the debate between the Keynesians and monetarists called into question the efficacy of fiscal policy as a discretionary tool to offset excessive fluctuations in aggregate demand or prices. By the 1980s the overriding concern on the part of the politicians was the persistence of government deficits and mounting pressure to slow the rapid accumulation of public debt. In addition, the expansion of social service programs, which are sensitive to economic conditions, added to the built-in flexibility of provincial budgets, which resulted in a rapid deterioration in the budget balance as unemployment rose. In short, by the 1980s public budgets – federal, provincial, and municipal

– exhibited a good deal of automatic counter-cyclical movement in response to increasing unemployment and recession.

Apparently, a recent return to more prosperous times, has not produced a swing toward budgets surpluses or even a balanced budget. Albert Sommers (1978), in a study of U.S. federal budget deficits, illustrated the deteriorating tendency for deficits to "self-correct." In the postwar period, 1947 to 1965, deficits tended to work their way back into a surplus following a period of economic slowdown. For the 1965 to 1976 period, however, no such "self-correcting" tendency was evident.

In its reassessment of provincial fiscal policy, the Ontario Treasury (1987) highlighted the fact that the provincial budget tended to be in a deficit even in periods of estimated full employment although the province did suggest that the assumptions underlying the definition of full employment needed to be reviewed. Nevertheless, because of the reoccurring deficits and the lack of a strong fiscal feedback to tax reductions or expenditure stimulation, "the Province is now working towards a balanced budget target by 1981" (18).

Of some concern, however, was the fact that the provincial government did fail to account for the fact that it had consistently included capital expenditures with its overall current expenditure plans. A strong case can be made to *exclude* such expenditures and include them as part of a capital budget (see Auld 1985; 1991). In a study of the Ontario deficit during the 1973–82 period, Auld (1984) demonstrated that if *net investments* were eliminated from the current budget, the Ontario budget was, at full employment, in a *surplus* position in every year but one. While there have been discussions of capital expenditure in budget speeches for years, it has been only very recently that this issue has been accorded the importance it deserves.

It would be an error of omission not to point out that the issue of federal versus provincial fiscal policy is very much part of the debate about the future of Canada. The 1979 task force on Canadian Unity report, *A Future Together*, recommended that "the annual conference of finance ministers should be used more actively to ensure the coordination of economic stabilization policies by providing a common assessment of the economy and a better knowledge of the total revenue, expenditures, and borrowing of the Canadian public sector as a whole" (Recommendation 24).

The theme is repeated, underscored, and perhaps more finely tuned in the recent federal government constitutional proposals. Chapter three of *Canadian Federalism and Economic Unity* (Canada 1991) is devoted to the need to manage macroeconomic fiscal policy in a more coordinated fashion. As an example of the problems that the lack of coordination can create, the document argues that during 1986–89, the increased spending of the Ontario government complicated the Bank of Canada's task of reducing inflation and increased costs to Canadians by exporting inflation pressures from Ontario to the rest of the economy, and national interest rates rose much more than would have been the case with a more appropriate Ontario fiscal policy. In turn the higher interest rates exacerbated the fiscal position of all governments and complicated the efforts of the federal government to control its deficit and debt.

The scope of this study and time constraints do not permit an in-depth debate on this and other related issues, but it should be noted that from 1985–86 to 1988–89 the Ontario government *reduced* its deficit each year and in 1988–89 produced an operating *surplus* of $2.6 billion. Just how Ontario exported its inflation and drove up interest rates is difficult to see from the federal document. The only reference, somewhat oblique, to provincial fiscal policy is the statement: "As economic conditions may vary across the country, the appropriate fiscal course of action may not be the same for all jurisdictions" (33).

In summary, it is important to remind ourselves of certain facts:

• the non-federal sector in Canada is large;
• the non-federal sector exhibits considerable built-in stability with respect to the business cycle;
• the bulk of public capital spending occurs at the provincial and local level and has a high "local" content;
• the business cycle is not homogeneous across Canada;
• regional expenditure multipliers are not that much smaller than national expenditure multipliers; and
• the "fiscal feedback" to the provinces in terms of new revenues due to expansionary policies is limited.

These facts, combined with a strong sense of provincial identity in many parts of Canada, indicate that while harmonization of fiscal policies is clearly desirable, it will not be an easy task to accomplish. Furthermore, given the external "checks" that exist (e.g., domestic and foreign financial markets), it is unlikely that any one province will undertake any extreme policies. The limiting factor, as far as deficits are concerned, is the method of financing the shortfall in revenue. Borrowing externally to finance a deficit may be beneficial in the short run, but the repayment of the principle and interest will be a drain on the provincial economy, thereby thwarting long-term economic growth and prosperity.

When confronted with the temptation to initiate tax and expenditure policies that will lead to a significant deficit in the operating account of the province, the treasurer should ask these questions:

- Will the expenditure and/or tax policies I am proposing contribute, in the long run, to the productivity and growth of the Ontario economy?
- Will the fiscal measures I intend to implement minimize the welfare effects of discretionary tax changes?
- Will the method of financing the deficit have a small impact only on short-term interest rates?
- Will the method of financing the deficit ensure that, as much as possible, the interest on the debt remains in Ontario, or at least in Canada?

If the answer is "yes" to the above questions, some provincial stimulus to prevent serious short-term unemployment is justified. What exactly is meant by "some" will depend on the "total" debt of the province and the current political climate.

Appendix A: Estimating the Full Employment Surplus

To estimate the full employment budget surplus (FEBS) in any given budget year, the *actual* budget is the starting point. Revenues are then adjusted upward if, in that year, unemployment is greater than the rate of unemployment at the estimated full employment GNP. If the economy is *not* in recession, corporate profits would be higher, consumer spending would be greater, and the level of personal income would be higher. Consequently, tax revenues would also be higher. Statistically estimated tax functions are employed to estimate the full employment levels of revenue. Expenditures are adjusted *downward* on the reasonable assumption that unemployment benefits (at the federal level) and social assistance payments would decline if the economy is at full employment.

At full employment then, the only way there can be a significant change in the budget result from one year to the next is when the government makes policy decisions to change a fiscal instrument such as a tax rate, the exemption level, or an expenditure program. If the FEBS declines from one year to the next, that downturn is a record of a discretionary policy designed to stimulate the economy, since it reflects a tax reduction, an increase in expenditure, or some combination of the two that results in the budget deficit's becoming larger or the surplus smaller.

Appendix B: Estimating the Weighted Budget Result

The weighted budget result is the net demand-creating or demand-reducing effect of the government budget. Each component of the budget (tax or expenditure item) is assigned a "responding" coefficient, reflecting the impact of that budget item on the domestic economy through an increase or decrease in real demand. For example, the component "interest on the public debt" is assigned a responding coefficient equal to the ratio of domestic to total outstanding debt. Interest paid to foreigners has very little impact on the domestic spending front. The responding coefficient on personal income tax is the marginal propensity to consume *minus* the marginal propensity to import. Expenditure items are assigned a positive sign and taxes a negative sign, and the aggregation of all the weighted items in the budget is the weighted budget.

Notes

The first draft of this paper was prepared for the Ontario Fair Tax Commission and completed in November 1992.

1 A fairly up-to-date summary and analysis of the debate concerning crowding out can be found in Wilton and Prescott (1982). For a recent attack on conventional stabilization policy and a call for more emphasis on incomes policies, see Fortin (1991).

2 This is often referred to as the Phillips curve, but it is somewhat misnamed. The Phillips curve was named after the British economist A.W. Phillips, who first isolated a distinct statistical relationship between the rate of unemployment and the rate of change in wages, not prices. The high correlation between wage and price changes and the need to target prices, not wages, in anti-inflationary policy, give rise to the policy trade-off between the two objectives.

3 We shall use the term "non-federal levels of government" to refer to the provincial-municipal/local sectors in Canadian government and the

state-local sectors in the United States. When specific references to either the provincial or the municipal is required, the level of government will be identified.

4 For example, in 1972, private fixed capital expenditure in Canada increased 9.3 per cent. In Ontario the increase was 7.2 per cent, in New Brunswick it was minus 14.3 per cent, and in Saskatchewan the increase was 29.9 per cent (Canada 1989).

5 The commission (1966) concluded that "the fact that the provinces do not control the money supply (and we do not believe they should) could make it difficult for them, under extreme conditions, to finance stabilizing increases in expenditure without raising taxes during periods of high unemployment" (vol. 2, 102).

6 It is interesting to note that, some years later, in a paper on regional economic stabilization, Pierre Fortin (1989a) concluded that, "provincial expenditures have shown no systematic or significant sensitivity to the swings in the business cycle."

7 Of particular interest is the fact that the debt issued by non-federal governments in Canada tends to be sold to non-residents, which may have interesting foreign exchange rate implications. For example, it is generally accepted that the massive public borrowing by provincial and local governments and their agencies in the early 1970s contributed to the rise of the value of the Canadian dollar at that time. This had the effect of lowering inflation by way of lower import costs and hampering the growth of exports. For detailed discussion of this and related issues, see, Wonnacott (1972) and Winer (1975). Sheikh and Winer (1977) examine the importance of non-federal governments in the overall scheme of federal stabilization policies using the Economic Council of Canada macroeconomic model.

8 In a more recent paper, Miller (1988) examines the potential effectiveness of regional fiscal policies in the 1981–82 recession using a model that relates the elasticity of the rate of unemployment to total government expenditures in each of five regions in Canada (British Columbia, the prairie provinces, Ontario, Quebec, and the Atlantic provinces). Miller concludes that the increase in government expenditures necessary to offset the unemployment in the 1981–82 recession would have had to be very large and that "more moderate countercyclical expenditure policies ... would not have been very effective" (301). In an Ontario Economic Council study, Robin Boadway and Jack Treddenick (1978) concluded that the bulk of the impact of fiscal changes in Ontario was felt in the province itself.

9 The author's research also points out that the "feedback" to the public

sector's revenue, as a result of a stimulus, is much higher for the federal than it is for the provincial budgets. An increase of $1.00 in public expenditure with no compensating increase in tax rates eventually improves federal revenues by $0.42 and provincial revenues by $0.18. In part, this rise is due to the decline in UIC payments, which improves the fiscal position of the federal government with no corresponding change at the provincial level.

10 Engerman (1965) reached the conclusion that "as long as stabilization measures are left to particular states, there can be no expectation of an optimal national policy, for there may be either smaller or larger changes in demand than would be considered desirable" (53).

11 When reviewing the research and policy discussions of provincial fiscal policy, there is virtually no mention of anti-inflationary policies. Increasing the full-employment budget surplus by way of tax increases or reduced public expenditures will not create the same monetary problems as would a deficit. The exchange rate implications are nevertheless still there, albeit with opposite signs. A *net redemption* of provincial debt would put downward pressure on the Canadian dollar and, under a floating exchange rate, impact on trade nationally. Under a fixed exchange rate regime, such action, if of sufficient magnitude, would require central bank intervention to stabilize the value of the currency. Politically, of course, tax increases at the provincial level would be far more unpopular than tax reductions.

12 The derivation of the weighted budget result and its application to the evaluation of fiscal policy is found in Appendix A. It should be noted that changes in the way revenues were shared between the federal and provincial governments during the 1960–67 period preclude an accurate measure of the impact of changes in certain tax revenues, notably, the personal and corporate income taxes.

13 A full description of the technique is found in Appendix B of this paper. In essence, the FEBS is the budget surplus (or a deficit possibly) that would exist if the economy were operating at full employment and there were no discretionary changes such as tax rates or government expenditure. In Ontario, this technique was first employed by the Ministry of Treasury and Economics to evaluate fiscal policy in 1970–71 (see McKeough 1971).

Bibliography

Advisory Commission on Intergovernmental Affairs. 1978. *Counter-Cyclical Aid and Economic Stabilization.* Washington, DC: ACIA

- 1979. *State-Local Finances in Recession and Inflation: An Economic Analysis*, Washington, DC: ACIA

Auld, D.A.L. 1969. *Fiscal Policy Performance in Australia: 1948–64*. Canberra: Australian National University Press

- 1975. "Counter-Cyclical Budget Effects in Ontario: Some Preliminary Results." *Canadian Tax Journal*, 23: 173–83

- 1978. "Decentralizing Fiscal Policy." In *Canadian Confederation at the Crossroads: The Search for a Federal-Provincial Balance*, ed. Michael Walker, 269–83. Vancouver: Fraser Institute

- 1980. "The Scope for Short-Run Fiscal Stabilization Policy Within Confederation." In *Fiscal Dimensions of Canadian Federalism*, ed. R.M. Bird, 91–110. Toronto: Canadian Tax Foundation

- 1984. "The Ontario Budget Deficit: A Cause For Concern?" In *Deficits: How Big and How Bad?* 78–106. Ontario: Ontario Economic Council

- 1987. "An Evaluation of Economic Management at the Provincial Level: the Case of Ontario." *Canadian Journal of Regional Science*, 5: 1–18

- 1991. "Compensatory Fiscal Policy: Evolution or Revolution?" In *Retrospectives on Public Finance*, ed. L. Eden, 306–22. Durham, NC: Duke University Press

Auld, D.A.L., and David Wilton. 1988. "The Impact of Progressive Income Taxation on Wage Inflation." *Canadian Journal of Economics*, 3: 279–84

Baratz, Morton S., and Helen T. Farr. 1959. "Is Municipal Finance Fiscally Perverse?" *National Tax Journal*, 12: 276–84

Barber, Clarence. 1966. *Theory of Fiscal Policy As Applied To a Province*. Toronto: Ontario Committee on Taxation

Barro, Robert J. 1984. *Macroeconomics*. New York: John Wiley

Blinder, Alan, and Robert Solow. 1973. "Does Fiscal Policy Matter?" *Journal of Public Economics*, 2: 319–37

Boadway, R., and J. Treddenick. 1978. "The Effects of Fiscal Policy Measures in Ontario." In *Input-Output Analyses of Fiscal Policy In Ontario*, ed. J. Bossons, 72–93. Toronto: Ontario Economic Council

Boskin, Michael. 1987. "Concepts and Measures of Federal Deficits and Debt and Their Impact on Economic Activity." NBER Working Paper No. 2332

Brennan, Geoffrey, and D.A.L. Auld. 1968. "The Tax-Cut as an Anti-Inflationary Measure." *Economic Record*, 44: 520–25

Brown, E. Cary. 1956. "Fiscal Policy in the Thirties: A Reappraisal." *American Economic Review*, 46: 857–79

Canada. 1966. Royal Commission on Taxation. *Report (Carter Report)*. Vol. 2. Ottawa: Queen's Printer

- 1979. The Task Force on Canadian Unity. *A Future Together*. Ottawa: Ministry of Supply and Services

- 1989. Department of Finance. *Quarterly Economic Review*, June: Table 22.1
- 1991. *Canadian Federalism and Economic Union: Partnership for Prosperity.* Ottawa: Ministry of Supply and Services

Carter Report. See Canada (1966).

Eisner, Robert. 1986. *How Real is the Federal Deficit?* New York: Free Press

Engerman, Stanley. 1965. "Regional Aspects of Stabilization Policy." In *Essays in Fiscal Federalism*, ed. Richard Musgrave, 7–62. Washington, DC: Brookings Institution

Feldstein, Martin. 1982. "Government Deficits and Aggregate Demand." *Journal of Monetary Economics*, 9: 1–20

Fortin, Pierre. 1982a. *Provincial Involvement in Regulating the Business Cycle: Justification, Scope and Terms.* Discussion Paper No. 213. Ottawa: Economic Council of Canada
- 1982b. *The Comparative Size of the Federal and Provincial Budgets and Economic Stabilization.* Discussion Paper No. 211. Ottawa: Economic Council of Canada

Gusen, Peter. 1978. *The Role of Provincial Governments in Economic Stabilization: The Case of Ontario's Auto Sales Tax Rebate.* Ottawa: Conference Board of Canada

Hansen, Alvin H., and Harvey Perloff. 1944. *State and Local Finance in the National Economy.* New York: Norton

Jones, B., Nancy Bardecki, and B. Hill. 1977. *Regional Stabilization Policy in Canada: The Ontario Record.* Ontario: Taxation and Fiscal Policy Branch, Treasury and Economics

Lynch, Kevin, and Jack Selody. 1981. *The Determinants of Fiscal Policy in Canada 1957–79.* Paper presented to the Canadian Economics Association Meetings, Halifax

Maxwell, James. 1958. "Counter-Cyclical Role of State and Local Governments." *National Tax Journal*, 11: 371–76

McKinnon, Ronald, and Wallace Oates. 1966. *The Implications of International Economic Integration for Monetary, Fiscal and Exchange-Rate Policy.* Princeton, NJ: Princeton University Press

Miller, F.C. 1980. "The Feasibility of Regionally Differentiated Fiscal Policy." *Canadian Journal of Regional Science*, 3: 13–27
- 1987. "The Natural Rate of Unemployment: Regional Estimates and Policy Implications." *Canadian Journal of Regional Science*, 10: 64–75
- 1988. "Regional Fiscal Policy and the Great Recession of 1981–2." *Canadian Journal of Regional Science*, 5: 287–302

Miller F.C., and D.J. Wallace. 1983. "The Feasibility of Regionally Differentiated Fiscal Policies." *Canadian Journal of Regional Science*, 5: 259–79

Modigliani, France, and Arlie Sterling. 1986. "Government Debt, Government Spending and Private Sector Behavior." *American Economic Review* 76: 1168–79

Mundell, R.A. 1961. "Employment Policy under Flexible Exchange Rates." *Canadian Journal of Economics and Political Science,* 29: 509–17

– 1963. "Capital Mobility and Stabilization Policy under Fixed and Flexible Exchange Rates." *Canadian Journal of Economics and Political Science,* 29: 475–85

Newcomer, Mabel. 1954. "State and Local Financing in Relation to Economic Fluctuations." *National Tax Journal,* 7: 97–109

Oates, W. 1968. "The Theory of Public Finance in a Federal System." *Canadian Journal of Economics,* 5: 37–54

– 1972. *Fiscal Federalism.* New York: Harcourt Brace Jovanovich

Ontario. Ministry of Treasury and Economics. 1987. *Re-assessing The Scope For Fiscal Policy in Ontario.* Toronto: Queen's Printer

Peacock, Alan T. 1965. "Towards a Theory of Inter-Regional Fiscal Policy." *Public Finance,* 2: 7–17

Peacock, A.T., and G.K. Shaw. 1978. "Is Fiscal Policy Dead?" *Banca Nazionale del Lavoro, Quarterly Review,* June: 107–22

Rabeau, Yves, and Robert Lacroix. 1979. "Economic Stabilization and the Regions: The Dilemma in Canada." *Proceedings in the Workshop on the Political Economy of Confederation.* Institute for Intergovernmental Relations. Ontario: Queen's University

Rafuse, Robert, Jr. 1965. "Cyclical Behaviour of State-Local Finances." In *Essays in Fiscal Federalism,* ed. Richard Musgrave, 63–121. Washington, DC: Brookings Institution

Reynauld, André. 1971. "Pour une politique de stabilisation régionale." *Administration publique du Canada,* 14: 344–53

Ricardo, David. 1951. *The Works and Correspondence of David Ricardo,* ed. P. Straffa and M.H. Dobb. Cambridge: Cambridge University Press

Robinson, T.R., and T.J. Courchene. 1969. "Fiscal Federalism and Economic Stability: An Examination of Multi-Level Public Finances in Canada, 1952–65." *Canadian Journal of Economics,* 2: 165–68

Sharp, Ansel. 1958. "The Counter-Cyclical Fiscal Role of State Governments During the Thirties." *National Tax Journal,* 11: 138–45

Sheikh, M.A. and S.L. Winer. 1977. "Stabilization and Non-Federal Behaviour in an Open Federal State: An Econometric Study of the Fixed Exchange Rate Canadian Case. *Empirical Economics,* 2: 195–211

Sommers, Albert. 1978. *The Balanced Federal Budget: An Orthodoxy in Trouble.* No. 36. Washington, DC: Conference Board

Wonnacott, P. 1972. *The Floating Canadian Dollar*. Washington, DC: American Enterprise for Public Policy Research

Wilson, Thomas. 1977. "The Province and Stabilization Policy." *Intergovernmental Relations*. Ontario: Ontario Economic Council

Wilton, David, and David Prescott. 1982. *Macroeconomics*, ch. 16. Toronto: Addison-Wesley

Winer, Stanley. 1975. "Monetary-Fiscal Influences in a Federal State: With Applications to the Post-War Canadian Economy." Unpublished PH D dissertation. Baltimore: Johns Hopkins University Press

– 1979. "Short-Run Monetary Fiscal Influences in a Federal State With Application to the Canadian Economy." *Public Finance Quarterly*, 7: 395–423

Notes on Contributors

Peggy B. Musgrave is Professor Emeritus of Economics, University of California, Santa Cruz.

Richard A. Musgrave is H.H. Burbank Professor Emeritus of Political Economy, Harvard University, and Adjunct Professor of Economics, University of California, Santa Cruz.

Albert Breton is Professor in the Department of Economics, University of Toronto.

Douglas G. Hartle is Emeritus Professor in the Department of Economics, University of Toronto.

Brian Erard is Professor in the Department of Economics, Carleton University.

François Vaillancourt is Professor in the Department of Economics and Centre de recherche et développement en économique, Université de Montréal.

Dr D.A.L. Auld is President, Loyalist College, and Professor of Economics, Trent University.

Commission Organization

Chair**
Monica Townson

Vice-Chairs
Neil Brooks*
Robert Couzin*

Commissioners
Jayne Berman
William Blundell
Susan Giampietri
Brigitte Kitchen*
Gérard Lafrenière
Fiona Nelson
Satya Poddar*

Executive Director
Hugh Mackenzie

Director of Research
Allan M. Maslove

Assistant Director of Research
Sheila Block

Executive Assistant to Research Program
Moira Hutchinson

Editorial Assistant
Marguerite Martindale,

  * Member of the Research Subcommittee
** Chair of the Research Subcommittee